PROMISING Paradise

CUBAN ALLURE AMERICAN SEDUCTION

Featuring images from
The Vicki Gold Levi Collection at The Wolfsonian–FIU

and essays by
Rosa Lowinger and Francis Xavier Luca

Jon Mogul, editor
Marlene Tosca, art director
Lynton Gardiner, photographer
Kara Pickman, copyeditor

The Wolfsonian–Florida International University
1001 Washington Avenue
Miami Beach, Florida 33139
wolfsonian.org

Promising Paradise: Cuban Allure, American Seduction is published by The Wolfsonian–FIU, and made possible by support from Vicki Gold Levi.

The Wolfsonian receives ongoing support from John S. and James L. Knight Foundation; State of Florida, Department of State, Division of Cultural Affairs and the Florida Council on Arts and Culture; Miami-Dade County Department of Cultural Affairs and the Cultural Affairs Council, the Miami-Dade County Mayor and Board of County Commissioners; and City of Miami Beach, Cultural Affairs Program, Cultural Arts Council.

Printed by Indice SL, Spain

First edition

ISBN 978-0-9968699-5-9

Library of Congress catalog record available at https://lccn.loc.gov/2018044526

Cover images

Front: Dancers outside Sans Souci, c. 1952, see p. 4.
Inside: View of outdoor seating at Tropicana's Bajo las Estrellas cabaret, c. 1955, see p. 17.
Back: Dirty Dick's Bar, c. 1927, see p. 11.

Promising Paradise

Cuban Allure
American Seduction

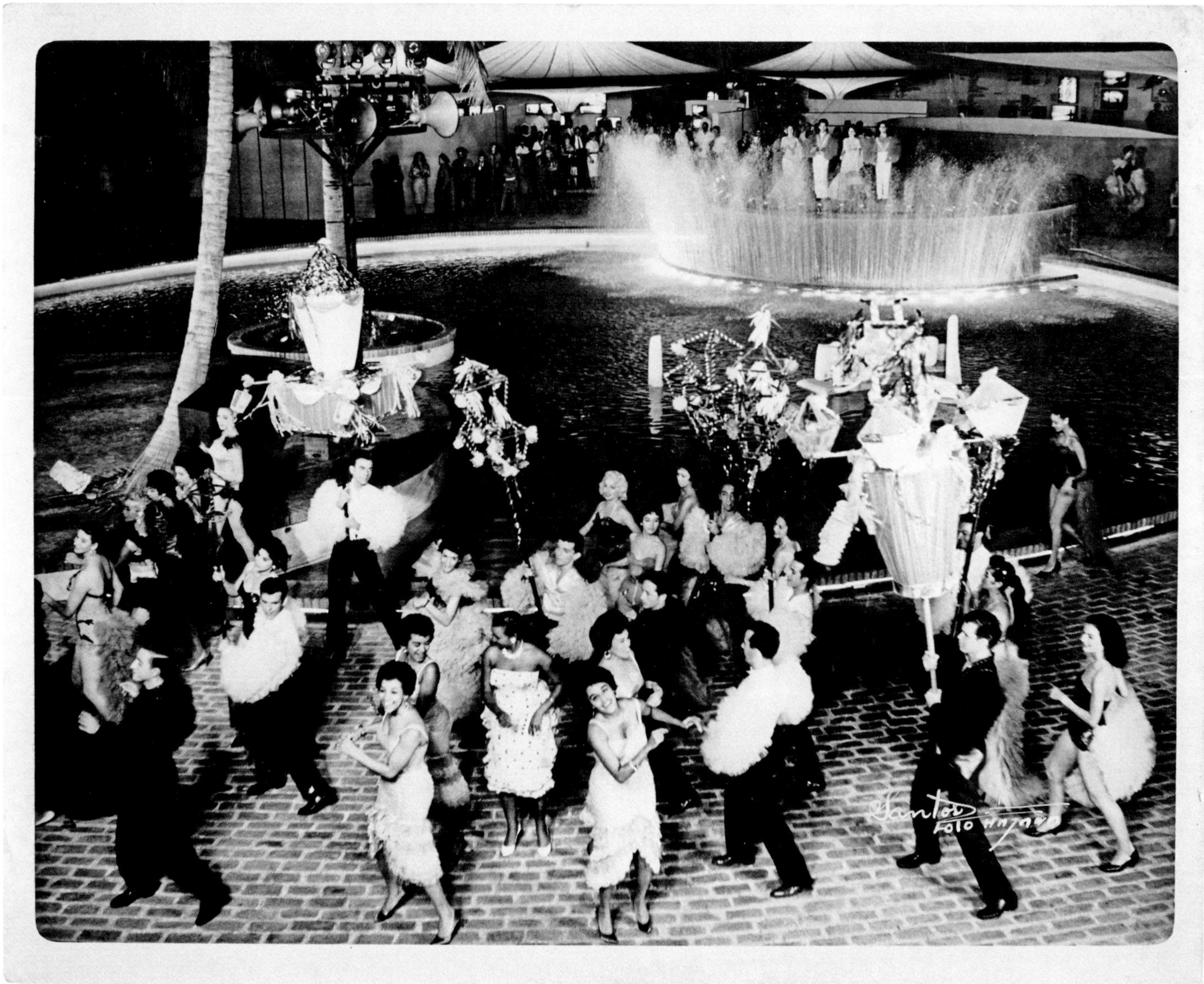

Photograph, **Dancers outside San Souci**, c. 1952
Gelatin silver print

The Wolfsonian–FIU, The Vicki Gold Levi Collection, XC2016.01.1.1136

Director's Foreword

Tim Rodgers, Director, The Wolfsonian–FIU

Thanks to our Miami Beach location, we at The Wolfsonian have a close-up view of Cuba's changing relationship with the United States. But we are more than witnesses to unfolding events. We are also, due to the generosity of one collector in particular, stewards of an important part of the legacy of that relationship. Vicki Gold Levi's 2016 promised gift of photographs, tourist materials, memorabilia, and other items offers rich evidence of the economic, social, and cultural entanglement between Cuba and the United States before the 1959 revolution. These materials were the backbone of our 2016 exhibition *Promising Paradise: Cuban Allure, American Seduction*, the first large-scale show at The Wolfsonian that focused specifically on Cuba, and they are the basis of this book as well.

The significance of Vicki's gift extends very far beyond the exhibition and the book. Together with her earlier gifts to our collection, these items form an archive of considerable importance for research on Cuban culture. They are available both in our library and in our digital catalog, and have already proven of great interest both to advanced scholars and to our students at Florida International University (FIU). The gift comes at a particularly opportune moment, in fact, as FIU is making a substantial investment in promoting Cuban studies, as evidenced in the CasaCuba initiative. The Vicki Gold Levi Collection at The Wolfsonian can be one of the key intellectual assets supporting this development.

The book, like the 2016 exhibition, results not only from Vicki's gift, but from collaboration between The Wolfsonian's chief librarian, Frank Luca, and Rosa Lowinger, an art and architectural conservator and expert on Cuban popular culture. I am most grateful to both of them for contributing incisive essays to this book, building on their very productive work as co-curators of the 2016 exhibition. In addition, the project benefited very much from the skill and hard work of a number of Wolfsonian staff members—most of all, Lynton Gardiner's photography, Marlene Tosca's art direction and design, and Jon Mogul's editorial oversight. I would also like to thank Kara Pickman for her work as copyeditor.

Vicki Gold Levi's generosity is not limited to the gift of her collection. She has also provided significant financial support for the *Promising Paradise* exhibition and publication, as well as for our summer 2019 installation about Cuban illustrator Conrado Walter Massaguer. For their support of the 2016 exhibition, I am also grateful to Dr. Alexander Levi; Bacardi USA, Inc.; Arthur Murray International; Terra Group; Trina Turk, Mr Turk; Brickell Bank; Marsh & McClennan; AIG; BankUnited; and the Cuban Research Institute at FIU.

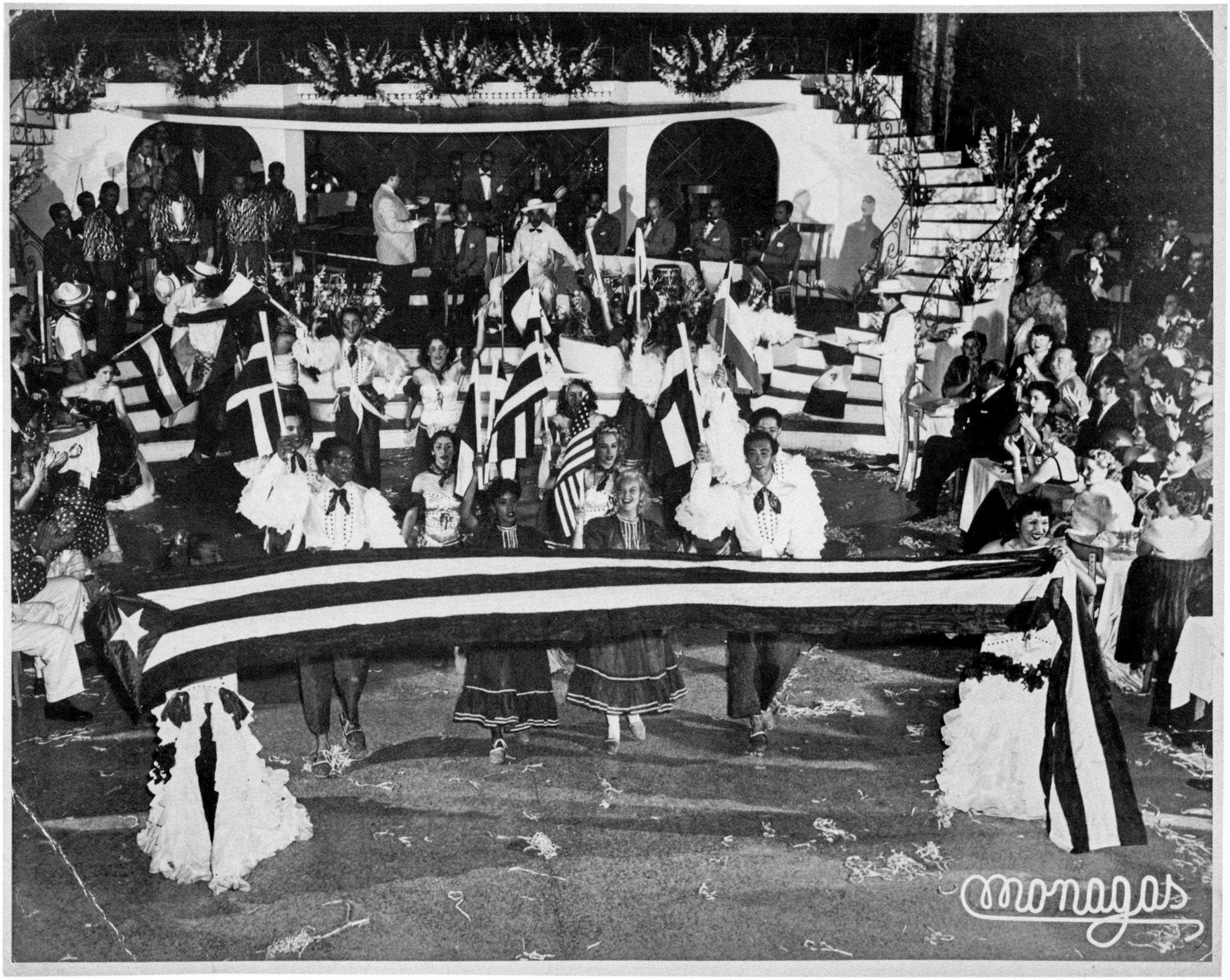

Photograph, **Performance at Sans Souci**, c. 1955
Monagas, photographer
Gelatin silver print

The Wolfsonian–FIU, The Vicki Gold Levi Collection, XC2016.01.1.1206

Note from the Collector

Vicki Gold Levi

I have been accused of being a hoarder, but I think of myself as a collector. Collecting images and artifacts has always been a passion of mine, a form of cultural anthropology. This passion started in my hometown, Atlantic City, and inspired a book about the city's history. I knew I had been infected by the collecting bug when I saw my plates, postcards, menus, chalk kewpie dolls, and Mr. Peanut relics on display at the Cooper Hewitt, Smithsonian Design Museum, part of an Atlantic City architecture exhibition. That experience inspired me to co-found the Atlantic City Historical Museum on the Boardwalk to house these treasures.

Strange as it sounds, Atlantic City led me to an exploration of Cuban culture. After buying a letter on eBay from a woman who rode the High Diving Horse, a water circus act in Atlantic City, I learned that she had taken the act to Cuba. Intrigued, I went on to find amazing advertising graphics on Cuba, and the link between these two places—the resort city on the Jersey coast, and the gem of the Caribbean—made Cuba a natural segue for me. I discovered a symbiotic relationship: not only did Americans export movies, architecture, and automobiles to the island, but Cuba sent its culture our way as well. Back in the 1950s, the Palladium Ballroom in New York City was bursting with energy as Puerto Ricans, Cubans, Jewish American "Mamboniks," and others danced the night away to the music of Machito, Tito Puente, and Tito Rodríguez.

The thrill of a new collectible lies in putting together pieces of a puzzle to discover a stimulating narrative. Following clues from letters, websites, books, and other collectors is exhilarating, especially when you unearth something completely unknown. Contributing to a body of knowledge that will inform those who come after you is a gratifying legacy.

I came to know Cuba through photographs of musicians, tobacco plantation workers, dancers, and Carnival performers, through travel brochures and hotel luggage labels, Art Deco magazine covers, and rum recipes. These poignant articles of Cuban life and tourism made the country come alive for me and led to a 2002 book, co-authored with famed art director Steven Heller, called *Cuba Style*. My fascination with Cuba did not end there. Since then I have traveled to Havana several more times and amassed 1,500 objects and photographs from all over the world, which I donated to The Wolfsonian–FIU. This gift resulted in the vibrant 2016 exhibition *Promising Paradise*, co-curated by Frank Luca and Rosa Lowinger and artfully designed by Richard Miltner. It is also the basis for this book.

My interest in Cuba remains very strong. I have most recently focused my attention on the works of Conrado Walter Massaguer, founder of *Social* magazine and a world-renowned illustrator. The future is uncertain, but I expect to keep collecting, and I believe that there is much more to discover about Cuban culture.

. . .

In the course of working on the *Promising Paradise* exhibition and book with my Wolfsonian collaborators, we have accumulated debts to many contributors and allies. I want to gratefully acknowledge the following: Marcos Ansia, Bacardi USA, Inc., Juan Bergaz Pessino, Ramon Cabral, Iliana Cepero, Cernuda Arte, Gerardo Chávez, Darrel Couturier, Geo Darder, Alina Diaz, Diana Diaz, Luis Diaz, Ramiro Fernández, Leonard Finger, Lutz Heinrich, Steven Heller, Sandra C. Jimenez, Elena Kurstin, Christian Larsen, Alex Levi, Sandra Levinson, Ricardo Linares, Gustavo López González, Alan Magluta, Hermes Mallea, Victor Martinez, Memorias Store (Havana), Sergio Mercenit, Luz Merino, Joelle Orr, Omer Pardillo Cid, Tony Ransola, Aurelia Reinhardt, Eduardo Luis Rodriguez, Gonzalo Rodriguez, Carole Rosenberg, Vic Ruggiero, Althea Silvera, Maria Elena Toraño, Olga Maria Touzet, Tony Ulloa, the late Julian Valdes, Jr., and Ruffino del Valle Valdés.

Special thanks to Marlene Tosca, who shaped the graphic identity of both the 2016 exhibition and this book, which is the culmination of three years of collaboration on this subject so dear to my heart.

Cuban Allure

The Draw of Rum, Rumba, and Roulette

Rosa Lowinger & Francis Xavier Luca

Ever since Christopher Columbus called Cuba the "loveliest land that human eyes have ever seen," foreigners have envisioned the largest island in the Caribbean as an alluring, tropical locale.[1] In the early to mid-twentieth century, U.S. investors and the newly established Cuban Tourist Commission promoted Cuba as an earthly paradise to attract North American vacationers.[2] Between 1919 and the 1959 revolution, Cuban artists, graphic designers, photographers, and performers shaped the young republic's image as a close-to-home but exotic destination offering access to ancient landmarks and modern amenities, and opportunities to indulge in drinking, dancing, and gambling. Posters, publicity photographs, Hollywood films, and promotional literature promised visitors warm winter breezes and beaches; the scent of tobacco and the flavor of rum; the rhythms of rumba, mambo, and Afro-Cuban jazz; the comfort of glamorous hotels; and the excitement of Havana's casinos, nightclubs, and other entertainment. In the 1920s and again in the 1950s, American tourists took advantage of cheap travel fares and thronged to Cuba's capital city, Havana, eager to see and experience for themselves the island that marketed itself as "so near and yet so foreign."

Close cooperation developed between the United States and Cuba in the wake of American intervention in the island's independence war in 1898, the subsequent occupation, and the establishment of the republic. While the sixteenth-century Spanish fortress El Morro remains Havana's most prominent landmark, the city's defining modern feature is the Malecón, a seaside promenade and seawall whose construction began during U.S. military rule in 1901 and was extended seven kilometers between 1902 and 1921. Sugar warehouses, cigar factories, office towers, social clubs, theaters, hotels, and private mansions—many built with the modern technique of steel-reinforced concrete—sprung up on the outskirts of the colonial district. These early twentieth-century structures included examples of every major architectural style of the period: Art Nouveau, neoclassical, neo-Gothic, neo-baroque, and eclectic. Habaneros were transforming their city, and Americans also saw the value of investing in the region, building amenities catering to wealthy Cubans and American tourists alike. As the First World War raged in Europe, American travelers looked for alternative places to vacation, and investors scouted Cuba's potential. With sugar prices at an all-time high during the war, the country experienced a construction boom that transformed its capital city. For example, in 1915 Harry ("Curly") Brown opened Oriental Park, a thoroughbred horse racetrack, in the Marianao suburb of Havana, adding to the upscale yacht, golf, and tennis clubs already in the neighborhood.[3]

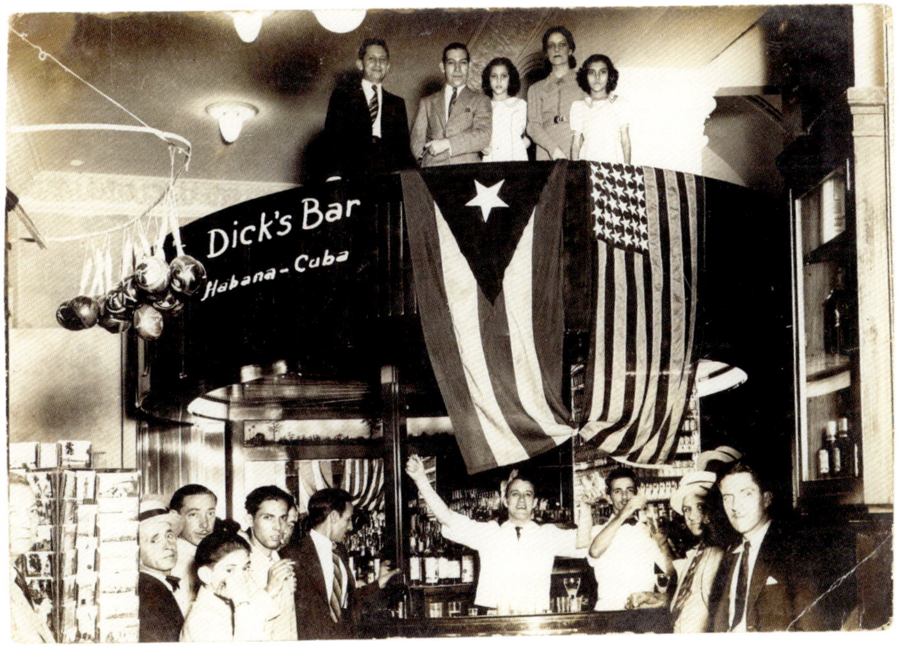

After the Great War ended, sugar prices dropped precipitously, and the "dance of the millions"—as the boom period was known—came to a crashing halt. Recognizing the need for economic diversification, Cuban politicians decided to attract additional American tourists to the island.[4] In 1919 Cuba's national legislature passed a bill that authorized the establishment of gambling ventures. Thus was born the Gran Casino Nacional de Marianao, along with Havana's fame as the "Monte Carlo of the Western Hemisphere."[5]

At the precise moment that Cuban politicians began courting American tourists, the U.S. government provided unexpected and inadvertent assistance. Passage of the Eighteenth Amendment and the Volstead Act prohibited the "manufacture, sale, or transportation of intoxicating liquors" in the United States. Threatened with a loss of livelihood, notable American saloon owners packed up and moved to Havana, competing with local bodegas that sold food and drink along with groceries and tobacco.[fig. 1] "Thirsty" American travelers flocked to Cuba aboard modestly priced steamships, and Havana's tourism boosters wasted no time in billing the island as a hassle-free place to sunbathe on sandy beaches, dance the rumba, try one's luck at the roulette tables, and drink the night away in some of the estimated seven thousand bars and saloons popping up all over the city.[6] Advertisements, postcards, press photographs, and sheet music cover art and lyrics left no doubt that Havana was the place for serious drinkers.[fig. 2]

Fig. 1
Photograph, **Dirty Dick's Bar**, c. 1927
Gelatin silver print

The Wolfsonian–FIU, The Vicki Gold Levi Collection, XC2016.01.1.1225

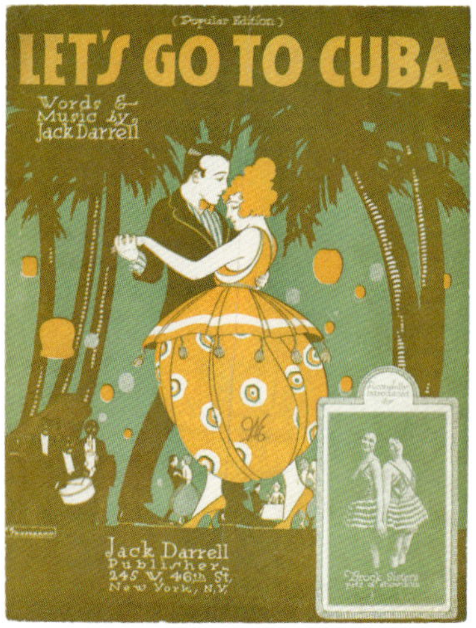

Fig. 2
Sheet music cover, ***Let's Go to Cuba (Before They Drink the Darn Place Dry)***, 1920
Jack Darrell, lyricist and composer
Jack Darrell Publishers, New York, publisher

The Wolfsonian–FIU, The Vicki Gold Levi Collection, XC2016.01.1.1224

During the era of Prohibition, lasting until 1933, illegal speakeasies in America infamously began serving cocktails concocted with cheap "bathtub" gin, so bitter that no amount of honey or fruit juice could mask the flavor—making Havana even more attractive for drinkers. As travel writer Basil Woon boasted in the 1920s, there was "no possibility of the liquor stocks in Havana ever running short."[7] Originally consumed by slaves on plantations, sailors, and pirates in the seventeenth century, rum was rebranded as a gentleman's drink by the Bacardí family, whose firm filtered, distilled, and aged it in oak barrels. With a base of rum and cola, the "Cuba libre" was invented in the wake of the Cuban War of Independence and remained popular well into the twentieth century; but the drink that won tourists over was the daiquiri, a lime, sugar, shaved ice, and rum cocktail named for the eastern sugar-mill town where it originated.[8]

The most popular of Havana's watering holes was a no-frills, dimly lit place with a long mahogany bar, located near the city center. Numerous legends purport to explain how the establishment earned its name; according to Woon, the proprietor, José ("Joe") García Rio, quarreled with a local journalist, who retaliated by running an editorial urging the city's sanitation commission to look into "a place on Zulueta Street which should be called 'Sloppy Joe's.'"[9] The name became an ironic marketing success, and advertisements for the bar were placed in every Cuban guidebook to ensure its popularity with American visitors. Another nearby bar and restaurant, El Floridita, was made famous by Ernest Hemingway, who declared its daiquiris the best in the country.

The wave of tourists that came with Prohibition spurred more American investment and Cuban highway and hotel construction. Within months of the law's enactment, the Biltmore hotel chain acquired the Spanish-Moorish Hotel Sevilla (1906), hiring the New York–based architecture firm Schultze and Weaver to expand it. The proprietors promoted the refurbished hotel with a "Winter in Cuba" campaign designed to entice revelers to ring in the New Year with champagne.[10] Another American firm, McKim, Mead and White, designed the grand Hotel Nacional de Cuba, which opened in December 1930 [fig. 3] Affording a commanding view of Havana Harbor, this hotel was operated by the American managers of the Plaza Hotel and eventually catered to so many American tourists and diplomats that locals nicknamed it *la embajada americana*.[11] Local architects also transformed Havana's skyline. Bacardí—Cuba's largest homegrown industrial enterprise—commissioned the firm Fernández, Castell, y Menéndez to design an office tower for their headquarters in Havana. Erected in three hundred days and completed in 1930, this Art Deco masterpiece clad in terracotta tiles stood as the city's tallest structure. Topped by a bronze rooftop ornament that featured the company's logo of a bat with outstretched wings, the building also included a paneled mezzanine bar where visitors could sample the company's brands free of charge.[12]

Affluent American visitors enjoyed playing golf and tennis, betting on horseraces, and lounging at stylish beach resorts by day, and spent their evenings dancing and sipping daiquiris at the rooftop garden of the Hotel Sevilla-Biltmore. Lent and Easter tended to fall at the height of the winter tourist season; however, by the 1920s the actual dates of the associated Carnival celebrations and parades were occasionally shifted a week or two in order to ensure the street festivals and processions took place during the tourist season's busiest weeks. Havana offered more hedonistic thrill-seekers year-round burlesque and striptease acts, and other more explicit entertainment venues where the "salaciously-inclined may witness startling scenes in the flesh or by means of moving pictures."[13] Habaneros also began encountering more budget-conscious travelers among the six hundred thousand Americans who came between 1928 and 1932.[14]

Cuban artists and graphic designers played an important role in both reflecting and shaping American and Cuban perceptions of each other during these early encounters. As North American visitors poured into Havana, the Cuban Tourist Commission hired local illustrators such as Conrado Walter Massaguer to portray them as debonair in their advertisements; on the covers of popular Spanish-language magazines, however, Massaguer and other artists caricatured the "migratory ducks" as less than handsome

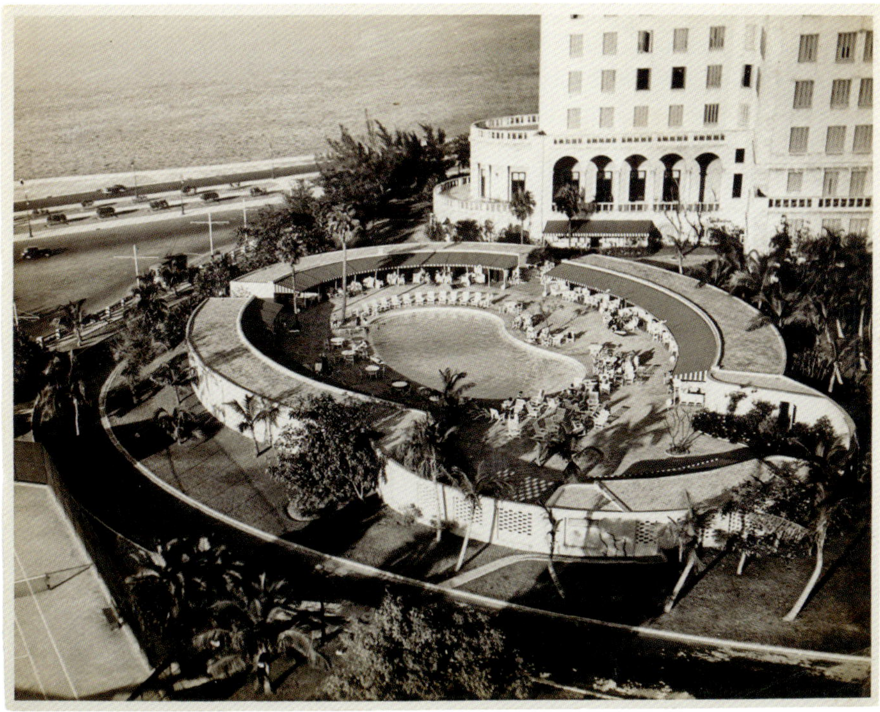

Fig. 3
Photograph, **Cabana Sun Club and swimming pool, Hotel Nacional de Cuba**, c. 1950
Henry Wallace, photographer
Gelatin silver print

The Wolfsonian–FIU, The Vicki Gold Levi Collection, XC2016.01.1.154

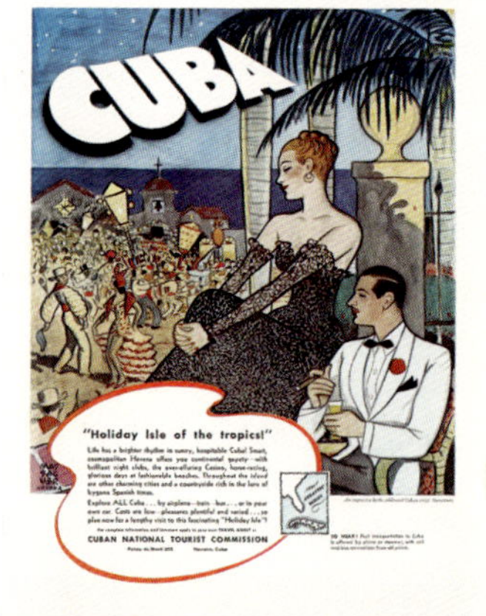

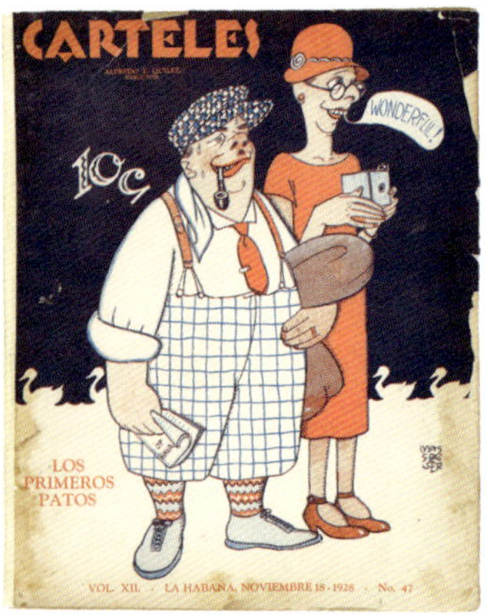

Fig. 4
Advertisement, ***Cuba: Holiday Isle of the Tropics***, 1939
Conrado Walter Massaguer (Cuban, 1889–1965), illustrator
Cuban National Tourist Commission, Havana, publisher

The Wolfsonian–FIU, The Vicki Gold Levi Collection, XC2002.11.4.216

Fig. 5
Periodical, ***Carteles***, November 18, 1928
Conrado Walter Massaguer (Cuban, 1889–1965), cover illustrator

The Wolfsonian–FIU, The Vicki Gold Levi Collection, XC2016.01.1.930

and graceful.[figs. 4, 5] Even as Cuban artists took part in the *afrocubanismo* movement that celebrated African-influenced music, dance, and other cultural traditions, many advertisements aimed at U.S. tourists employed derogatory images of blacks, or ignored them altogether and instead focused on the island's Spanish heritage.[15] Magazines designed for Cuban readers often acknowledged American racial prejudices, while simultaneously playing on their own national stereotypes about the sensuality of voluptuous mulatta women.

The repeal of Prohibition in 1933, combined with the economic woes of the Great Depression and growing social strife on the island, undermined tourism; the onset of the Second World War delivered the coup de grâce. Still, Cuban travel literature and Hollywood movies continued to depict a fanciful, exoticized locale. Those marketing efforts bore fruit in the 1950s, when, following another drop in sugar prices after the Korean War, Cubans tempted a second, larger wave of visitors back to the island. Middle-class Americans, journeying on long-distance commercial airliners and inexpensive ferries, which even allowed them to take their own cars, flooded into Havana to experience its glamorous nightlife for themselves.

Since the 1930s Cuba's artists, writers, composers, and architects had been consumed with defining the nation's cultural identity.[16] Their solution was to integrate tradition and modernity, drawing from their Spanish and Afro-Cuban heritage and selectively borrowing from Europe and the United States. Architects were at the forefront of this movement. Using engineering innovations that allowed walls to be liberally perforated, encased in glass, or treated merely like curtains to keep out the elements, they adapted the tenets of International Style modernism promoted by Le Corbusier to create a uniquely exuberant Cuban visual vocabulary that shaped the buildings of the postwar construction boom.

In 1952 Fulgencio Batista assumed the presidency by military coup and soon began redirecting funds from the Banco Nacional, Banco de Fomento Agrícola e Industrial de Cuba, and Banco de Desarrollo Económico y Social into the construction of hotels for tourists. These banks provided nearly half the capital expended in new hotel construction during the rest of the decade. Batista offered casino concessions to any developer who committed one million dollars or more to a project—an offer readily taken up by American organized crime figures, including Meyer Lansky, an old friend and business associate of Batista. Extraordinary modern venues rose on the island, resulting in a near doubling of hotel room capacity between 1955 and 1958.[17] The most lavish of these was the Havana Riviera (1957), which was financed by Lansky, designed by the Miami architects Polevitzky and Partners, and decorated by the Los Angeles hotel firm Albert Parvin and Associates.[fig. 6]

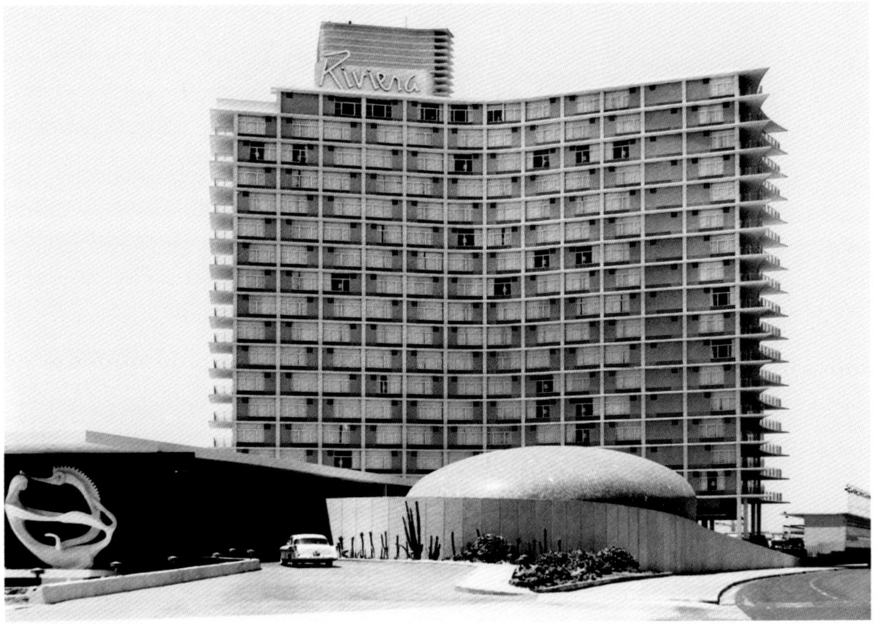

Next came the Havana Hilton (1958), financed by the Cuban hospitality industry union and designed by Welton Becket of Los Angeles with the Cuban firm Arroyo and Menéndez. Other new hotels included the Hotel Capri (1957) and the Comodoro (1955), owned by Tampa mobster Santo Trafficante, Jr.

In the mid-twentieth century, nightlife was once again the lifeblood of Havana. But while alcohol had been the draw of the 1920s, gambling, music, and dance were the primary attractions in the 1950s, and the island became a popular honeymoon destination. In every neighborhood, cabarets and bars featured local bands, dancers, and touring headliners that promoted the rapid-fire, modern musical rhythms of the era, most notably mambo and its more easily danceable cousin, the cha-cha-cha. Havana's top-tier clubs presented extravagant revues with stars such as Tony Bennett, Harry Belafonte, and Cab Calloway, and large casts of dancers and showgirls. With music provided by forty-piece swing bands alternating with Cuban conjuntos, these establishments operated off casino revenues.

The gambling venues were nearly universally owned or operated by American gangsters and catered to an upper echelon of Cuban society, who used them to celebrate weddings, anniversaries, and *quinceañeras*. Earlier, gambling on the island often had been wracked with corruption, including crooked gaming and a bait-and-switch game known as "razzle-dazzle."[18] Scams of this nature generated negative opinions among high rollers, and in 1952 the *Saturday Evening Post* published an article that excoriated rigged gaming

Fig. 6
Photograph, **Havana Riviera**,
c. 1958
Gelatin silver print

Ransola Ruggiero Collection, Miami Beach, Florida

in Cuba's nightclubs. Batista responded by placing the top-tier clubs under the oversight of an American gambler with a well-known, albeit underground, reputation for running clean gaming—his old friend Lansky. Advertisements for both Sans Souci's and Tropicana's casinos soon claimed affiliation with "Lefty" Clark, a low-level mobster linked to Lansky and narcotics trafficking. The casinos at both the Parisien and Montmartre, a swanky club that catered to American high rollers in the Vedado district, were openly under Lansky's and his brother Jake's control.[fig. 7] Tampa crime boss Trafficante ran operations at Sans Souci in conjunction with Norman Rothman, a South Florida gangster. The Hotel Capri even hired actor George Raft, who helped promote early Cuban tourism with his starring role in *Rumba* (1935) and later played mob roles in Hollywood movies, to greet guests.[fig. 8]

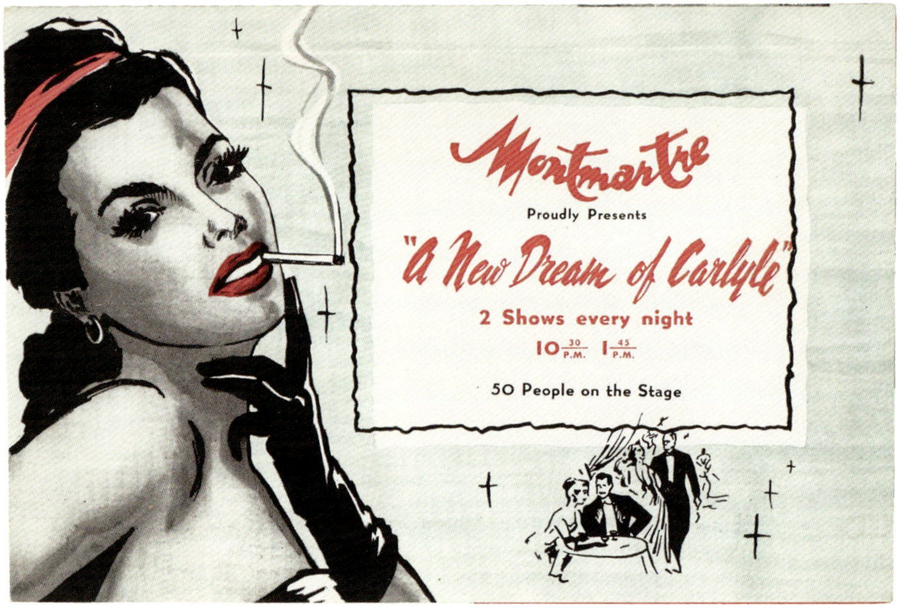

Founded in the late 1930s, Tropicana was the most famous nightclub of the era. Located in the gardens of a suburban mansion, it had a lush tropical setting. Martín Fox purchased the property in 1952 and added buildings designed by the American-educated Cuban architect Max Borges Recio that are considered masterpieces of thin-shell concrete construction; an indoor nightclub called Arcos de Cristal (Crystal Arches) was featured in the 1955 exhibition *Latin American Architecture since 1945* at the Museum of Modern Art, New York.[19] [fig. 9] It was complemented in 1953 by an outdoor performance space, Bajo las Estrellas (Under the Stars), where showgirls paraded on catwalks set among trees.[fig. 10] Though Tropicana was the only club both owned and operated by Cubans, Trafficante was a close friend of the owner, Fox, as was Lansky associate and Riviera casino manager Dino Cellini.[20]

Fig. 7
Brochure, ***Montmartre***,
c. 1953
Rodriguez Peña, Atalaya,
Cuba, printer

The Wolfsonian–FIU, The Vicki Gold Levi Collection, XC2016.01.1.789

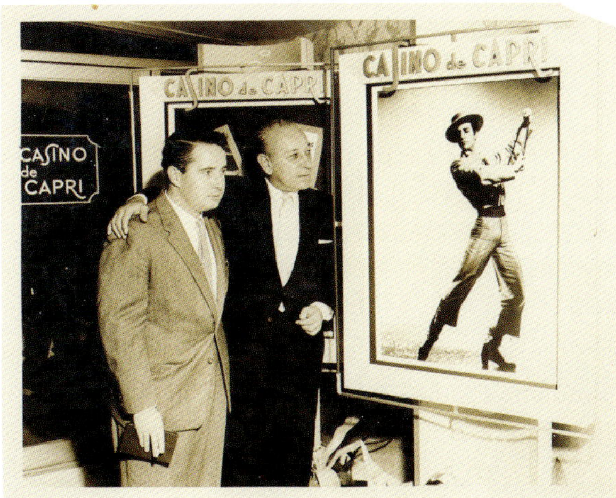

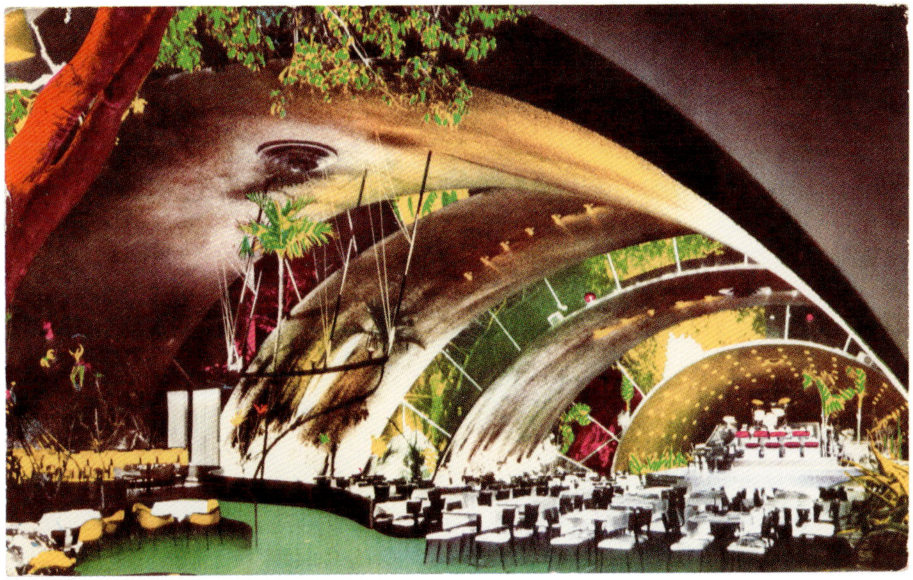

Fig. 8
Photograph, **Casino de Capri host George Raft** (right) **looks at poster image of himself in the 1934 film** ***Bolero***, c. 1958
Alberto Korda (Cuban, 1928–2001), photographer
Gelatin silver print

The Wolfsonian–FIU, The Vicki Gold Levi Collection, XC2016.01.1.132

Fig. 9
Postcard, ***Tropicana Night Club, Havana, Cuba, Showing Beautiful Crystal Arch***, 1954
Mario L. Guardiola, Havana, publisher
Curt Teich, Chicago, printer

The Wolfsonian–FIU, Gift of Francis Xavier Luca and Clara Helen Palacio Luca, XC2015.12.3.1

Fig. 10
Photograph, **View of outdoor seating at Tropicana's Bajo las Estrellas (Under the Stars) cabaret**, c. 1955
Vicente Muñiz (Cuban, 1917–2007), photographer
Gelatin silver print

The Wolfsonian–FIU, The Vicki Gold Levi Collection, XC2016.01.1.1351

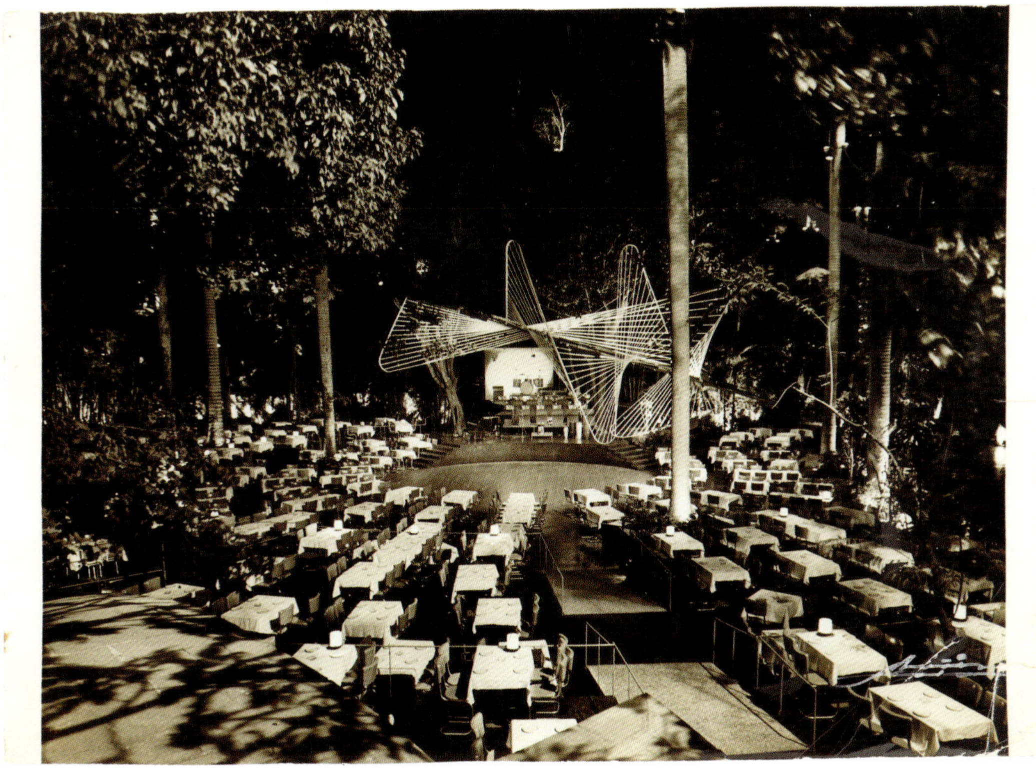

The club's early shows featured Josephine Baker and conga master Chano Pozo. Later performances presented celebrities Xavier Cugat, Carmen Miranda, Celia Cruz, and Nat King Cole. Soon everyone who went to Cuba went to Tropicana. Joan Crawford was photographed there with PepsiCo chairman Alfred Steele on their honeymoon, and Liberace, who held a dinner there for Cuba's press corps at a massive piano-shaped table, treated the crowd to an impromptu onstage mambo. Other notable stars photographed there included Marlon Brando, Steve Allen, Ava Gardner, and Frank Sinatra.[fig. 11]

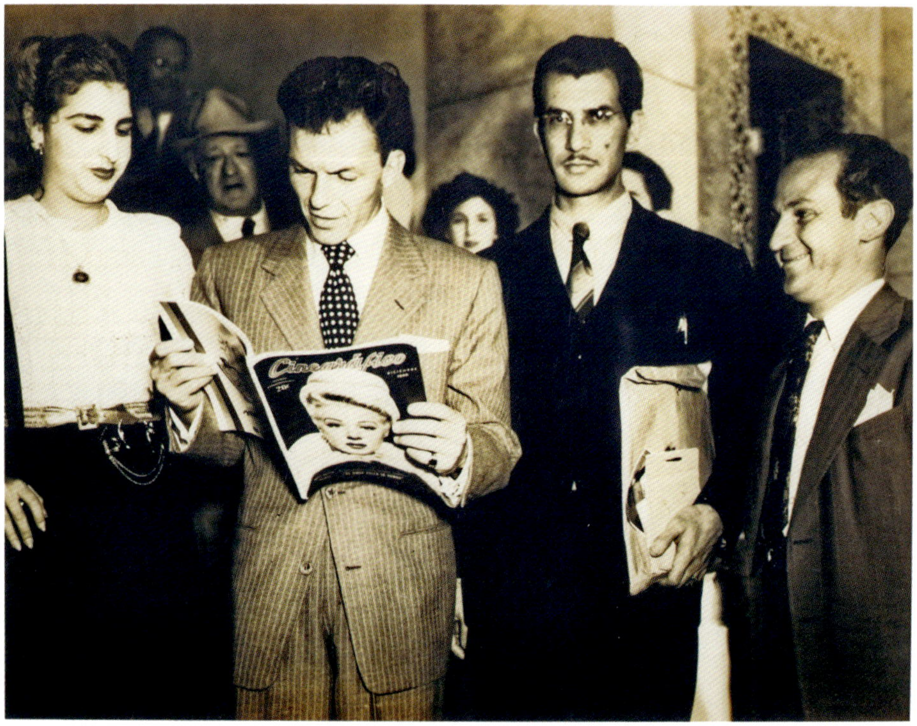

The true allure of Tropicana lay in the brilliance of its choreographer Roderico ("Rodney") Neyra. A past performer at Havana's notorious Shanghai burlesque theater, Rodney staged two original nightly revues at Tropicana every three months, with themes that ranged from Spanish zarzuelas to Mexican folklore and the Japanese tea ceremony. He was the first to stage reenactments of Santeria ceremonies for a tourist public, complete with authentic Yoruba religious *batá* drummers, and to include a nightly ballet performance in a cabaret revue. Rodney's lavish productions, with their elaborate sets, costumes of imported fabrics, and expensive makeup, were only possible thanks to proceeds from Fox's casino and his controlling interests in *la bolita* (a popular extralegal lottery).[21]

Fig. 11
Photograph, **Singer and actor Frank Sinatra**, c. 1946
Gelatin silver print

The Wolfsonian–FIU, The Vicki Gold Levi Collection, XC2016.01.1.223

Tropicana's house band was Armando Romeu's orchestra, an American-style big band that drew its inspiration from Stan Kenton and included musicians Bebo Valdés and Chico O'Farrill, who would go on to have extraordinary careers of their own. The greats of Cuban music played nightly—Olga Guillot, Rita Montaner, Bola de Nieve, Celeste Mendoza, Miguelito Valdés, Benny Moré, and Dizzy Gillespie's *conguero* collaborator, Pozo.

While the casino-cabarets attracted travelers, the era's most authentic modern dance and music were to be found in the dozens of smaller, after-hours nightclubs that dotted the city. Though primarily frequented by locals, these too began to see their share of tourists in the 1940s and '50s. Clubs like Johnny's Dream Club, the Ali Bar Club (where the great bolero singer Moré had a regular gig), and beachfront locales like the Pennsylvania, Panchín, and Rumba Palace often opened after the larger venues had closed.[fig. 12] Like Paris in the 1890s and Berlin in the 1920s, Havana in the midcentury became a popular destination for American honeymooners and hedonists, a "what happens here, stays here" city, with clubs, bars, and burlesque houses that catered to every taste, price range, and predilection. It was Las Vegas before Las Vegas was ever imagined.

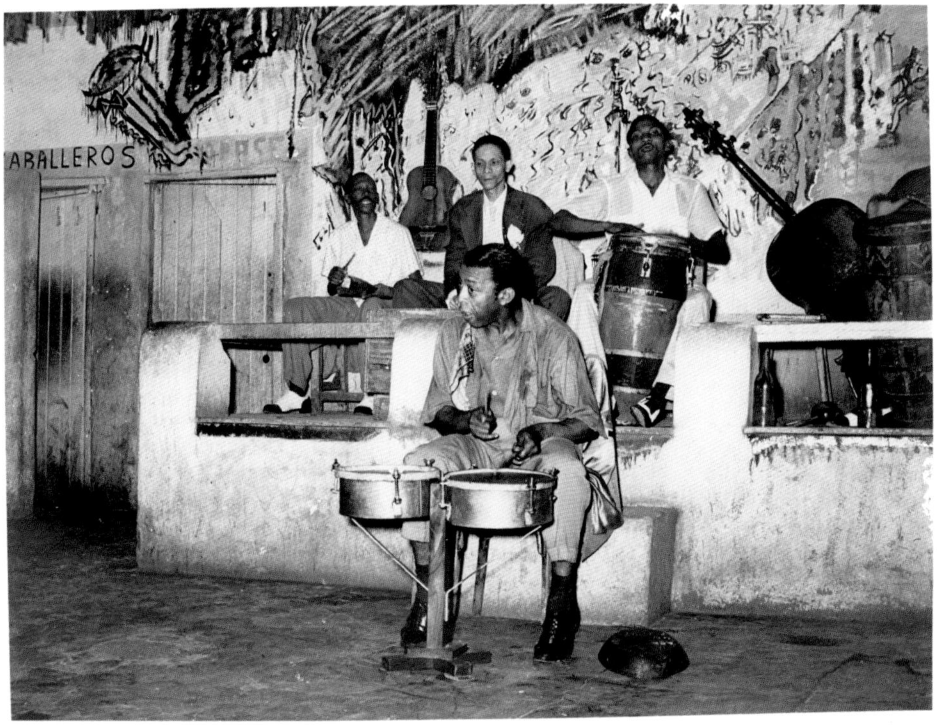

Fig. 12
Photograph, **Silvano Shueg Hechevarría** ("Chori") **playing drums at the Rumba Palace**, c. 1955
Inkjet print

The Wolfsonian–FIU, The Vicki Gold Levi Collection, XC2016.01.1.764.1

NOTES

1 Cuba's tourism promoters did not miss the opportunity to exploit Columbus's quotation. See for example the brochure, ***Cuba: The Loveliest Land that Human Eyes Have Ever Seen*** (Havana: Cuban National Tourist Commission, c. 1923). For Columbus's first reactions to sighting Cuba, see: Christopher Columbus, "Journal of the First Voyage of Columbus," in ***The Northmen, Columbus and Cabot, 985–1503: The Voyages of the Northmen; The Voyages of Columbus and of John Cabot***, ed. Julius E. Olson and Edward G. Bourne (New York: Charles Scribner's Sons, 1906), 131; online edition at americanjourneys.org/aj-062/.

2 Rosalie Schwartz, ***Pleasure Island: Tourism and Temptation in Cuba*** (Lincoln: University of Nebraska Press, 1999), xx–xxi; Christine Skwiot, ***The Purposes of Paradise: U.S. Tourism and Empire in Cuba and Hawai'i*** (Philadelphia: University of Pennsylvania Press, 2010), 77.

3 Dick Cluster and Rafael Hernández, ***The History of Havana*** (New York: Palgrave Macmillan, 2008), 135–36.

4 Ibid., 135.

5 Schwartz, ***Pleasure Island***, 30–31.

6 Basil Woon, ***When It's Cocktail Time in Cuba*** (New York: Horace Liveright, 1928), 37.

7 Ibid., 38.

8 Ibid., 38–39.

9 Ibid., 43–44.

10 Schwartz, ***Pleasure Island***, 44.

11 This nickname appears in personal communication from several Cuban Americans who formerly resided in nearby Vedado, including Rosa Lowinger's parents.

12 Allan Shulman, ***Building Bacardí: Architecture, Art & Identity*** (Coral Gables, Florida: Coral Gables Museum, 2012), 9–10.

13 T. Philip Perry, ***Terry's Guide to Cuba, Including the Isle of Pines, with a Chapter on the Airways and the Ocean Routes to the Island: A Handbook for Travelers***, rev. ed. (New York: Houghton Mifflin, 1929), 200.

14 Schwartz, ***Pleasure Island***, 68.

15 Eduardo Luis Rodríguez, ***The Havana Guide, Modern Architecture 1925–1965*** (New York: Princeton Architectural Press, 2000), vi.

16 Ibid.

17 Schwartz, ***Pleasure Island***, 152–54.

18 Lester Velie, "Suckers in Paradise: How Americans Lose Their Shirts in Caribbean Gambling Joints," ***Saturday Evening Post***, March 28, 1953, 181.

19 Henry-Russell Hitchcock, ***Latin American Architecture since 1945*** (New York: Museum of Modern Art, 1955), 108–9.

20 Rosa Lowinger and Ofelia Fox, ***Tropicana Nights: The Life and Times of the Legendary Cuban Nightclub*** (New York: In Situ, 2016), 28, 178.

21 Ibid., 42–49.

American Seduction

The Cuban Stamp on U.S. Popular Culture

Rosa Lowinger & Francis Xavier Luca

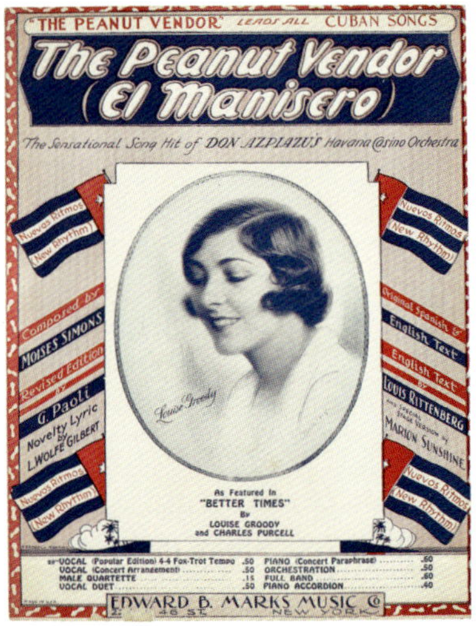

Fig. 1
Sheet music cover, ***The Peanut Vendor* (El Manisero)**, 1930
Marion Sunshine and L. Wolfe Gilbert, lyricists
Moisés Simons, composer
Lawrence Kempton, arranger
Edward B. Marks Music Co., New York, publisher

The Wolfsonian–FIU, The Vicki Gold Levi Collection, XC2016.01.1.987

Cuba and the United States were both shaped by the close cultural ties they established between 1919 and 1959. As Havana marketed itself as a sophisticated "Monte Carlo of the Western Hemisphere" to attract tourists, Cuban performers were creating rhythms and dances that swept through the United States and Europe and transformed popular music.

By the 1920s Havana resounded with septets, sextets, and smaller conjuntos that played in bars and open-air cafés, many in the vicinity of the Hotel Sevilla-Biltmore, which was frequented by American tourists. Among those who heard these groups was George Gershwin, who visited Cuba in 1932 and that year included four bars of composer Ignacio Piñeiro's hit song "Échale salsita" (c. 1930) in his fifth symphonic work, *Cuban Overture*.[1] Havana's orchestras and musical stars were also heard on Cuban radio stations that opened in 1922, only two years after Pittsburgh's KDKA became the first commercial radio station in the United States. As American musical scouts began arriving on the island, many of these artists were regularly playing on Broadway.

The American craze for Cuban music is often linked to the song "El manisero" (The Peanut Vendor), composed by Moisés Simons.[fig. 1] It debuted in the United States on April 26, 1930, when the house orchestra of Havana's Gran Casino Nacional de Marianao, led by Justo ("Don") Azpiazu, presented it at the Palace Theatre on Forty-Seventh Street and Broadway in New York. The song became an overnight hit. Azpiazu staged it again that year before a sold-out crowd at New York's RKO Coliseum, with the band in ruffled-sleeved Cuban shirts using cocktail shakers filled with lead shot as maracas and the silky-voiced lead singer Antonio Machín making his entrance pushing a peanut cart. Probably few Americans understood the salacious double entendre of the lyrics, which not-so-subtly urged women to taste the vendor's peanut cone; nonetheless, the first American recording, released by RCA Victor, sold over a million copies. Dozens of American musicians, including Louis Armstrong, Guy Lombardo, Stan Kenton, and Duke Ellington, recorded their own versions.

Though the rhythm of "El manisero" was a *son pregón* (a type of song based on the call and response of street vendors' cries), the music and the dance style that went along with it became known as "rhumba." Actual Cuban *rumba* (in Cuba there is no *h* in the word) entailed a series of fast Afro-Cuban rhythms danced to percussion. American-style rhumba was essentially a foxtrot set to Latin music.[2] Its most ardent promoter was Spanish-born Cuban bandleader Xavier Cugat, who in 1931 was hired to lead the house orchestra at New York's Waldorf Astoria. "[Rhumba] made those who usually only listened get up and dance," wrote Cugat in his 1948 autobiography *Rumba Is My Life*.[3] The dance style quickly became an American staple, taught by schools including Arthur Murray. At the 1933 Chicago World's Fair, the Cuban dance pair René and Estela (René Rivero Guillén and Ramona Ajón) helped popularize it with shows that integrated some of traditional Afro-Cuban rumba's more elaborate steps into the American version of the genre.

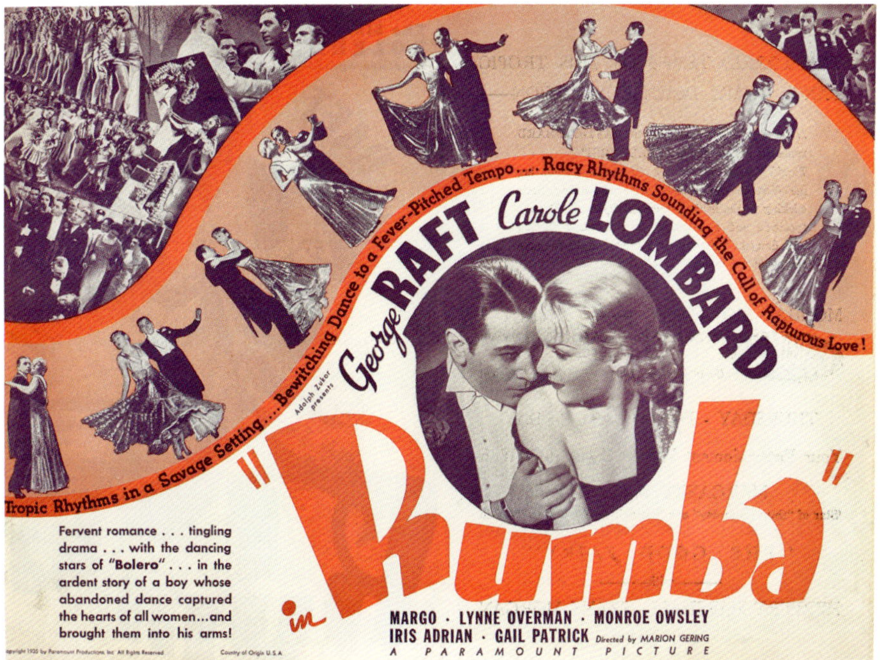

The rhumba craze soon extended to Hollywood, where dozens of movies set in Havana were produced for American audiences in the 1930s through '50s. Most of these films were light on plot and heavy on music and dance numbers. Many featured Cuban stars like Cugat and two of his discoveries—the vivacious performer Miguelito Valdés, who introduced the conga rhythm to the American stage, and a "young, mild-mannered handsome Cuban vocalist from Santiago [de Cuba] named Desi Arnaz."[4]

One of the earliest Cuban-themed films was director W. S. Van Dyke's *The Cuban Love Song* (1931). The story follows an aristocrat serving in the U.S. Marine Corps (Lawrence Tibbett) who falls in love and fathers an illegitimate child with a Cuban street vendor played by Lupe Vélez. In one scene, Vélez provides her paramour—and the American audience—with a fictionalized origin of "The Peanut Vendor," telling him it began as a lullaby whose lyrics she adapted to help sell her peanuts; her crooning costar turns the song into a duet.

Marion Gering's *Rumba* (1935) tells the story of a love affair between a wealthy American tourist (Carole Lombard) and a poor but ambitious dancer, played by George Raft, who aspires to open a nightclub of his own. Snubbed by the socialite, he plans to seduce and abandon her in revenge—that is, until the couple's romantic impulses take over. [fig. 2] In a life-imitating-art moment, Raft would later become the greeter at the Hotel Capri's casino in Havana.

Fig. 2
Leaflet, ***Rumba***, 1935
Paramount Productions, Inc., Hollywood, publisher

The Wolfsonian–FIU, The Vicki Gold Levi Collection, XC2016.01.1.726

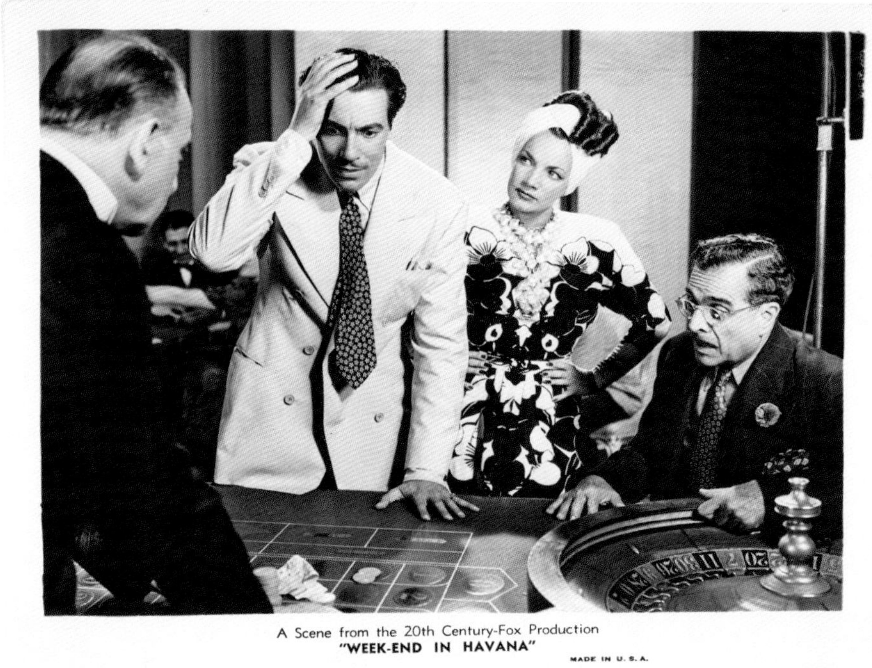

At the nadir of the Great Depression and in the same year that Prohibition was repealed, 1933, Hollywood released Ray Enright's *Havana Widows*—a ribald comedy with plenty of sexual innuendo and themes that would not have passed the censors once the Hays Code was enforced. In the film, Joan Blondell and Glenda Farrell portrayed New York chorus girls who travel to Cuba to find and fleece a millionaire, having been informed that the place is swarming with them. Once on the island, the gold diggers meet up with a shady lawyer (who is inebriated or passed-out drunk throughout the movie), but their plans go awry when one of them falls in love with their target's son.

Walter Lang's romantic comedy *Week-End in Havana* (1941) featured Alice Faye, John Payne, Brazilian singer Carmen Miranda, and Cuban American actor Cesar Romero in a thinly disguised advertisement for travel to Cuba aimed at Americans of modest means. The story centers on an uptight cruise line executive who must entertain a department store sales girl whose vacation plans are disrupted when his company's vessel runs aground. Flying her to Cuba on a Pan Am "clipper ship," the executive puts her up in a first-class hotel and hires a Cuban gambler and gigolo to entertain her, much to the consternation of the singer portrayed by Carmen Miranda.[fig. 3] All ends well once the executive and salesclerk realize their love for each other. Released on October 17, the film was unfortunate in its timing, as the Japanese attack on Pearl Harbor less than two months later forced Americans to shelve their vacation plans until the postwar period.

Fig. 3
Film still, ***Week-End in Havana***, c. 1941
Gelatin silver print

The Wolfsonian–FIU, The Vicki Gold Levi Collection, XC2016.01.1.29

While Hollywood depicted a frothy version of Cuba, the island's artists were busy creating new sounds that would once again redefine world music. In 1942 New York–based Cuban composer and bandleader Mario Bauzá wrote "Tanga," the first song to fuse jazz with the Cuban clave rhythm. Bauzá later introduced *conguero* Chano Pozo to jazz icon Dizzy Gillespie, and the latter two penned "Manteca" (1947), which would become a standard in the nascent genre known as Afro-Cuban or Latin jazz.[5] From 1946 into the '60s, Bauzá and his brother-in-law Frank ("Machito") Grillo's band, Machito and His Afro-Cubans, was the house orchestra at New York's Palladium club, where they helped popularize mambo.[fig. 4] A music and dance style with rapid-fire syncopation and jazz-fueled improvisation, mambo was created separately in the mid-1940s by two Cuban composers, Arsenio Rodríguez and Israel ("Cachao") López, and was spread internationally by bandleader Dámaso Pérez Prado.

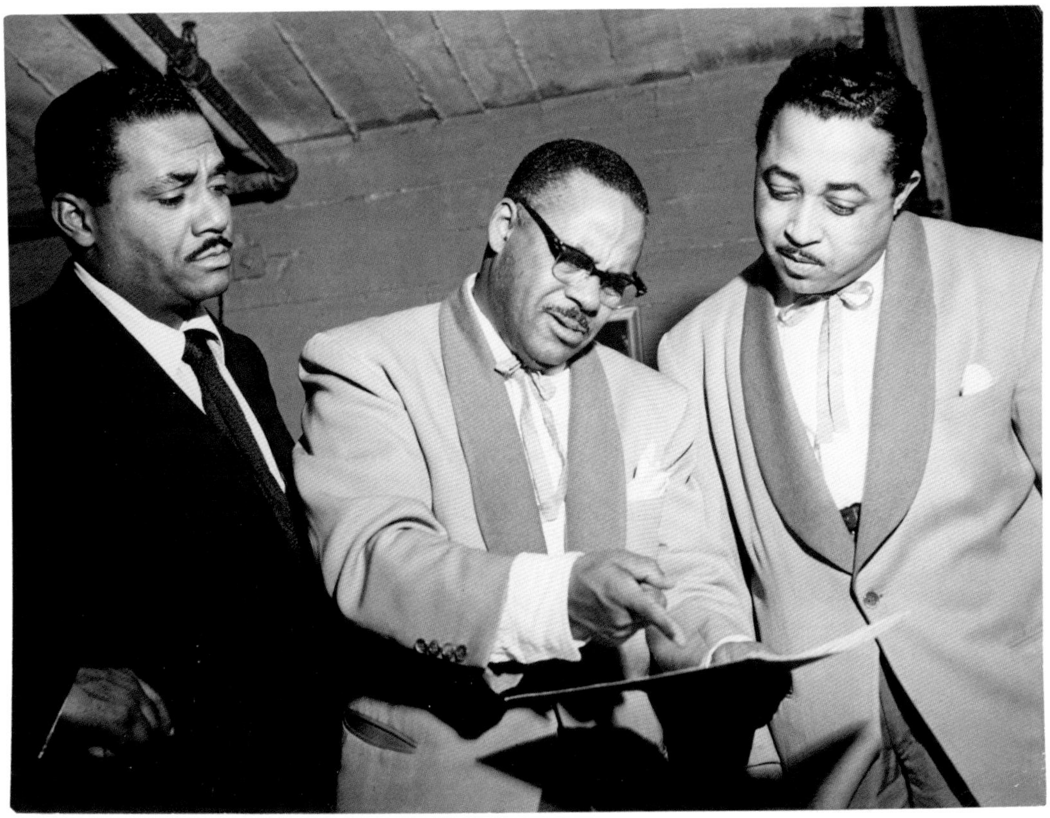

Fig. 4
Photograph, **Machito, Mario Bauzá, and René Hernández** (left to right), 1937
Gelatin silver print

The Wolfsonian–FIU, The Vicki Gold Levi Collection, XC2016.01.1.256

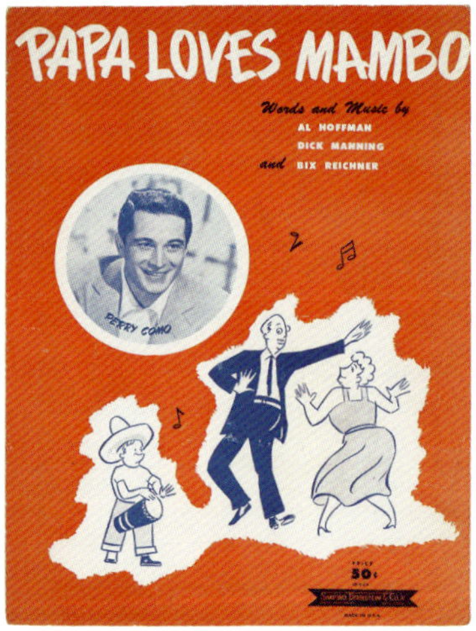

Fig. 5
Sheet music cover, ***Papa Loves Mambo***, 1954
Al Hoffman, Dick Manning, and Bix Reichner, composers and lyricists
Shapiro, Bernstein & Co., New York, publisher

The Wolfsonian–FIU, The Vicki Gold Levi Collection, XC2016.01.1.1230

By the early 1950s American dance charts were filled with mambo songs, including Perry Como's "Papa Loves Mambo" and Rosemary Clooney's "Mambo Italiano" (both 1954).[fig. 5] Vaughn Monroe's "They Were Doin' the Mambo" was reported to be RCA Victor's bestselling record in 1954, the same year that *Newsweek*, *Time*, and the *New York Times Magazine* published articles on "mambomania."[6] Novices flocked to dance academies to learn the style, and dozens of books decoded its impossibly complex moves. In 1953 composer Enrique Jorrín and his Orquesta América introduced a simplified rhythm that was more strongly marked and less syncopated. The tune came to be known as cha-cha-cha after the shuffling sound made by the dancers' feet.[7] The popularity of rhumba, Afro-Cuban jazz, mambo, and cha-cha-cha inspired Cuban-themed nightclubs across the United States.

Postwar Hollywood spotlighted these old and new Cuban rhythms in musicals such as Richard Whorf's *Luxury Liner* (1948), starring the Xavier Cugat Orchestra and American actress Jane Powell, who performed "The Peanut Vendor" with operatic trills. Promoting Franklin D. Roosevelt's Good Neighbor Policy south of the border, John H. Auer's *Pan-Americana* (1945) featured Cugat's protégé Miguelito Valdés and popularized the Afro-Cuban homage to the Santeria deity Babalú Ayé through a song written by Margarita Lecuona—"a not-very-close relation" of the famous Cuban composer, Ernesto Lecuona.[8] In the 1950s the same tune became the signature of Ricky Ricardo, the fictional bandleader played by Desi Arnaz in the successful American television series *I Love Lucy* (1951–57). Arnaz's first film appearance was in *Holiday in Havana* (1949).[fig. 6] Capitalizing on the popularity of the 1950 Broadway musical *Guys and Dolls*—itself used to promote travel to Cuba—MGM produced and Joseph L. Mankiewicz directed a film version, which was released in 1955 and starred Marlon Brando, Jean Simmons, Frank Sinatra, and Vivian Blain. In it, Brando plays a high-rolling gambler who bets he can convince an uptight missionary to dine with him in Havana, the "sin capital of the hemisphere." The tropical atmosphere, drinking, and dancing inevitably loosen her inhibitions, transforming the pair into lovers.[figs. 7, 8] The director of *Rock Around the Clock*, Fred F. Sears, released the film *Cha-Cha-Cha Boom!* (1956), in which an American talent scout brings Pérez Prado to New York, where he introduces mambo to the dance-club scene. The gritty film noir *Affair in Havana* (1957), directed by Laslo Benedek, is remembered mostly today for a scene in which young Cuban singer Celia Cruz made her Hollywood debut.

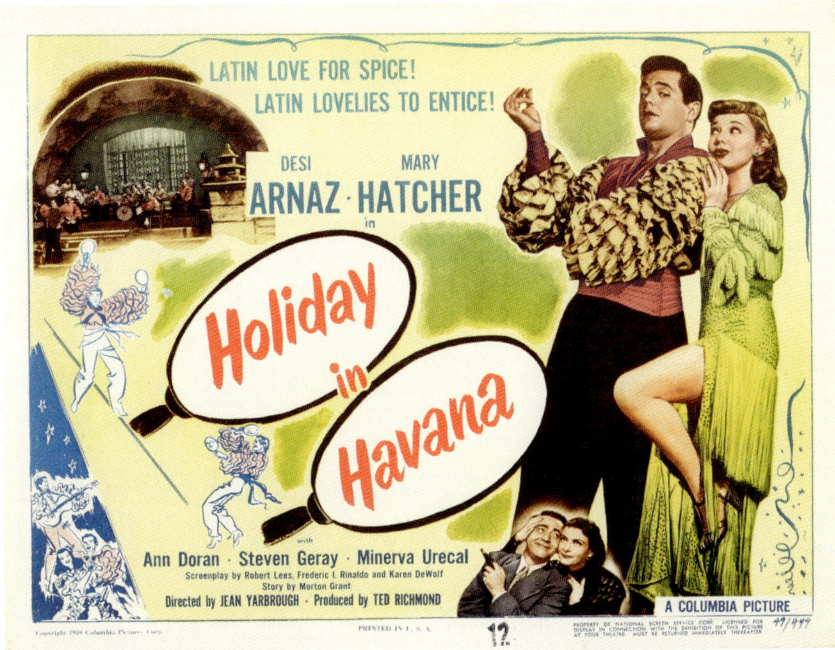

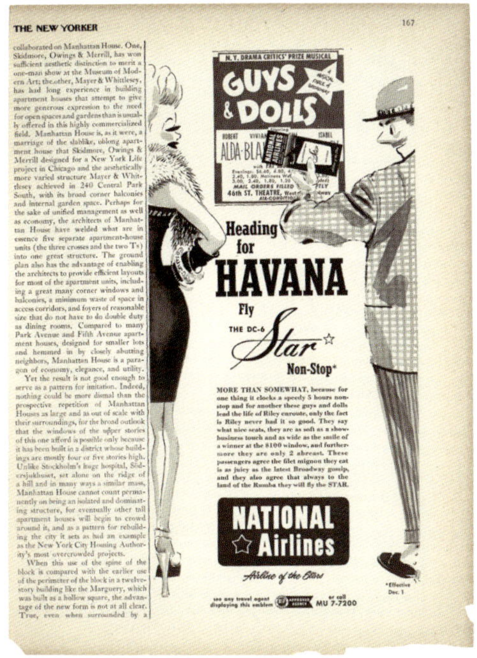

THE NEW YORKER

167

collaborated on Manhattan House. One, Skidmore, Owings & Merrill, has won sufficient aesthetic distinction to merit a one-man show at the Museum of Modern Art; the other, Mayer & Whittlesey, has had long experience in building apartment houses that attempt to give more generous expression to the need for open spaces and gardens than is usually offered in this highly commercialized field. Manhattan House is, as it were, a marriage of the slablike, oblong apartment house that Skidmore, Owings & Merrill designed for a New York Life project in Chicago and the aesthetically more varied structure Mayer & Whittlesey achieved in 240 Central Park South, with its broad corner balconies and internal garden space. Perhaps for the sake of unified management as well as economy, the architects of Manhattan House have welded what are in essence five separate apartment-house units (the three crosses and the two T's) into one great structure. The ground plan also has the advantage of enabling the architects to provide efficient layouts for most of the apartment units, including a great many corner windows and balconies, a minimum waste of space in access corridors, and foyers of reasonable size that do not have to do double duty as dining rooms. Compared to many Park Avenue and Fifth Avenue apartment houses, designed for smaller lots and hemmed in by closely abutting neighbors, Manhattan House is a paragon of economy, elegance, and utility.

Yet the result is not good enough to serve as a pattern for imitation. Indeed, nothing could be more dismal than the prospective repetition of Manhattan Houses as large and as out of scale with their surroundings, for the broad outlook that the windows of the upper stories of this one afford is possible only because it has been built in a district whose buildings are mostly four or five stories high. Unlike Stockholm's huge hospital, Södersjukhuset, set alone on the ridge of a hill and in many ways a similar mass, Manhattan House cannot count permanently on being an isolated and dominating structure, for eventually other tall apartment houses will begin to crowd around it, and as a pattern for rebuilding the city it sets as bad an example as the New York City Housing Authority's most overcrowded projects.

When this use of the spine of the block is compared with the earlier use of the perimeter of the block in a twelve-story building like the Marguery, which was built as a hollow square, the advantage of the new form is not at all clear. True, even when surrounded by a

Fig. 6
Lobby card, ***Holiday in Havana***, 1949
Columbia Pictures Corporation, Los Angeles, publisher

The Wolfsonian–FIU, Gift of Francis Xavier Luca and Clara Helena Palacio Luca, XC2016.02.3.2

Fig. 7
Advertisement, ***Heading for Havana: Fly the DC-6 Star NonStop***, from *The New Yorker*, November 17, 1951
National Airlines, Miami, publisher

The Wolfsonian–FIU, The Vicki Gold Levi Collection, XC2016.01.1.899

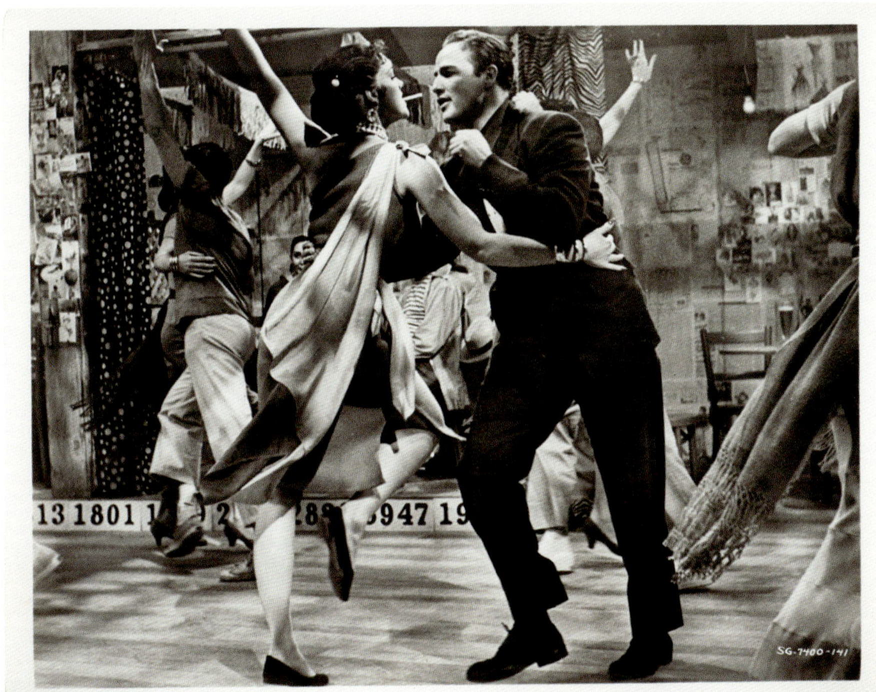

Fig. 8
Film still, ***Guys and Dolls***, 1955
Gelatin silver print

The Wolfsonian–FIU, The Vicki Gold Levi Collection, XC2016.01.1.900

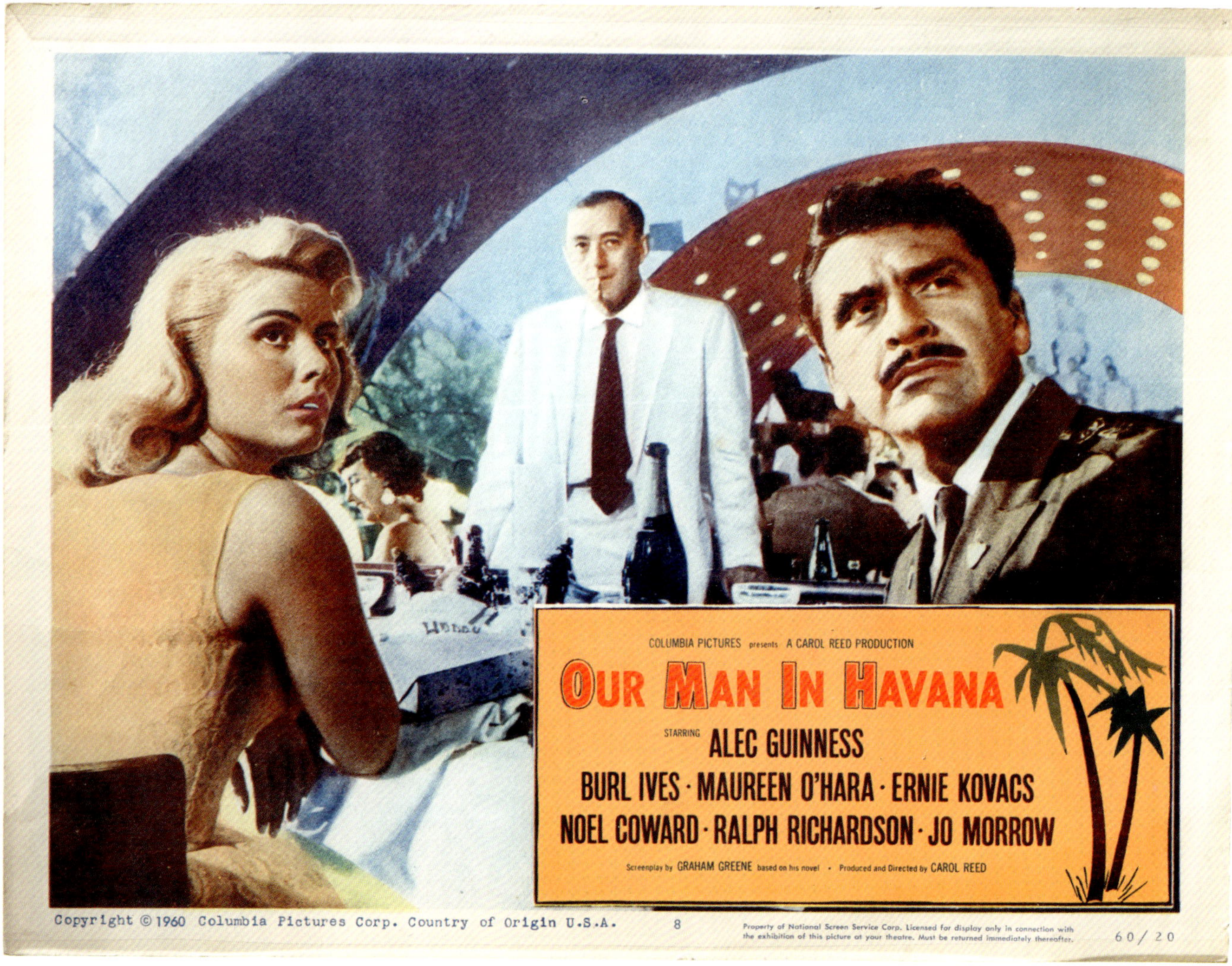

Fig. 9
Lobby card, ***Our Man in Havana***, 1960
Columbia Pictures Corporation, Los Angeles, publisher

The Wolfsonian–FIU, Gift of Francis Xavier Luca and Clara Helena Palacio Luca, XC2016.04.5

As the 1950s came to a close and Cuban revolutionaries threatened the Batista regime's hold over the country, Hollywood continued to produce films set in America's favorite vacation spot. More plot-driven than their musical forebears, these pictures focused on the country's reputation as a kleptocracy. Joseph Pevney's *The Big Boodle* (1957) featured Errol Flynn as a Havana casino croupier falsely accused of counterfeiting. Determined to clear his name, he exposes the true criminals: corrupt bankers with connections to important government officials. *Our Man in Havana* (1959), by Carol Reed, one of the last films set in Cuba before Batista's overthrow, is a British Cold War comedy thriller in which a vacuum cleaner salesman is recruited as a spy, yielding tragic yet humorous results. One scene was shot on location in Tropicana cabaret's famous Arcos de Cristal—a fitting end for films encouraging tourism to the island.[fig. 9]

By 1959, when the revolution led by Fidel Castro abruptly ended U.S. diplomatic ties and tourism, Cuba had already transformed the American music and dance scene and integrated into Hollywood cinema. Expatriates had flocked to the United States even before the nineteenth-century Cuban independence wars and founded immigrant communities, which were subsequently replenished and enlarged by exiled groups fleeing Gerardo Machado's dictatorship in the 1920s and '30s and the Castro regime from the '60s forward. Rumba, Afro-Cuban jazz, conga, mambo, and cha-cha-cha had made an indelible stamp on American culture, and Cuban performers such as Celia Cruz remained immensely popular. Successive waves of salsa, timba, and Cubatón music steadily have added to the American musical mosaic. The Buena Vista Social Club ensemble has helped revive U.S. interest in Cuba's earlier music traditions, and a spate of new films and television shows have focused on Havana then and now—including *Dirty Dancing: Havana Nights* (2004), *The Lost City* (2005), *Chico and Rita* (2010), *Una noche* (2012), *Papa: Hemingway in Cuba* (2015), and the Netflix series *Cuatro estaciones en La Habana* (2016). Despite the more than fifty years of hostility and strained relations that followed the Cuban revolution, Cuban culture has continued to impact the United States.

NOTES

1 Howard Pollock, ***George Gershwin: His Life and Work*** (Berkeley: University of California Press, 2007), 536–38.

2 Xavier Cugat, ***Rumba Is My Life: American Autobiography*** (n.p.: Reprint Services, 1949), 161.

3 Ibid., 101.

4 Ibid., 118.

5 Both *tanga* and *manteca* are old-fashioned Cuban slang words for marijuana.

6 See, for example, "Mambomania," ***Newsweek***, August 16, 1954, 54.

7 Helio Orovio, ***Cuban Music from A to Z*** (Durham, NC: Duke University Press, 2004), 50.

8 Gustavo Pérez Firmat, "Latunes: An Introduction," ***Latin American Research Review*** 43, no. 2 (2008): 192–3; Ned Sublette, ***Cuba and Its Music: From the First Drums to the Mambo*** (Chicago: Chicago Review Press, 2004), 447, 467–68.

Plates

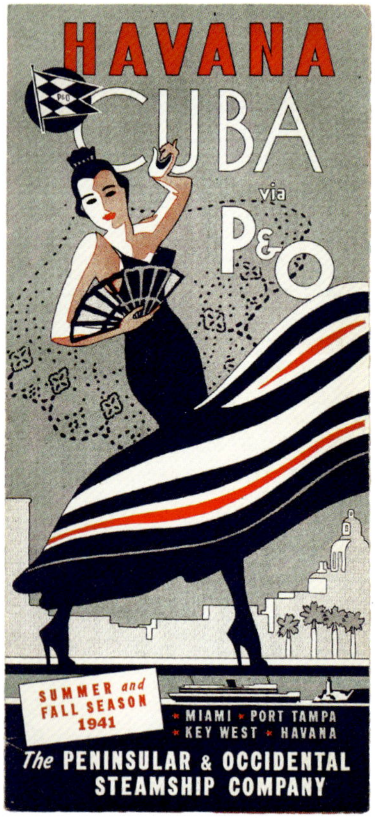

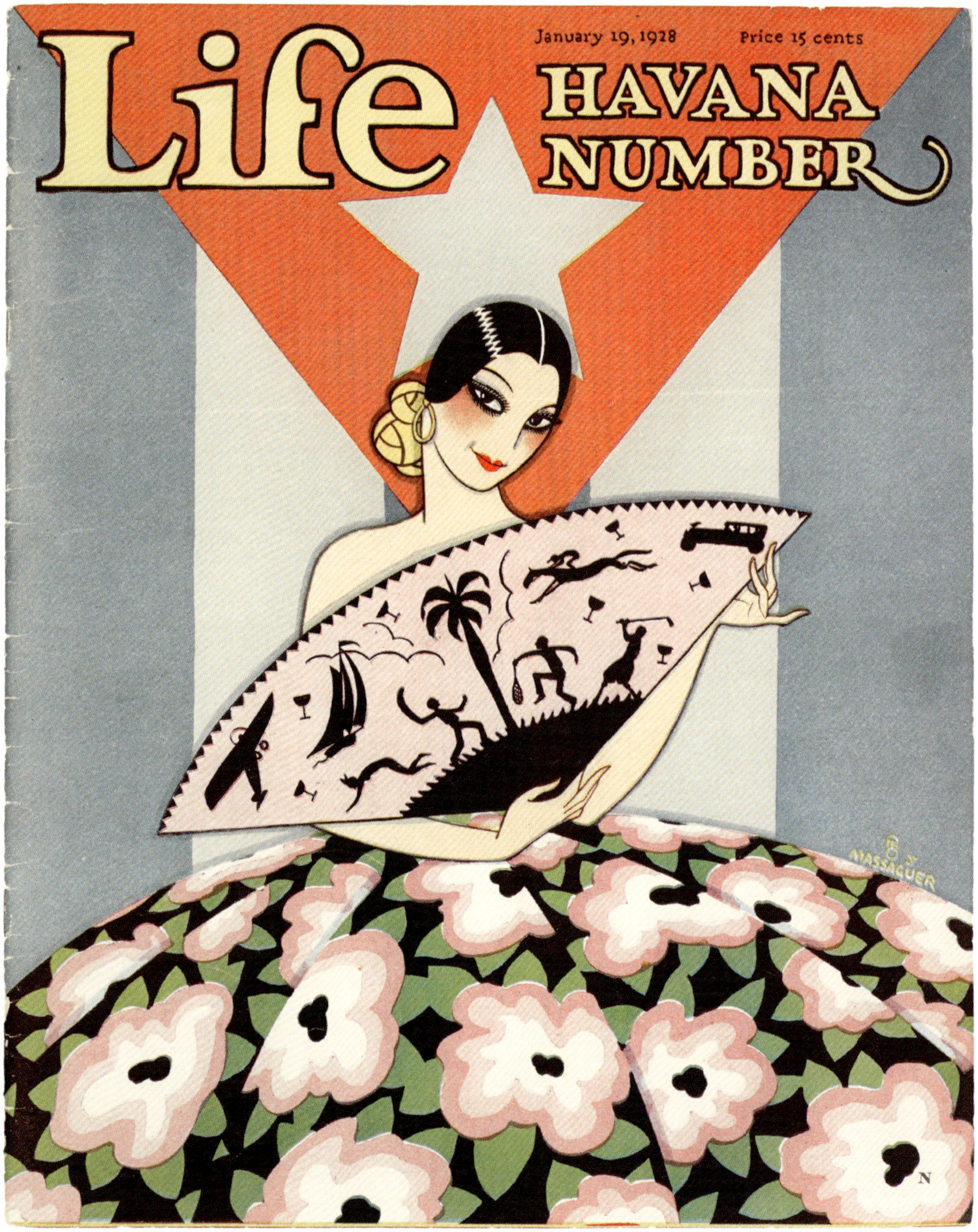

Brochure, *Havana, Cuba via P&O*, c. 1940
Peninsular & Occidental Steamship Company, Miami, publisher

The Wolfsonian–FIU, The Vicki Gold Levi Collection, XC2016.01.1.1344

Periodical, ***Life***, January 19, 1928
Conrado Walter Massaguer (Cuban, 1889–1965), cover illustrator
Life Publishing Co., New York, publisher

The Wolfsonian–FIU, The Vicki Gold Levi Collection, XC2002.11.4.384

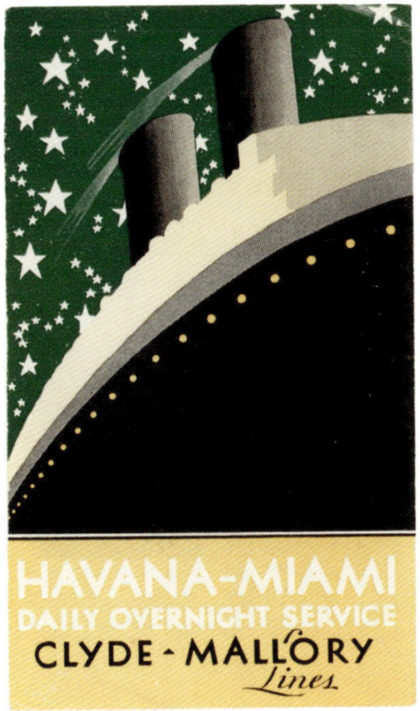

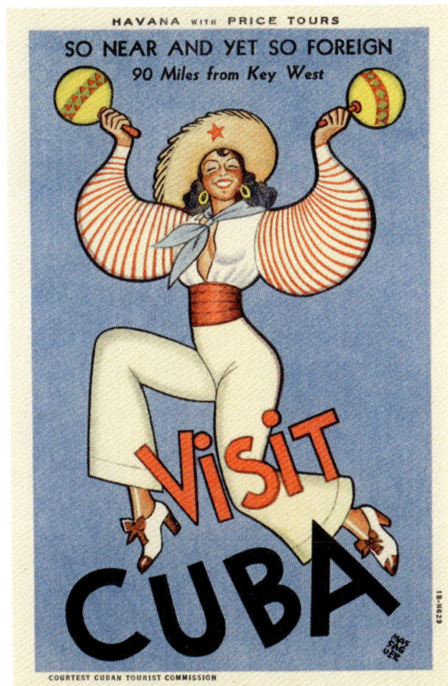

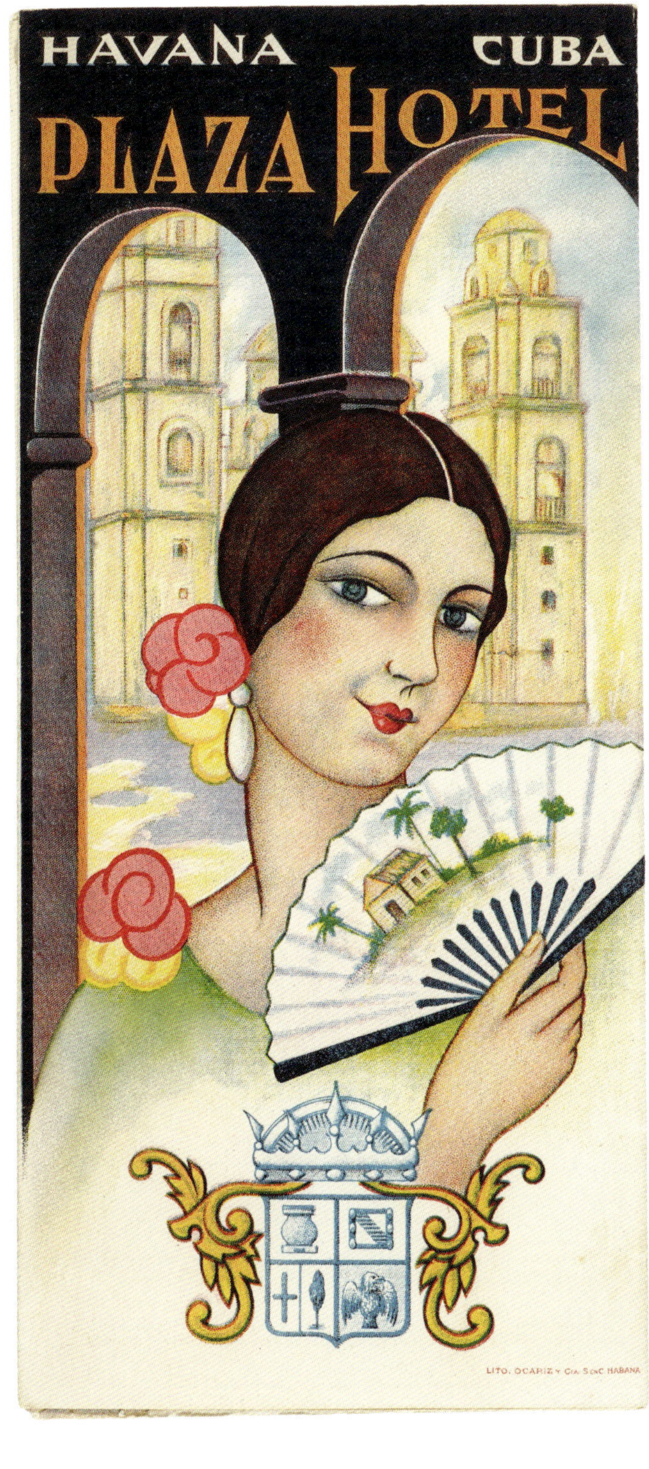

Advertisement, ***Havana-Miami, Daily Overnight Service***, 1929
Clyde-Mallory Lines, New York, publisher

The Wolfsonian–FIU, The Mitchell Wolfson, Jr. Collection, XB1991.523

Postcard, ***Visit Cuba***, c. 1935
Conrado Walter Massaguer (Cuban, 1889–1965), illustrator
Cuban Tourist Commission, Havana, publisher

The Wolfsonian–FIU, The Vicki Gold Levi Collection, XC2002.11.4.17

Brochure, ***Plaza Hotel, Havana, Cuba***, c. 1930
Ocariz Cia., Havana, printer

The Wolfsonian–FIU, The Vicki Gold Levi Collection, XC2016.01.1.1047

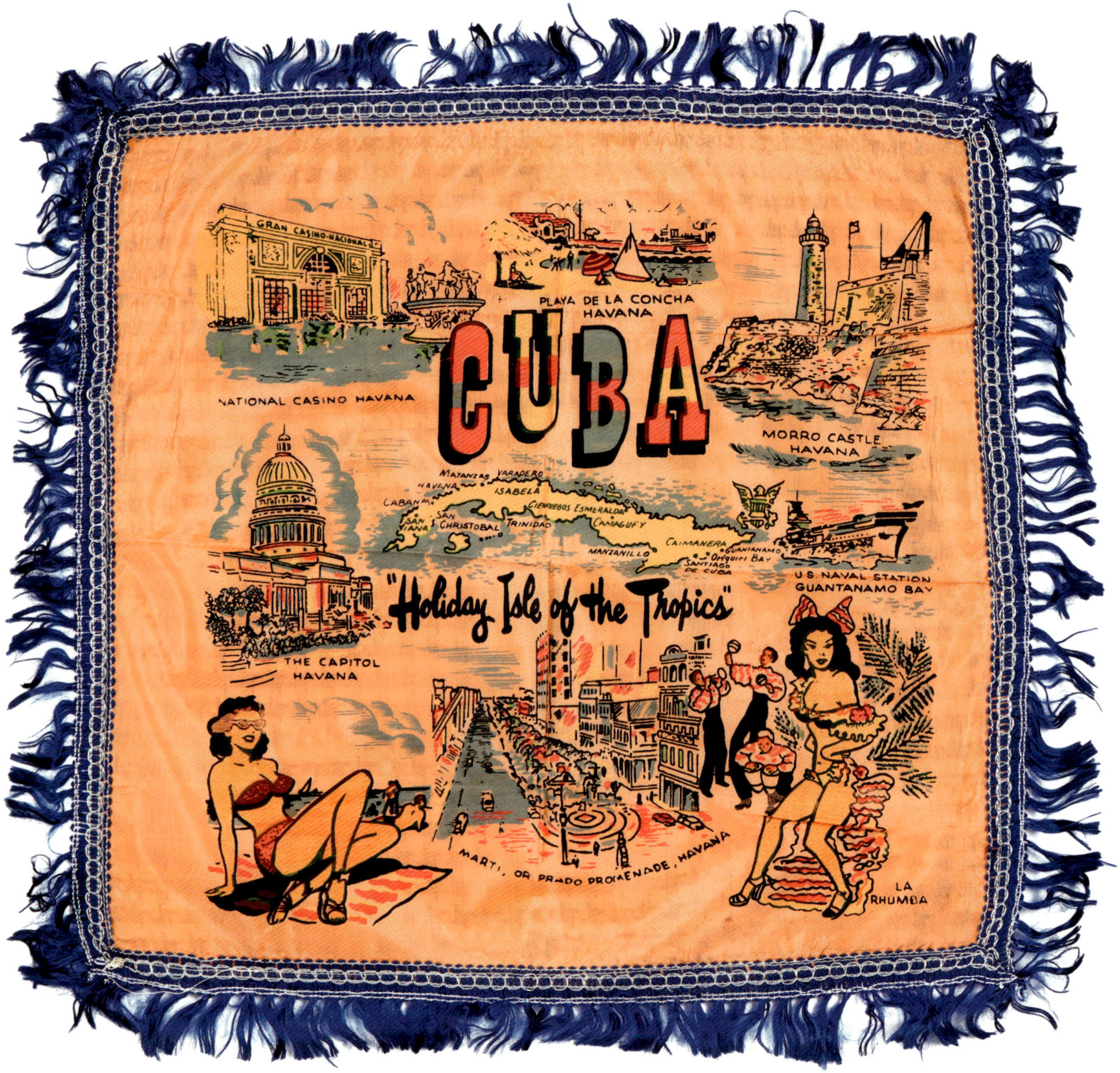

Pillowcase, ***Cuba: "Holiday Isle of the Tropics,"*** c. 1950

The Wolfsonian–FIU, Gift of Leonard Finger, XC2016.12.9.1

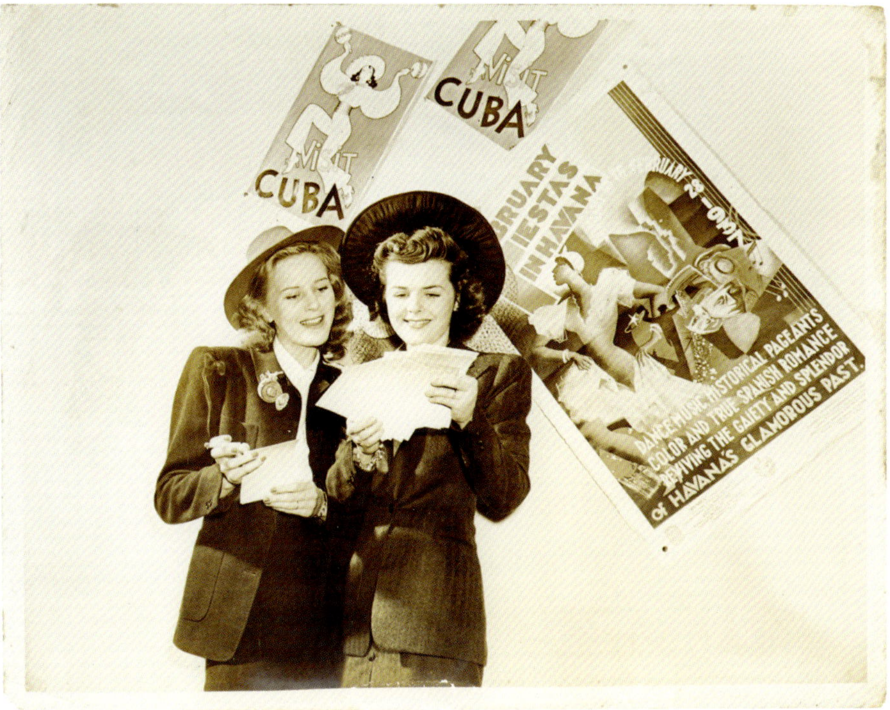

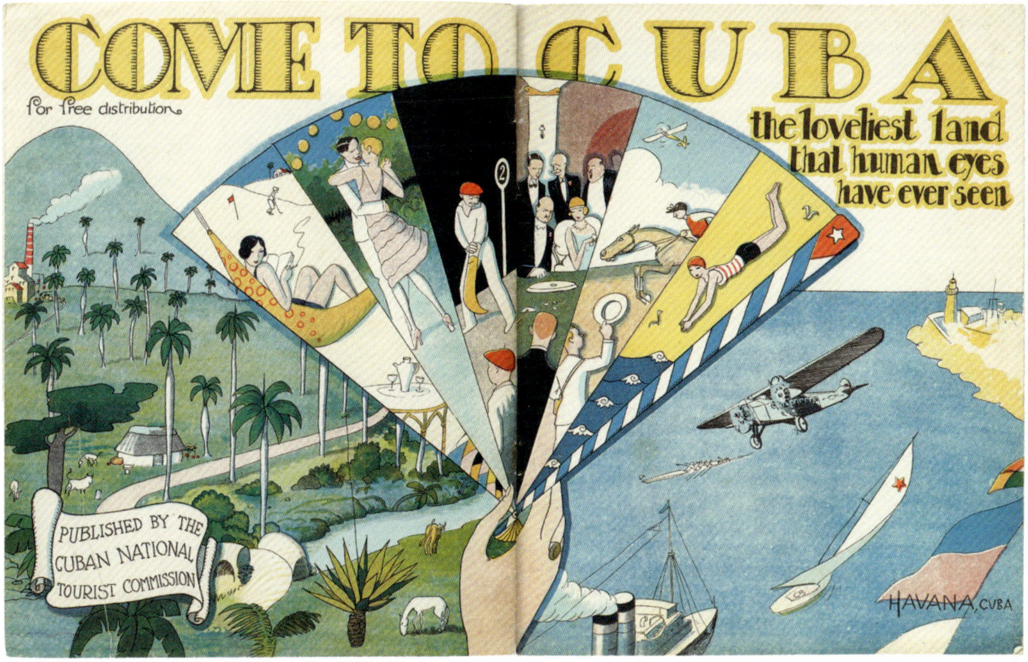

Photograph, **Two women in front of Visit Cuba posters**, c. 1935
Schuyler Crail, photographer
Gelatin silver print

The Wolfsonian–FIU, The Vicki Gold Levi Collection, XC2016.01.1.17

Brochure, ***Come to Cuba: The Loveliest Land that Human Eyes Have Ever Seen***, c. 1930
Conrado Walter Massaguer (Cuban, 1889–1965), cover illustrator

The Wolfsonian–FIU, The Vicki Gold Levi Collection, XC2016.01.1.1232

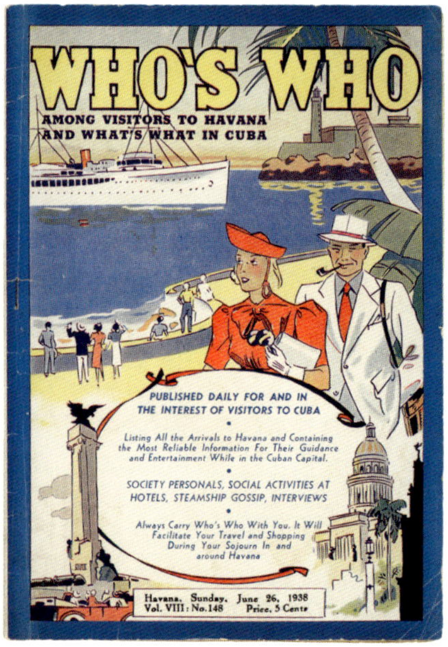

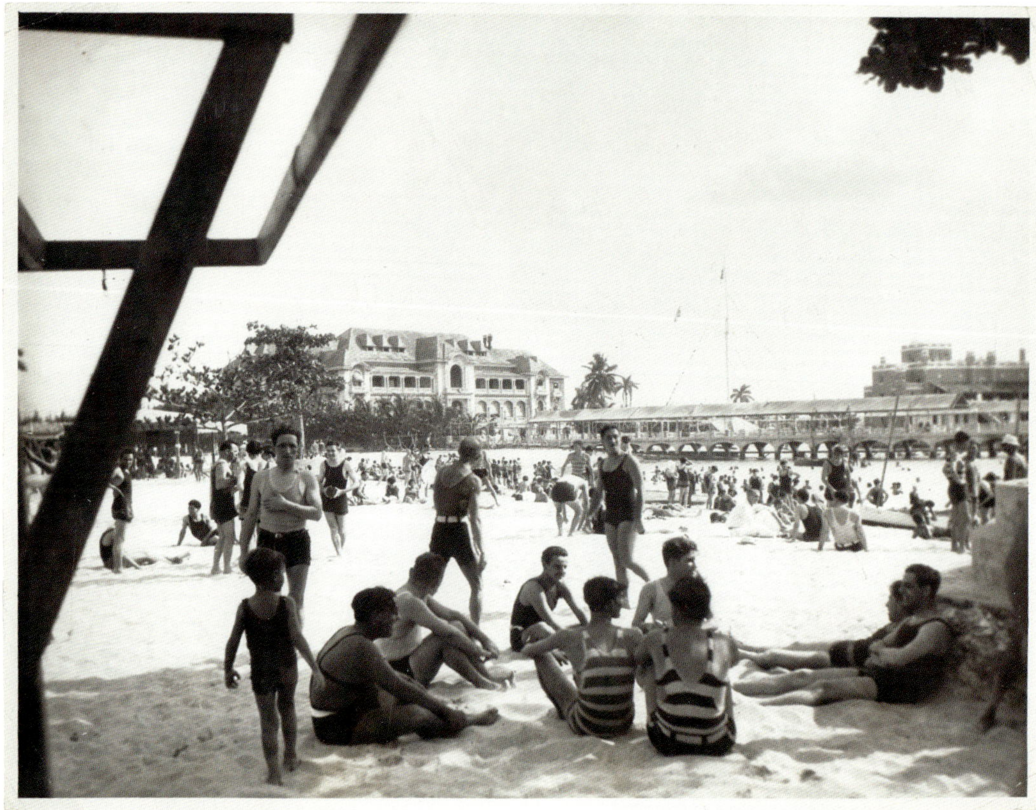

Periodical, ***Who's Who among Visitors to Havana and What's What in Cuba***, June 26, 1938
M. M. Stone, Havana, publisher

The Wolfsonian–FIU, The Vicki Gold Levi Collection, XC2002.11.4.399

Photograph, **Havana beach**, c. 1933
Gelatin silver print

The Wolfsonian–FIU, The Vicki Gold Levi Collection, XC2016.01.1.464

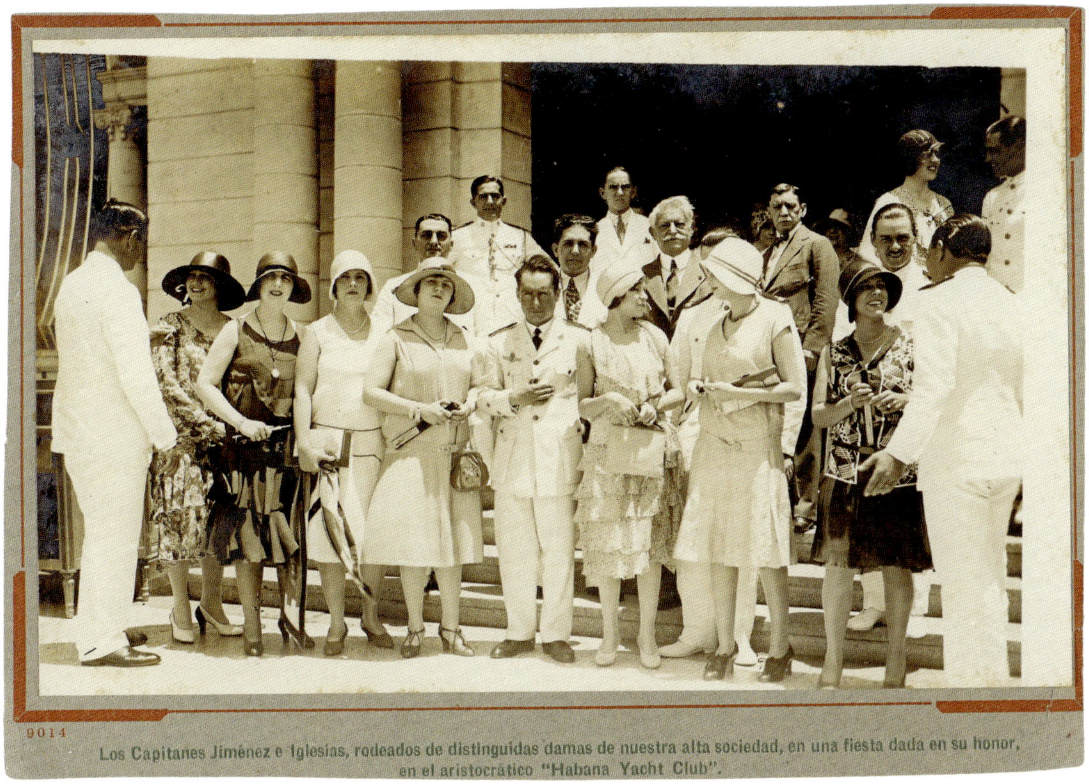

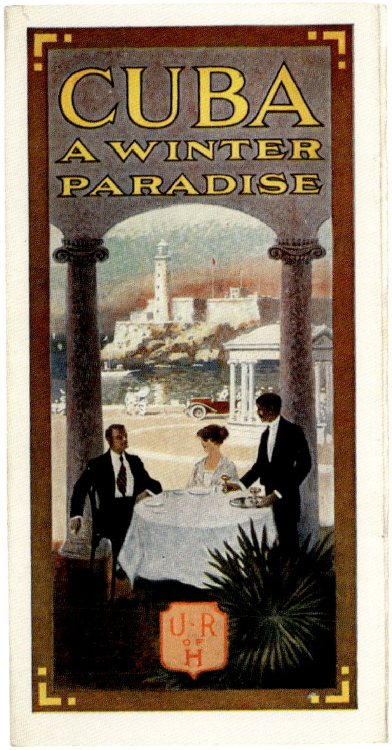

Photograph, **American socialites at the Havana Yacht Club**, c. 1926
Gelatin silver print

The Wolfsonian–FIU, The Vicki Gold Levi Collection, XC2016.01.1.77

Brochure, ***Cuba: A Winter Paradise***, c. 1916
United Railways of Havana, publisher

The Wolfsonian–FIU, The Vicki Gold Levi Collection, XC2016.01.1.1030

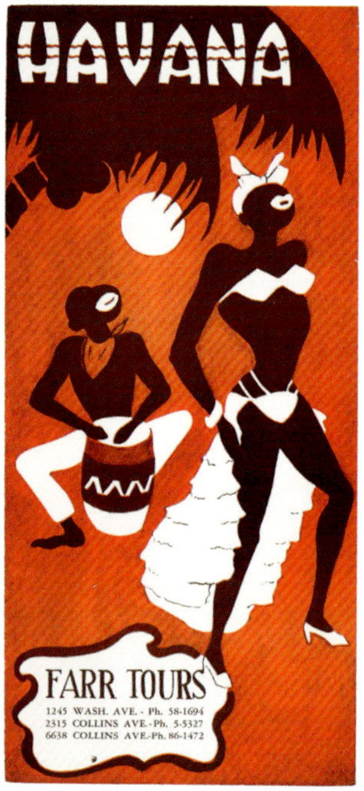

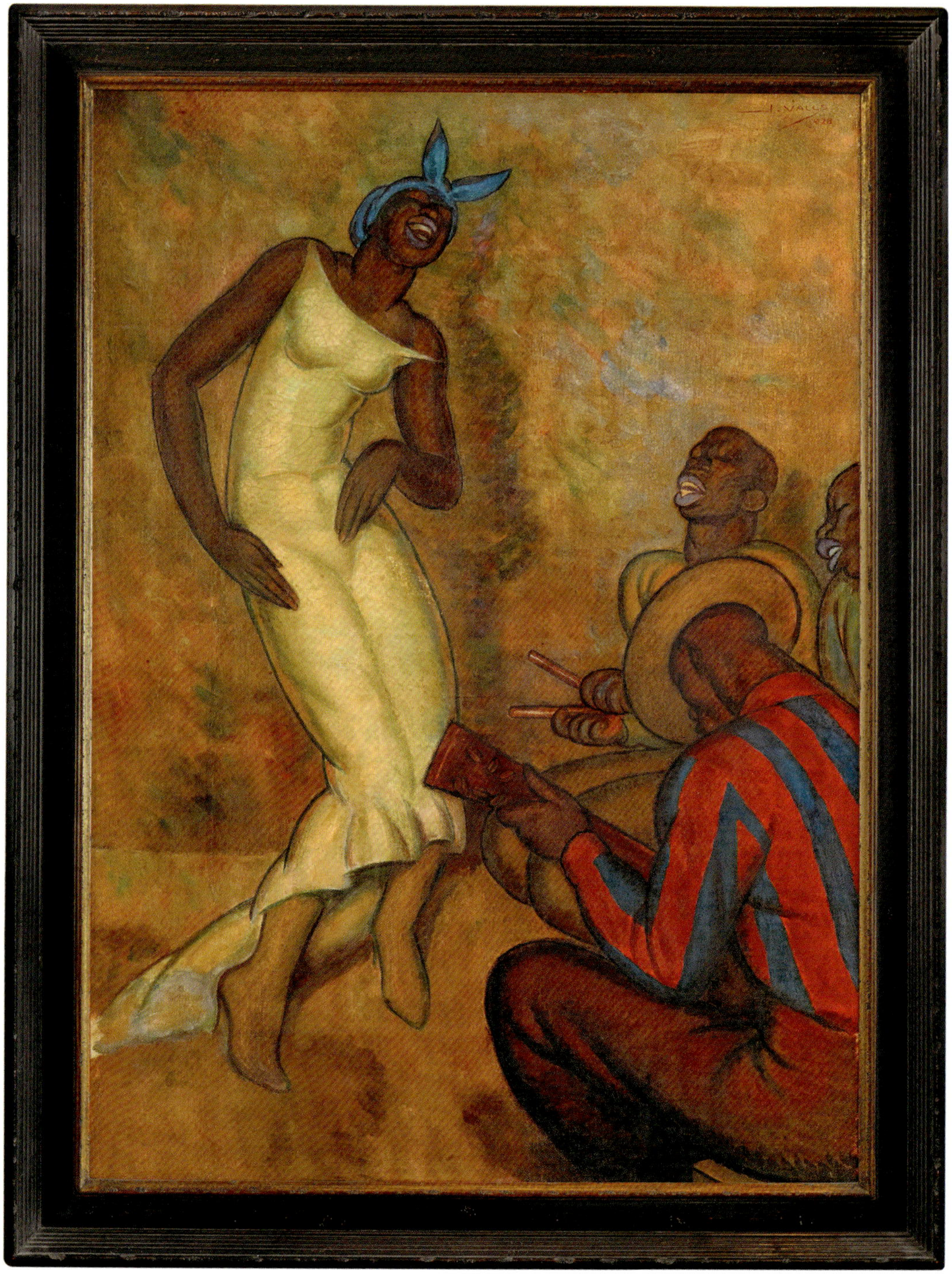

Brochure, ***Havana***, 1950
Farr Tours, Miami Beach, publisher

The Wolfsonian–FIU, The Vicki Gold Levi Collection, XC2016.01.1.1029

Painting, ***La rumba*** (also known as ***Bailando rumba***), 1928
Jaime Valls (Díaz) (Cuban, b. Spain, 1883–1955), artist
Oil on canvas

Ransola Ruggiero Collection, Miami Beach, Florida

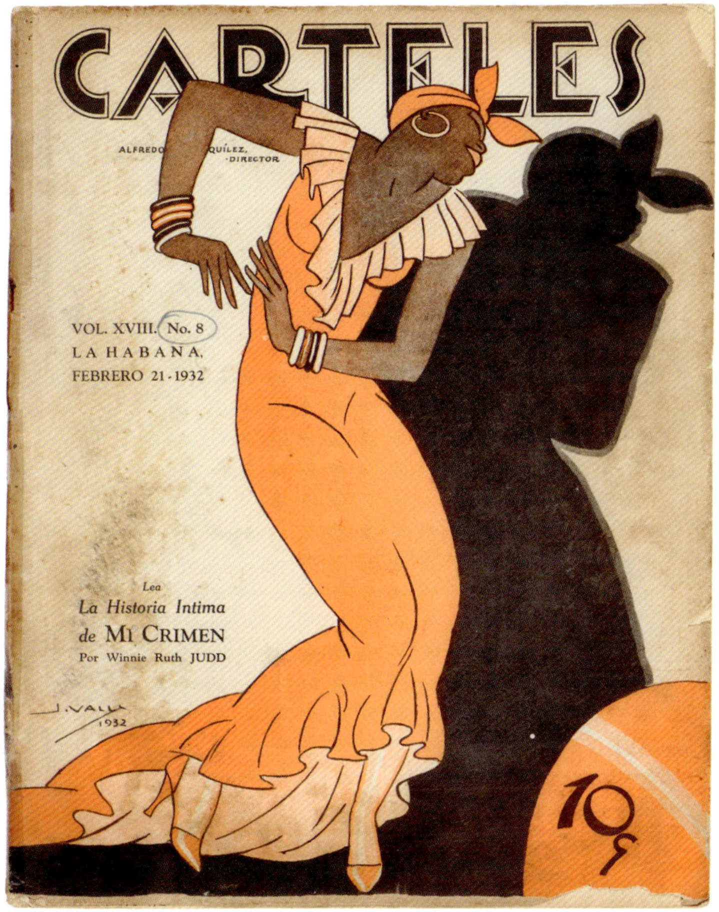

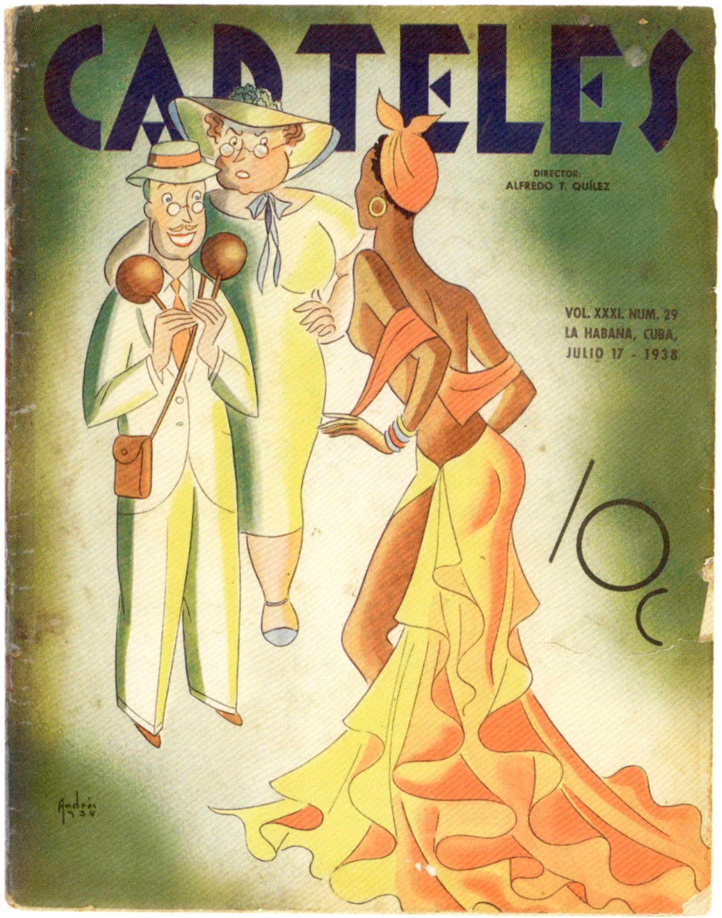

Periodicals, *Carteles*

February 21, 1932
Jaime Valls (Díaz) (Cuban, b. Spain, 1883–1955), cover illustrator

July 17, 1938
Andrés García Benítez (Cuban, 1916–1981), cover illustrator

The Wolfsonian–FIU, The Vicki Gold Levi Collection, XC2002.11.4.314.3, XC2016.01.1.929

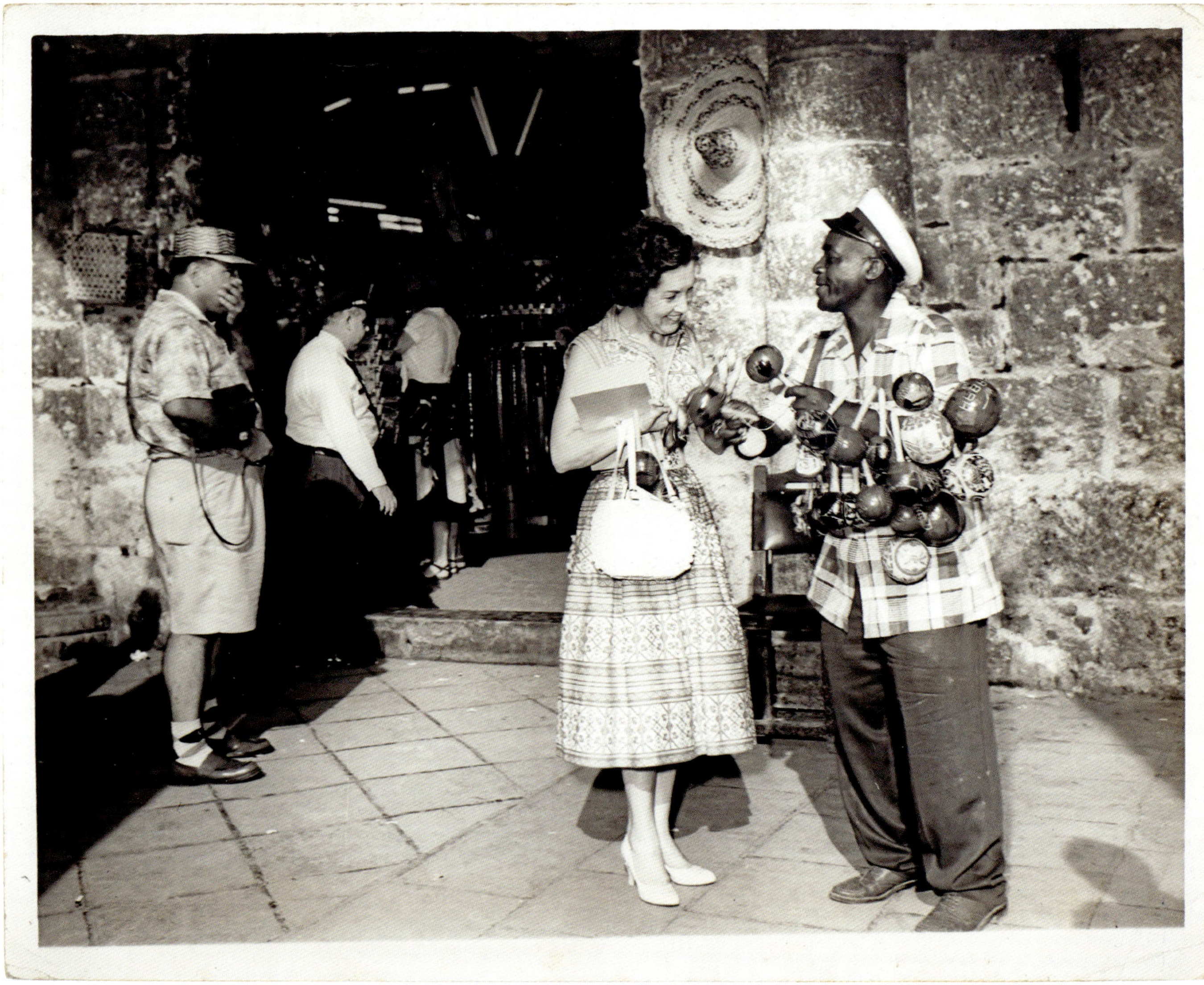

Photograph, **Vendor selling maracas to tourists**, c. 1955
Gelatin silver print

The Wolfsonian–FIU, The Vicki Gold Levi Collection, XC2016.01.1.342

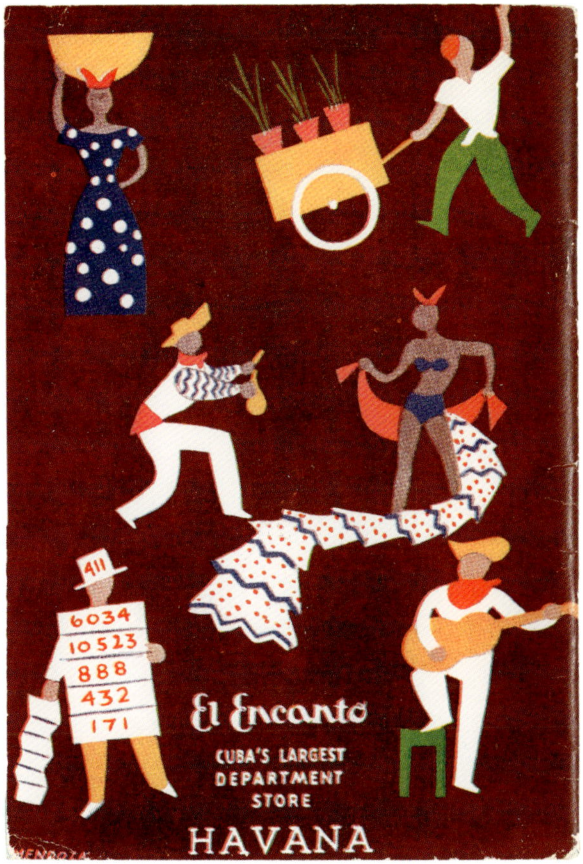

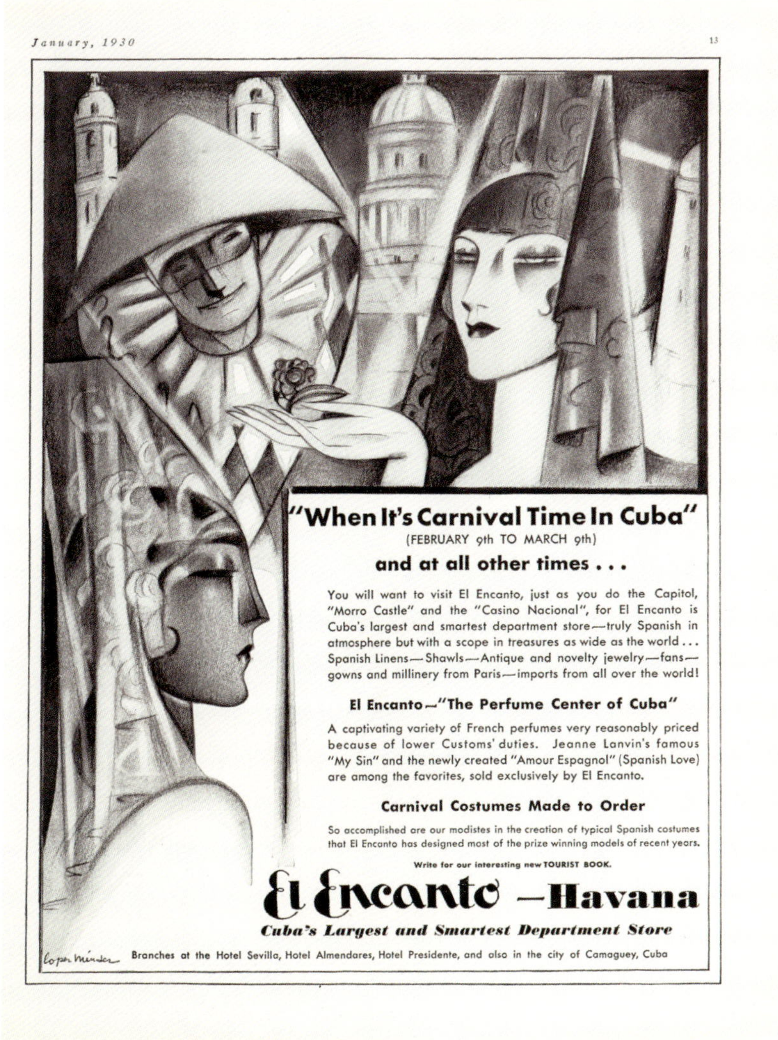

Brochure (back cover), ***Key to Havana, El Encanto***, c. 1931
El Encanto, Havana, publisher
Cardenas, Havana, printer

The Wolfsonian–FIU, The Vicki Gold Levi Collection, XC2016.01.1.7

Advertisement, **"When It's Carnival Time In Cuba": El Encanto, Havana**, from *House & Garden*, January 1930
López Méndez, illustrator
El Encanto, Havana, publisher

The Wolfsonian–FIU, The Vicki Gold Levi Collection, XC2016.01.1.74

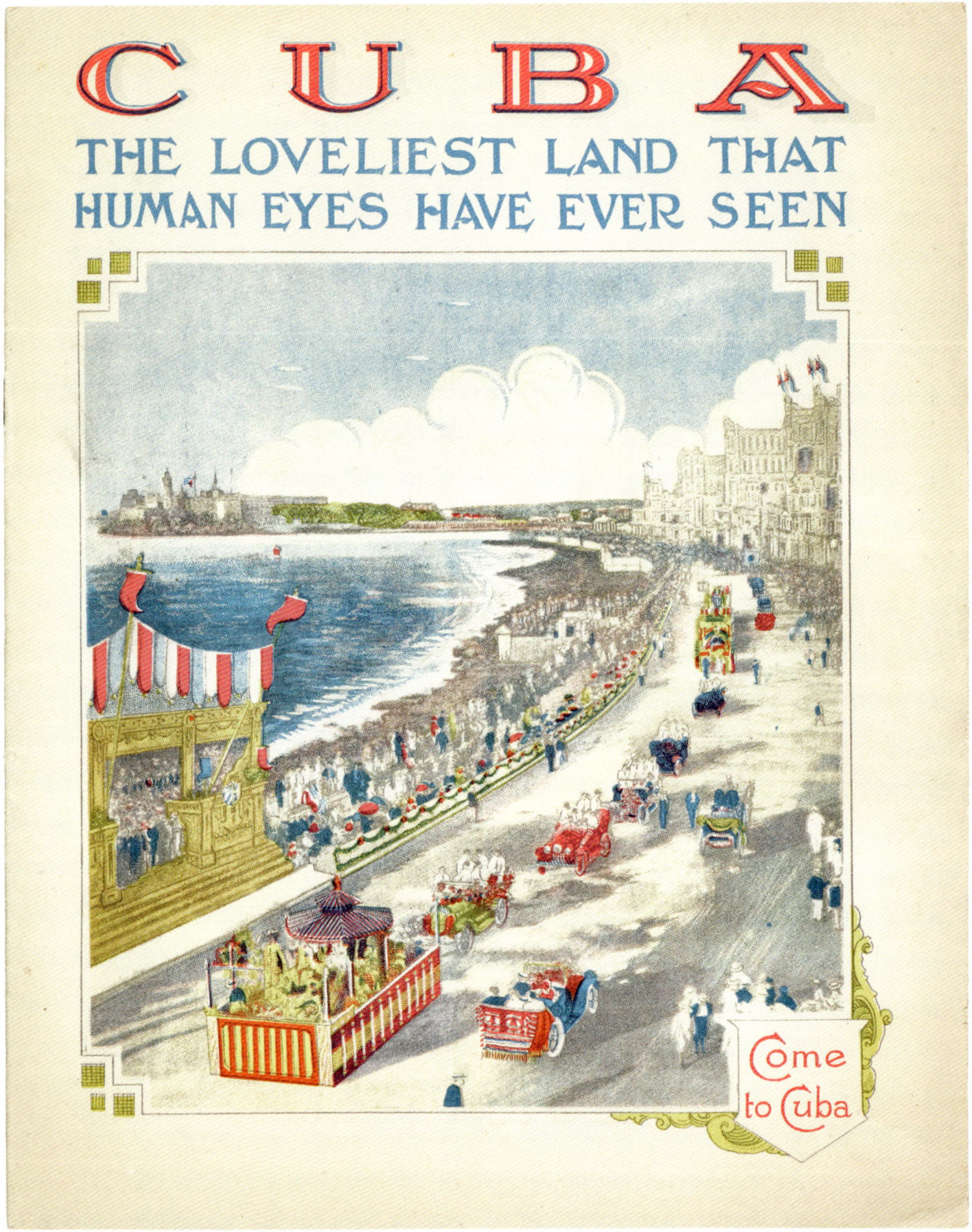

Guidebook, ***Cuba: The Loveliest Land that Human Eyes Have Ever Seen***, c. 1923
Cuban National Tourist Commission, Havana, publisher
Sindicato de Artes Graficas de la Habana, engraver and printer

The Wolfsonian–FIU, The Vicki Gold Levi Collection, XC2002.11.4.220

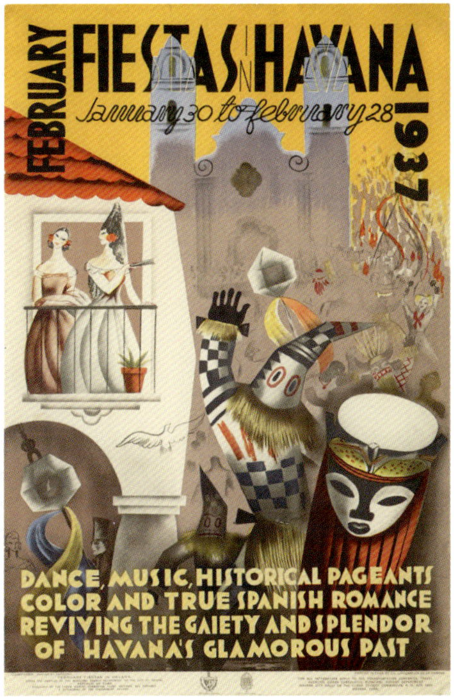

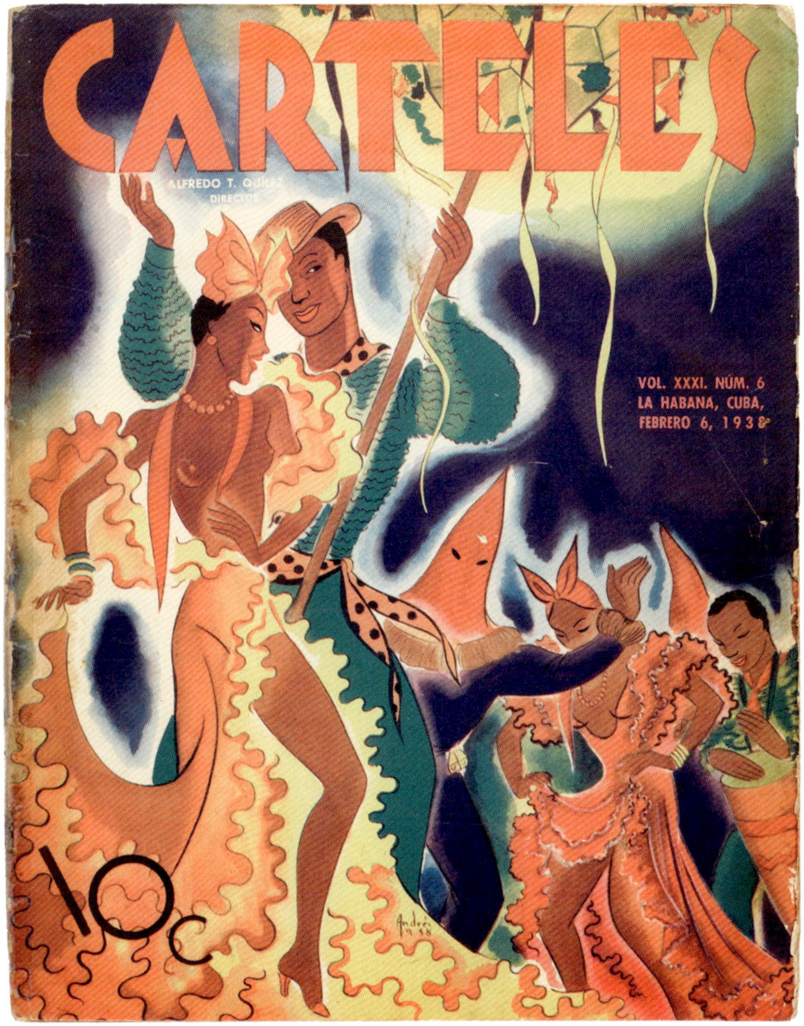

Poster, ***February Fiestas in Havana***,
c. 1937
Karreño (Mario Carreño; Cuban,
1913–1999), designer
Cuban National Tourist Commission,
Havana, publisher
Cia. Litográfica de la Habana,
Havana, printer
Offset lithograph

The Wolfsonian–FIU, The Mitchell Wolfson, Jr.
Collection, TD1990.276.4

Periodical, ***Carteles***,
February 6, 1938
Andrés García Benítez (Cuban,
1916–1981), cover illustrator

The Wolfsonian–FIU, The Vicki Gold Levi
Collection, XC2016.01.1.691

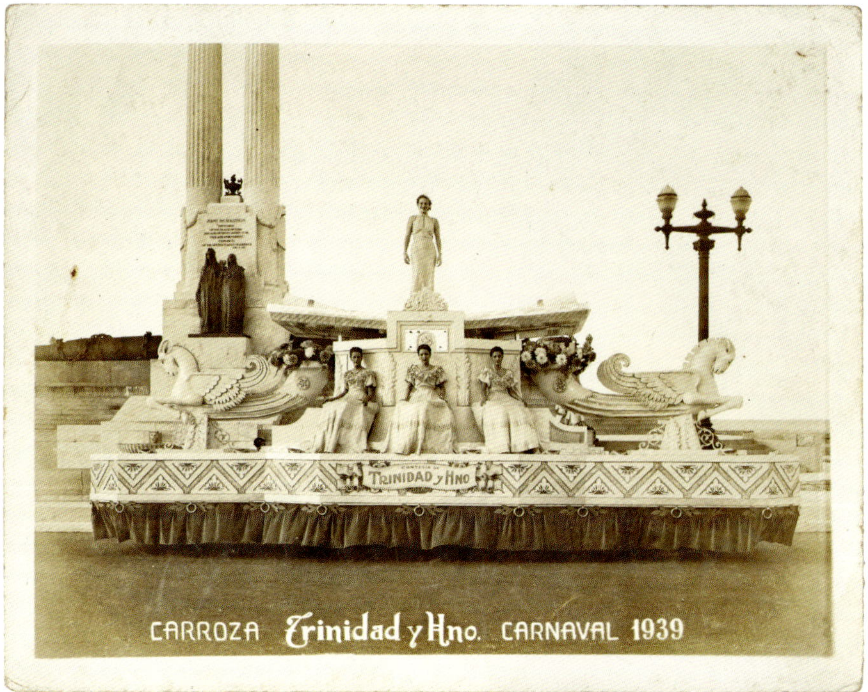

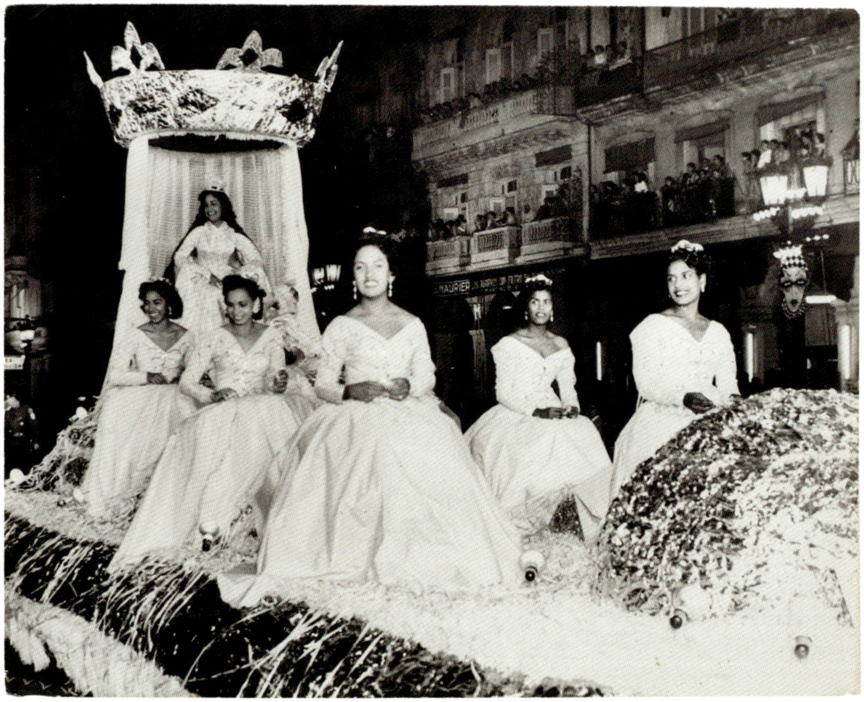

Photographs
Gelatin silver prints

Trinidad y Hno. cigar company Carnival float passing in front of USS Maine monument on the Malecón, 1939

Sociedad de Color Carnival float on the Paseo del Prado, 1955

The Wolfsonian–FIU, The Vicki Gold Levi Collection, XC2016.01.1.1146, .677

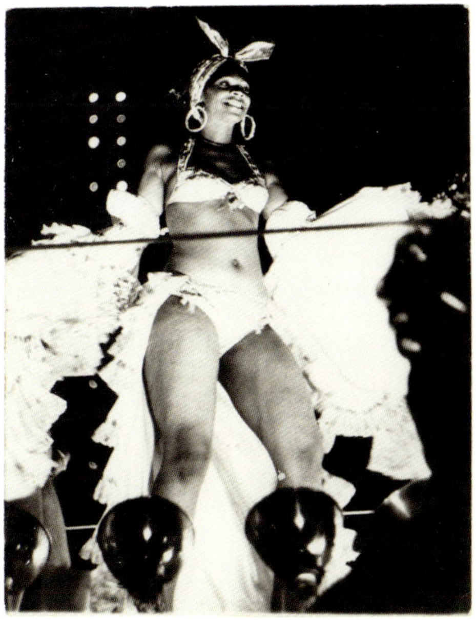

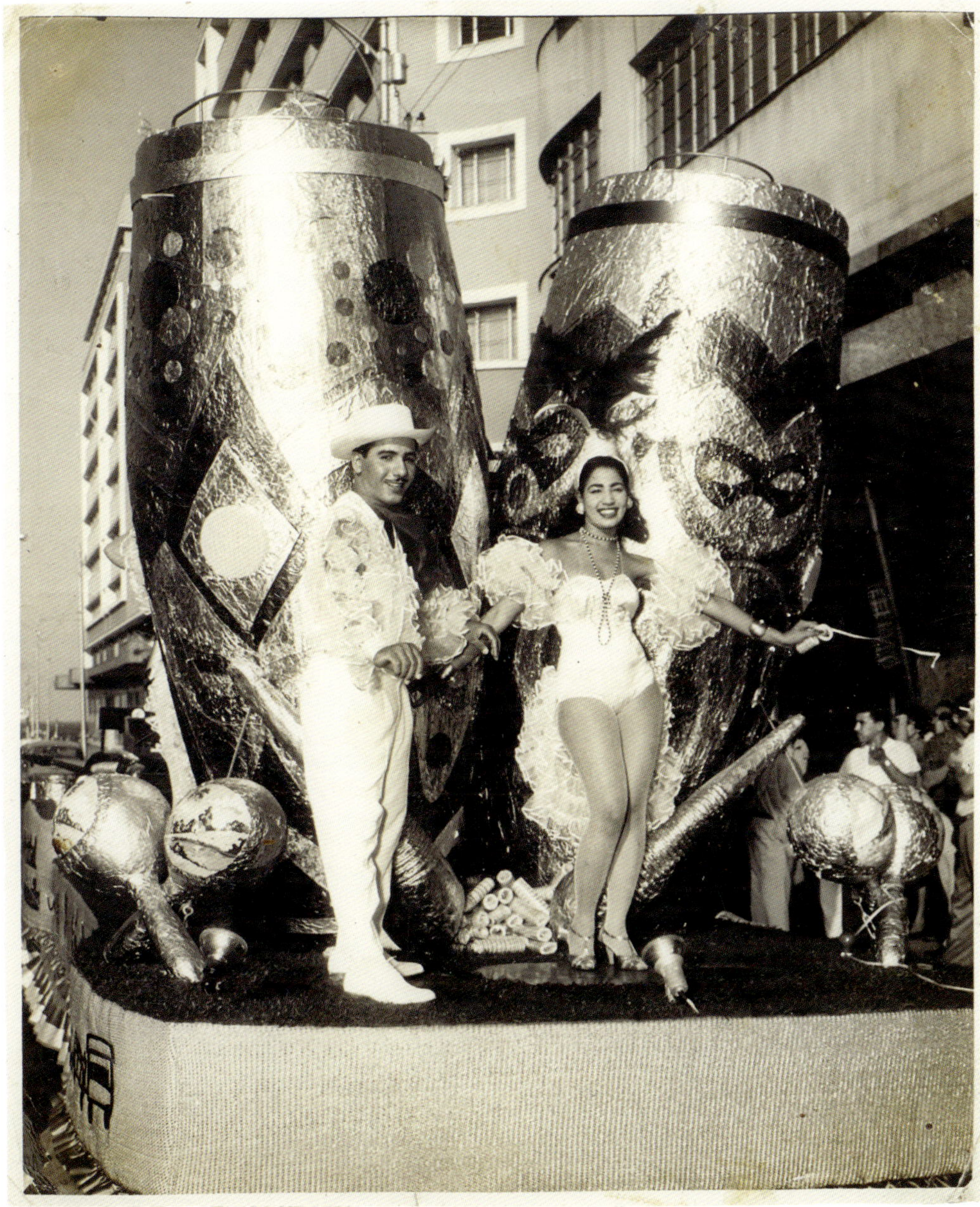

Photographs
Gelatin silver prints

Carnival dancer, c. 1955

Carnival float, 1955
Cooperativa Fotografia, photographer

The Wolfsonian–FIU, The Vicki Gold Levi Collection, XC2016.01.1.1227, .1221

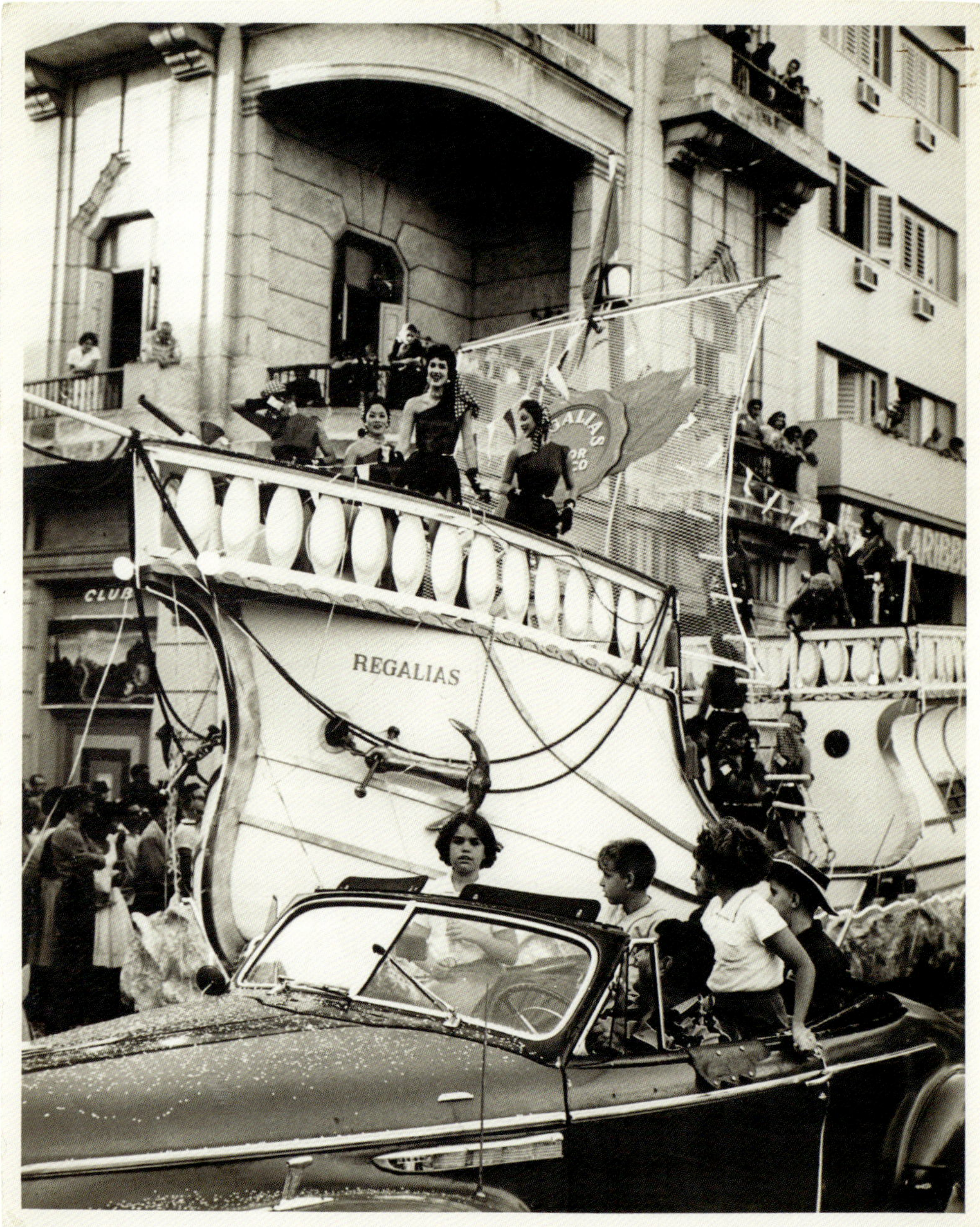

Photograph, **Cigarros Regalias Carnival float**, c. 1955

Gelatin silver print
The Wolfsonian–FIU, The Vicki Gold Levi Collection, XC2016.01.1.675

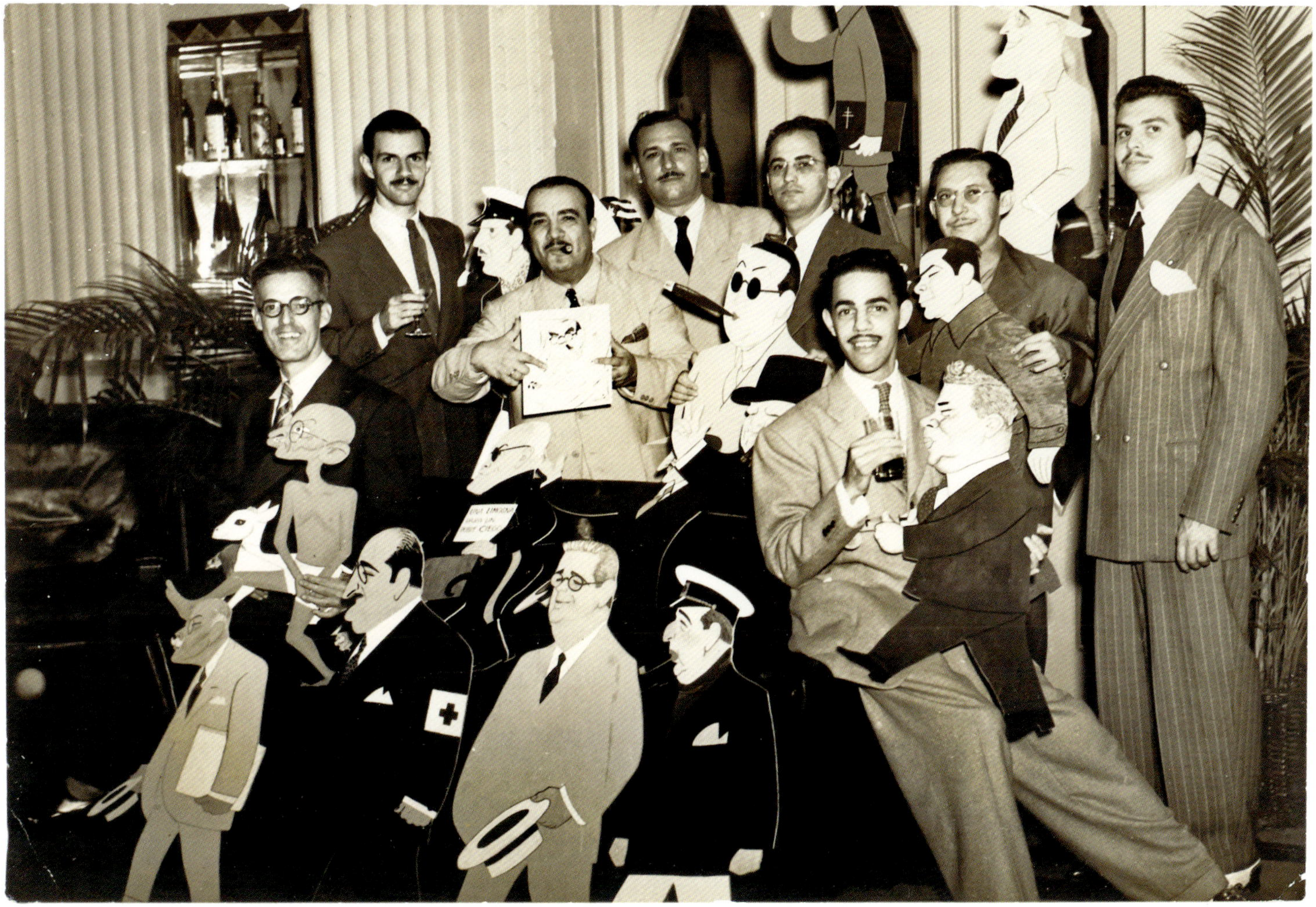

Photograph, **Cocktail party celebrating the birthday of Conrado Walter Massaguer** (third from left), March 14, 1943
Gelatin silver print

The Wolfsonian–FIU, The Vicki Gold Levi Collection, XC2016.01.1.463

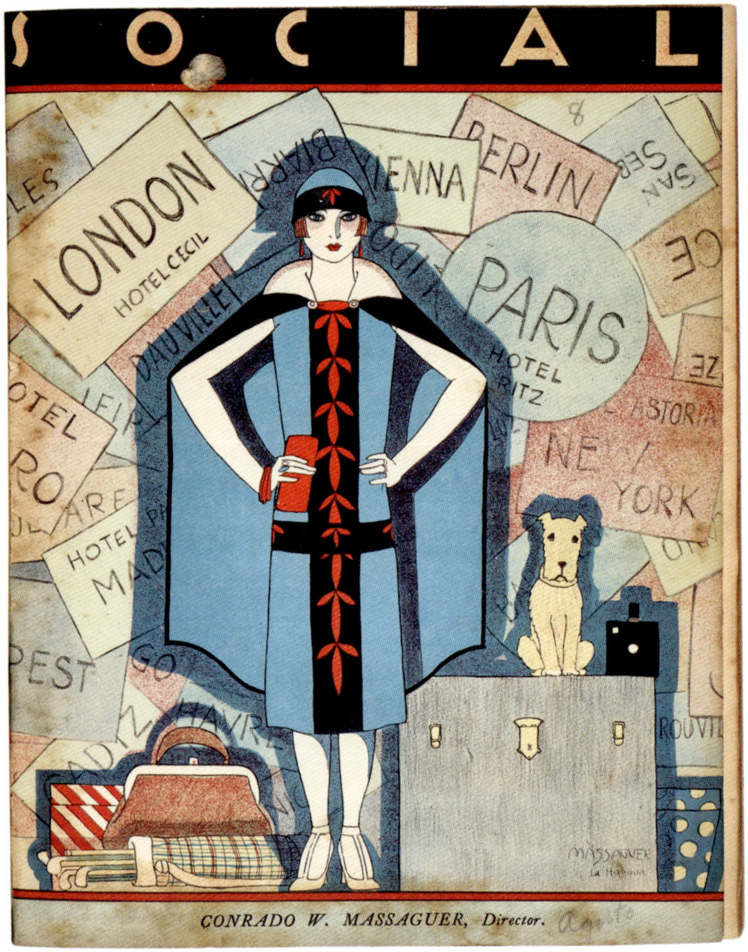

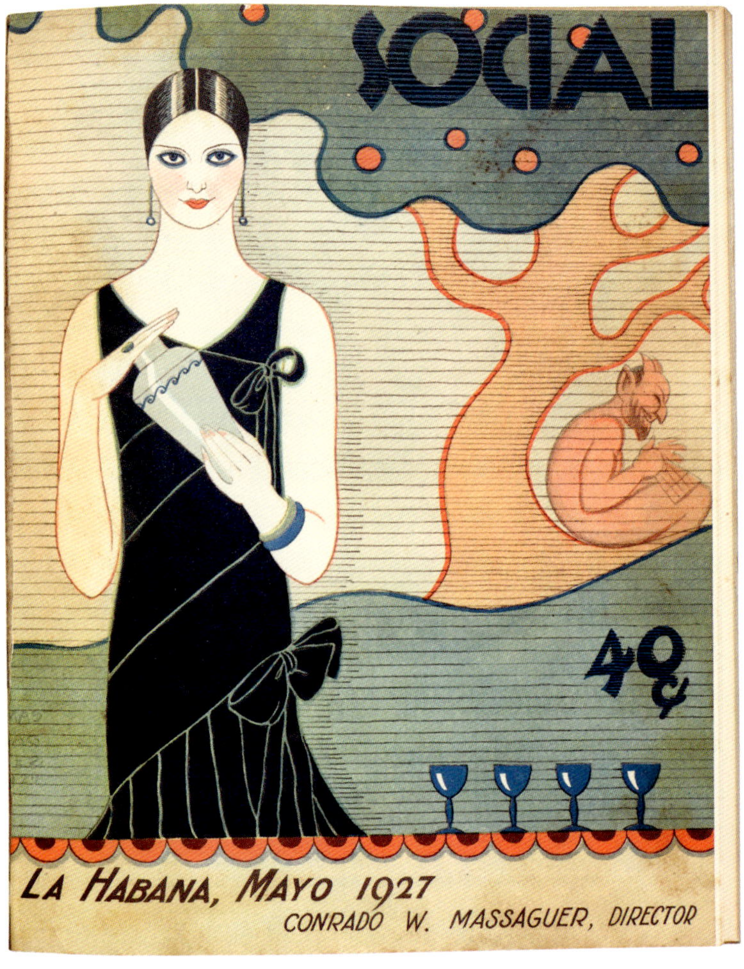

Periodicals, *Social*,
October 1924 and May 1927
Conrado Walter Massaguer (Cuban, 1889–1965), cover illustrator

The Wolfsonian–FIU, Mitchell Wolfson, Jr. Loan, XM2000.115.22, XM2000.45.3

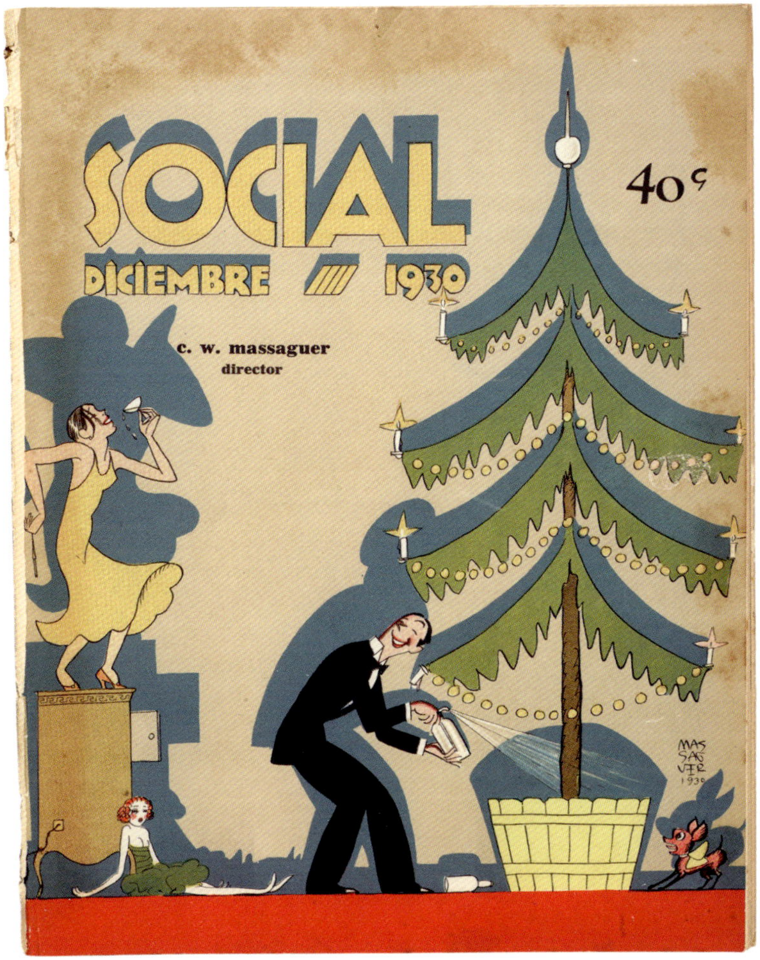

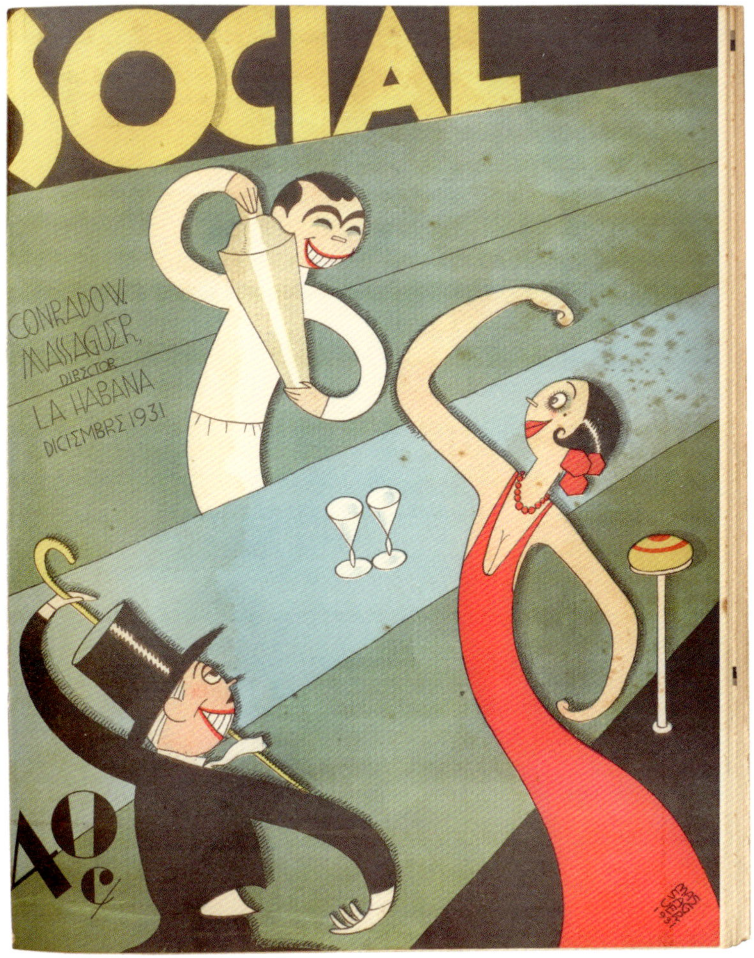

Periodicals, ***Social***,
December 1930 and December 1931
Conrado Walter Massaguer (Cuban, 1889–1965), cover illustrator

The Wolfsonian–FIU, Mitchell Wolfson, Jr. Loan, XM2000.45.10, XM2000.115.23

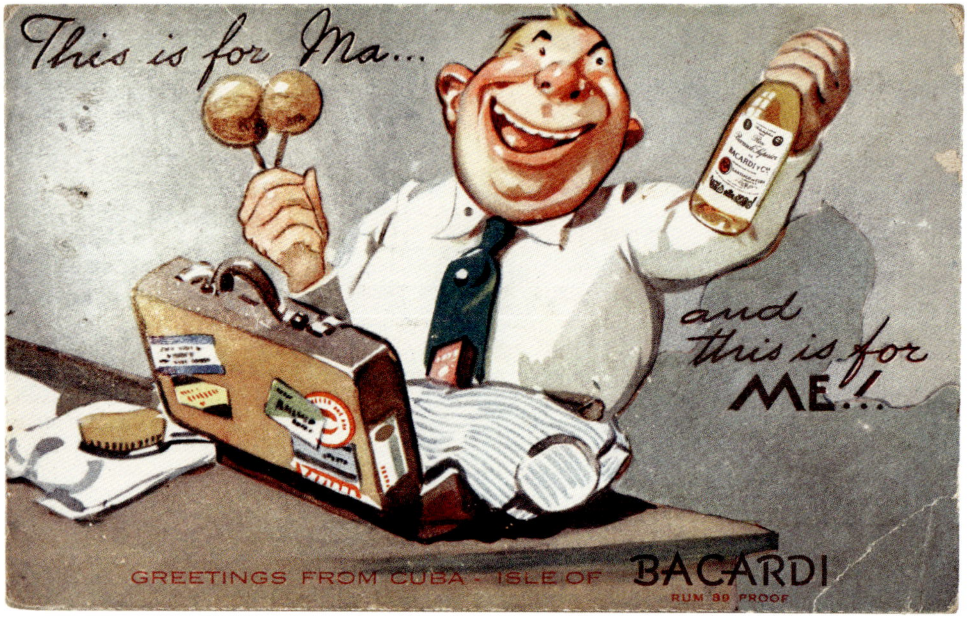

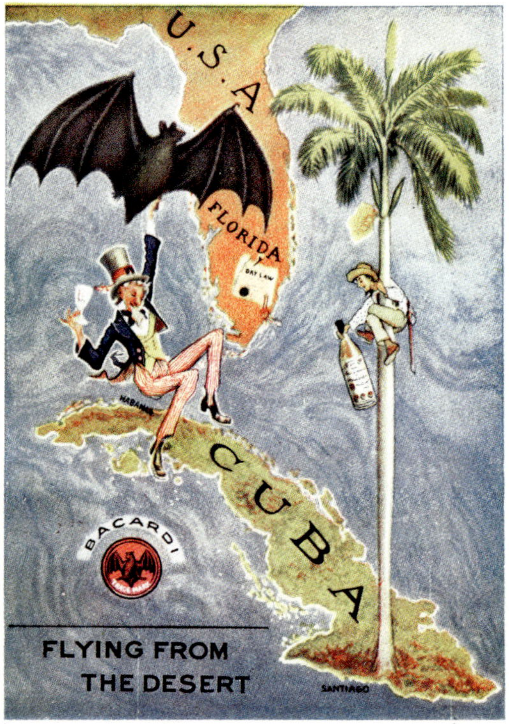

Postcards
Bacardí, Havana, publisher

This Is for Ma...and This Is for Me!!, c. 1930

Flying from the Desert, c. 1930
Compañia litográfica de la Habana, Havana, printer

The Wolfsonian–FIU, The Vicki Gold Levi Collection, XC2002.11.4.120, .118

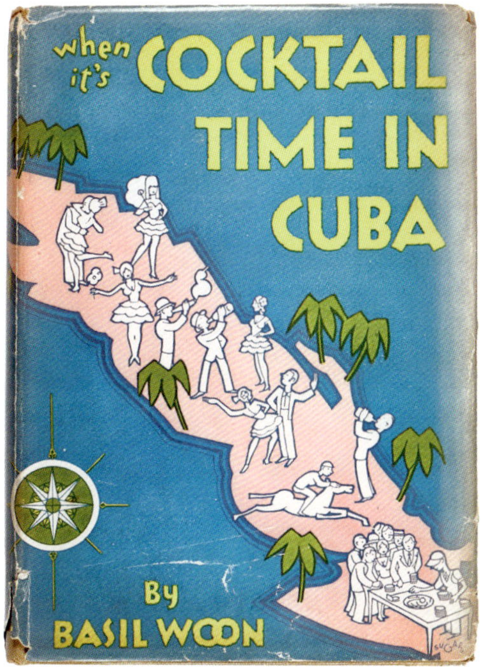

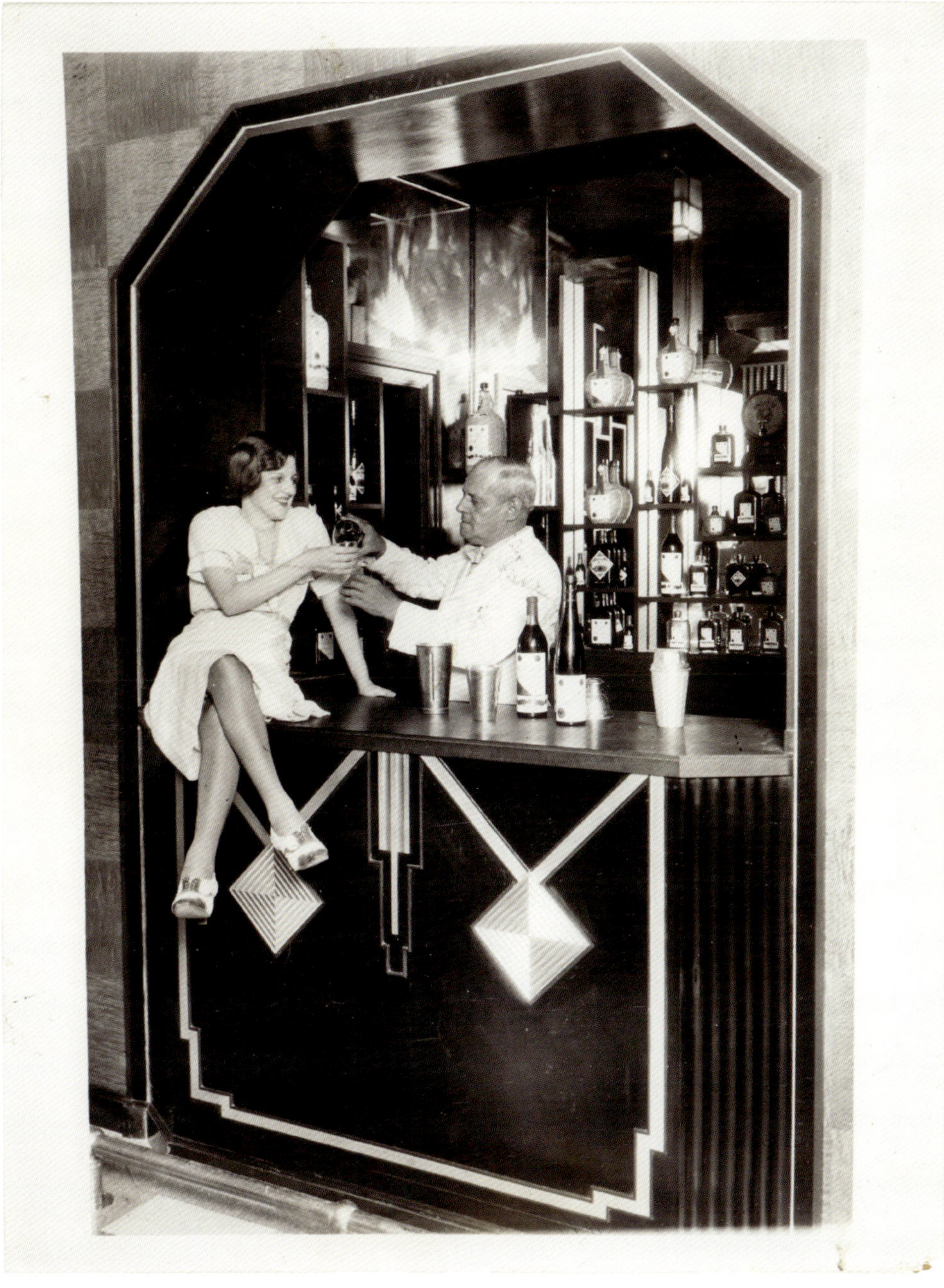

Book, ***When It's Cocktail Time in Cuba***, 1928
Basil Dillon Woon (American, b. Great Britain, 1893–1974), author
H. Liveright, New York, publisher

The Wolfsonian–FIU, The Vicki Gold Levi Collection, XC2016.01.1.1359

Photograph, **Mezzanine bar in the Edifico Bacardí**, 1931
Gelatin silver print

The Wolfsonian–FIU, The Vicki Gold Levi Collection, XC2016.01.1.65

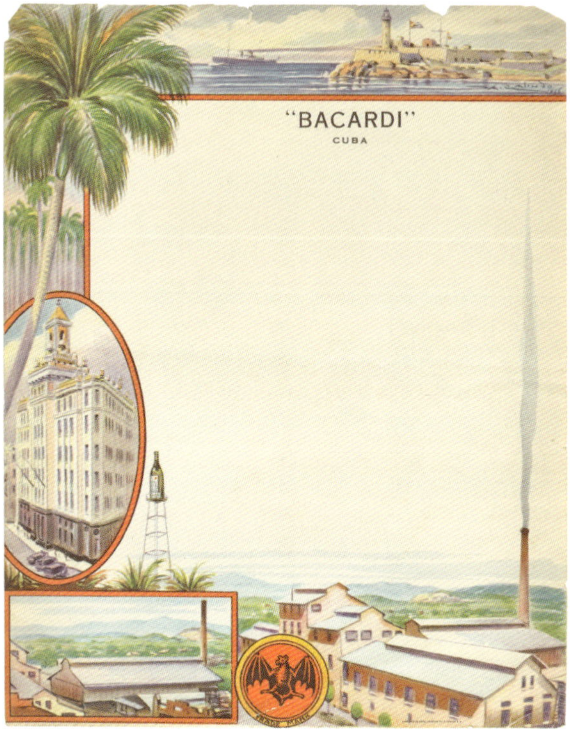

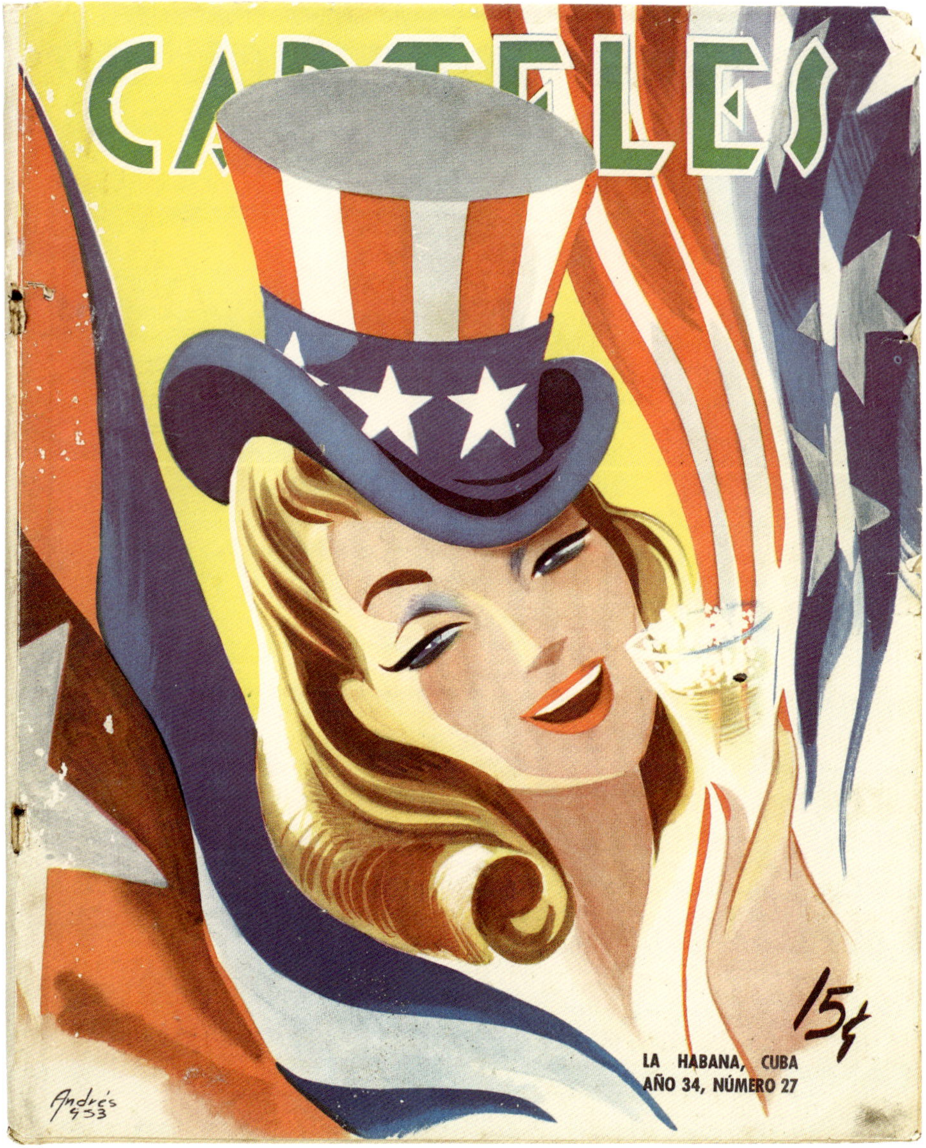

Stationery, **"Bacardí" Cuba**, c. 1935
Bacardí, Havana, publisher

The Wolfsonian–FIU, The Vicki Gold Levi Collection, XC2016.01.1.1168

Periodical, ***Carteles***, July 5, 1953
Andrés García Benítez (Cuban, 1916–1981), cover illustrator

The Wolfsonian–FIU, The Vicki Gold Levi Collection, XC2016.01.1.808

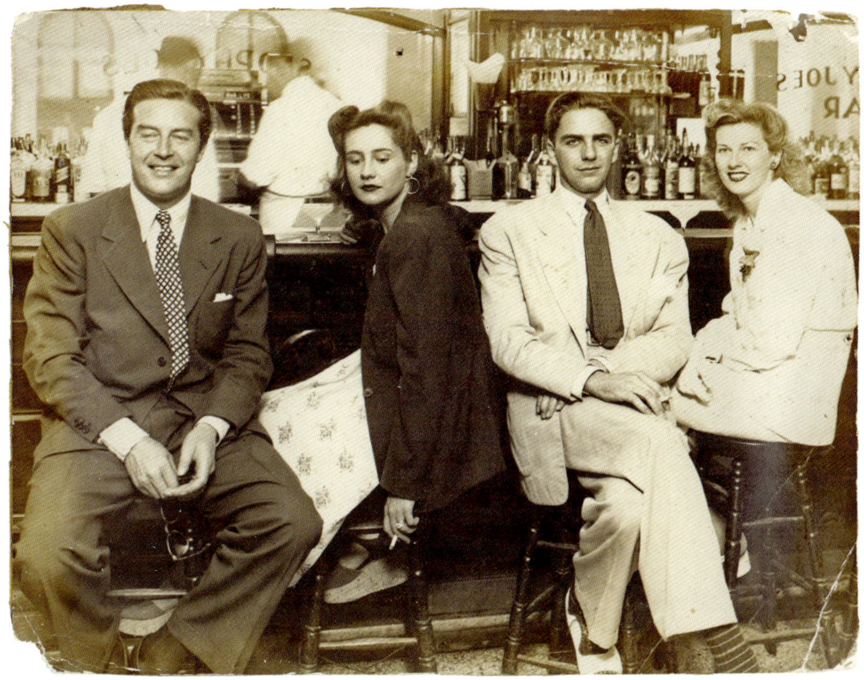

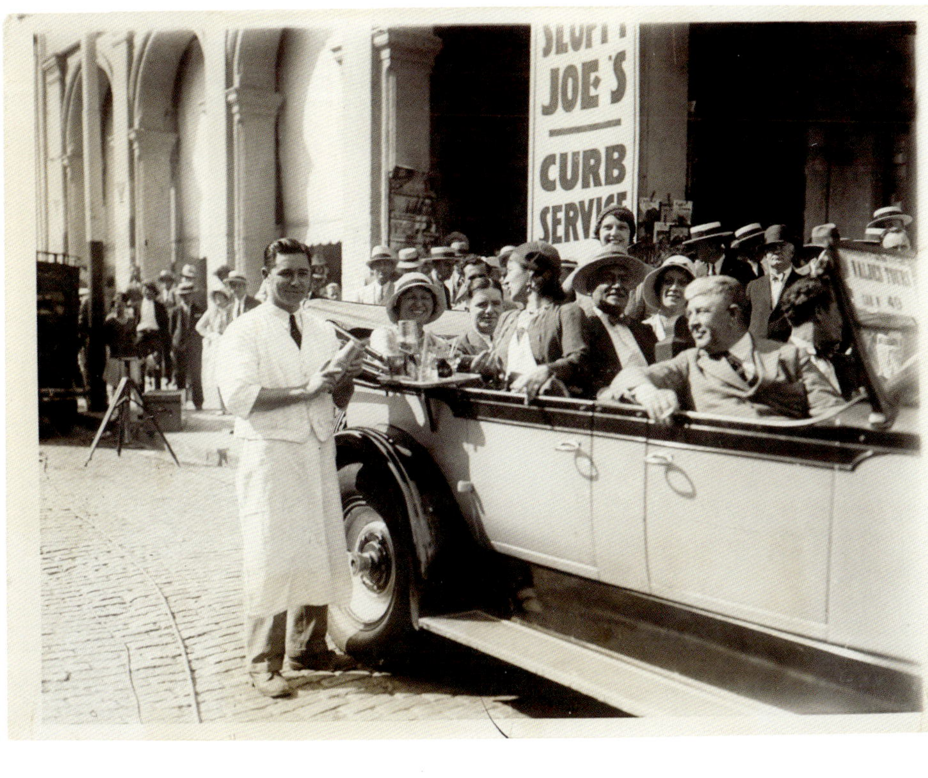

Photographs
Gelatin silver prints

Actors Robert Taylor and Barbara Stanwyck (left and center), **Sloppy Joe's Bar**, c. 1940

Sloppy Joe's Bar curb service, c. 1925

The Wolfsonian–FIU, The Vicki Gold Levi Collection, XC2016.01.1.1155, .788

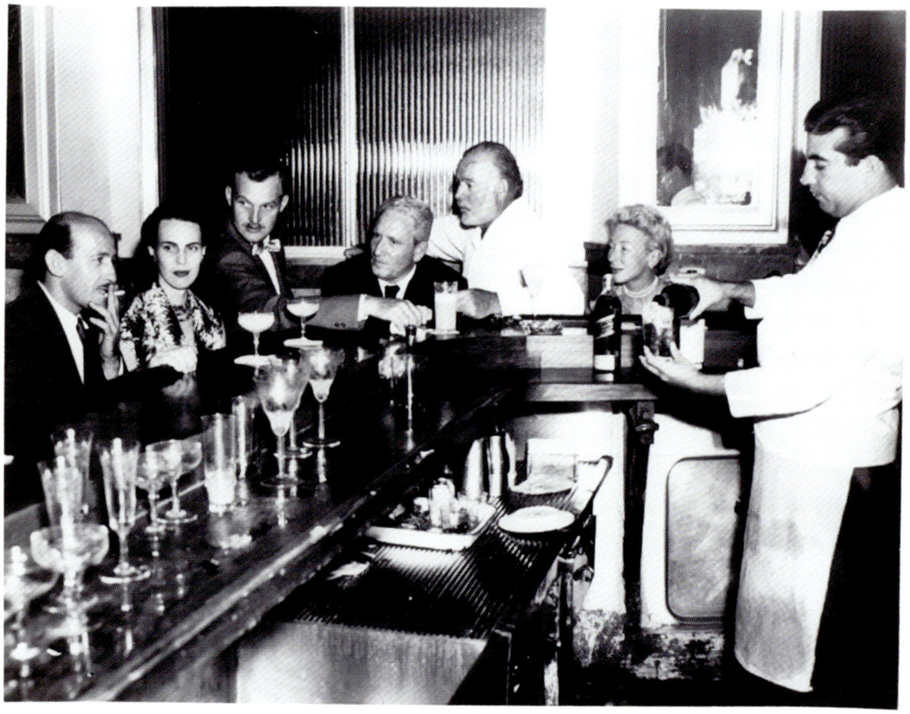

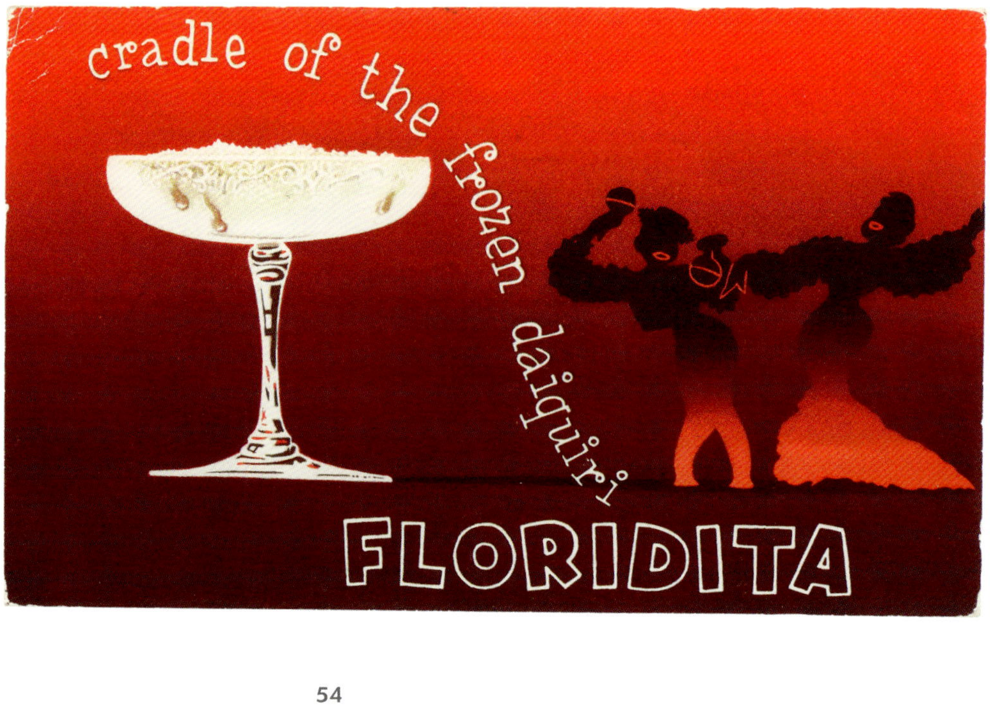

Photograph, **Spencer Tracy** (center) **with Ernest and Mary Welsh Hemingway** (to Spencer's right) **at Floridita**, c. 1956
Inkjet print

The Wolfsonian–FIU, The Vicki Gold Levi Collection, XC2016.01.1.323

Postcard, ***Cradle of the Frozen Daiquiri, Floridita***, c. 1955
Floridita, Havana, publisher

The Wolfsonian–FIU, The Vicki Gold Levi Collection, XC2002.11.4.71

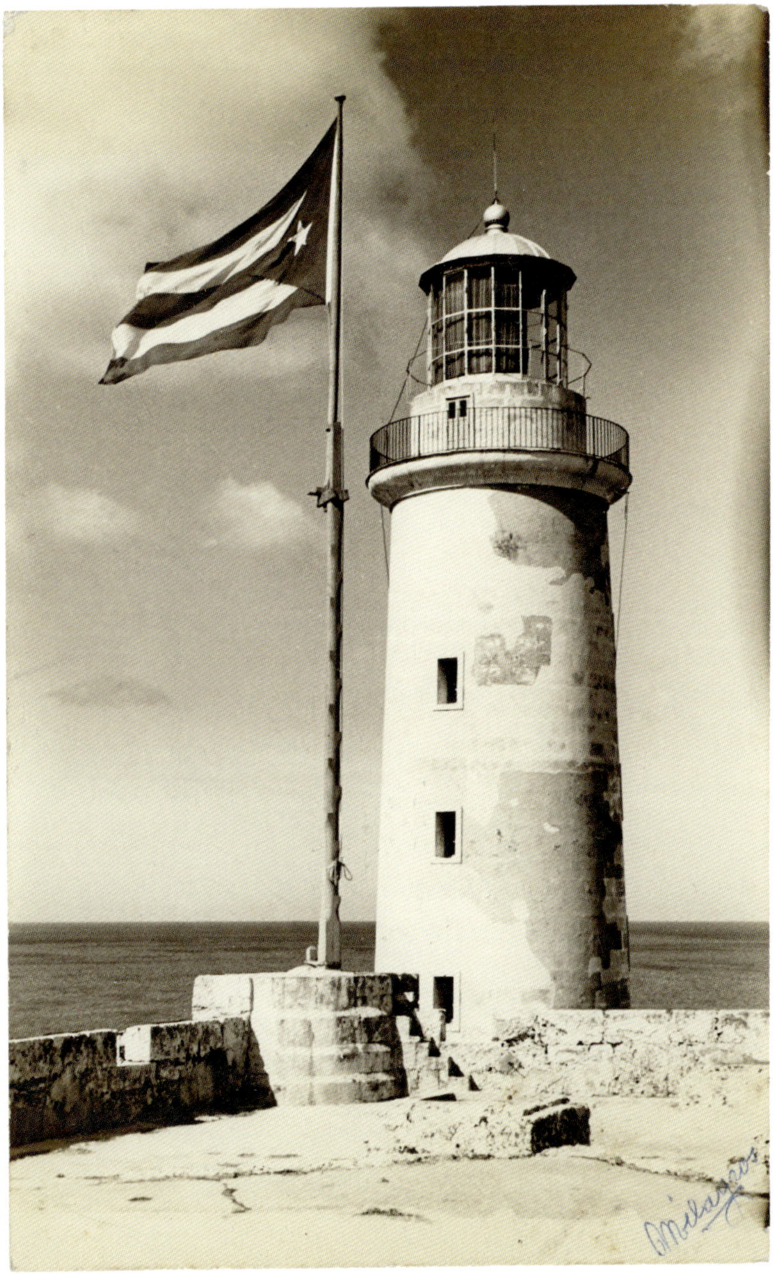

Photograph, **Lighthouse tower, Castillo del Morro, Havana Harbor**, c. 1949
Milagros, photographer
Gelatin silver print

The Wolfsonian–FIU, The Vicki Gold Levi Collection, XC2016.01.1.702

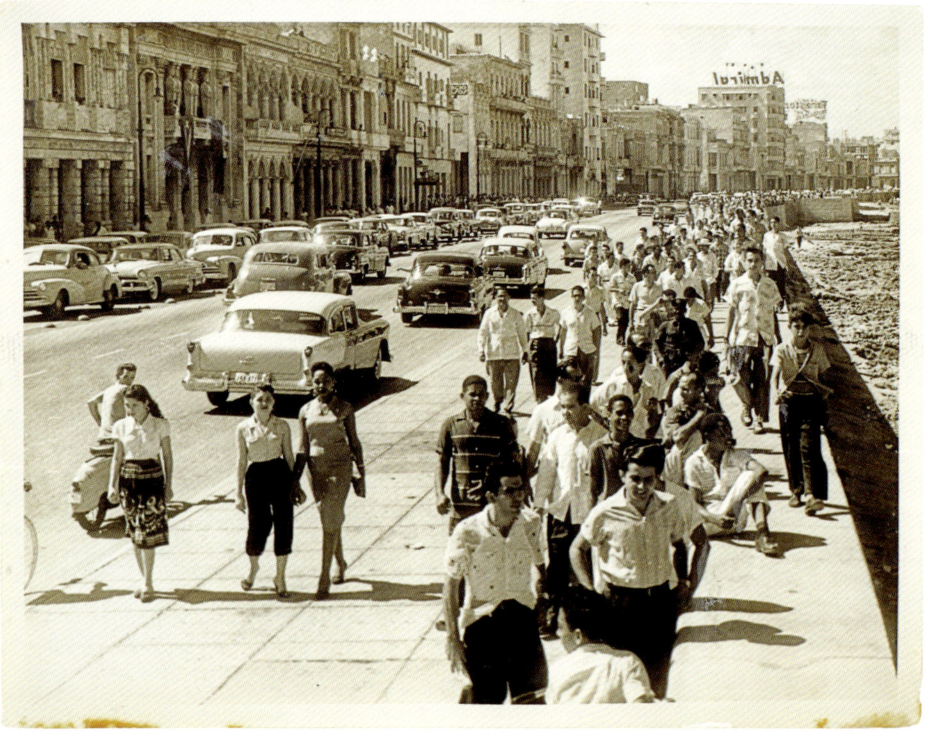

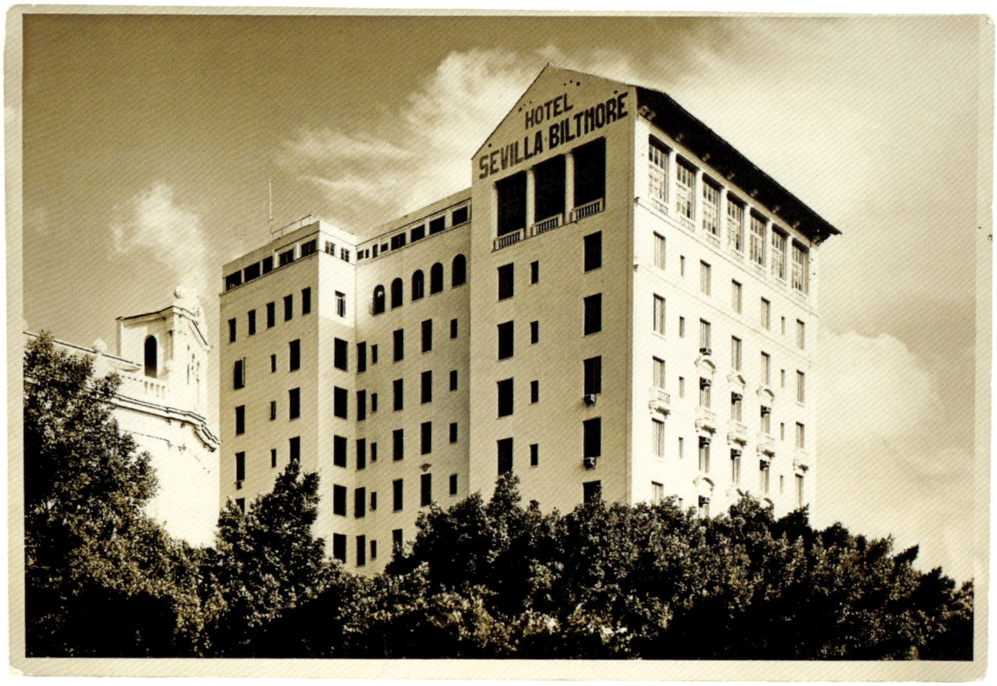

Photographs
Gelatin silver prints

Automobiles and pedestrians on the Malecón, c. 1955

Hotel Sevilla-Biltmore, c. 1950
Organización Fotomarin, photographer

The Wolfsonian–FIU, The Vicki Gold Levi Collection, XC2016.01.1.240, .467

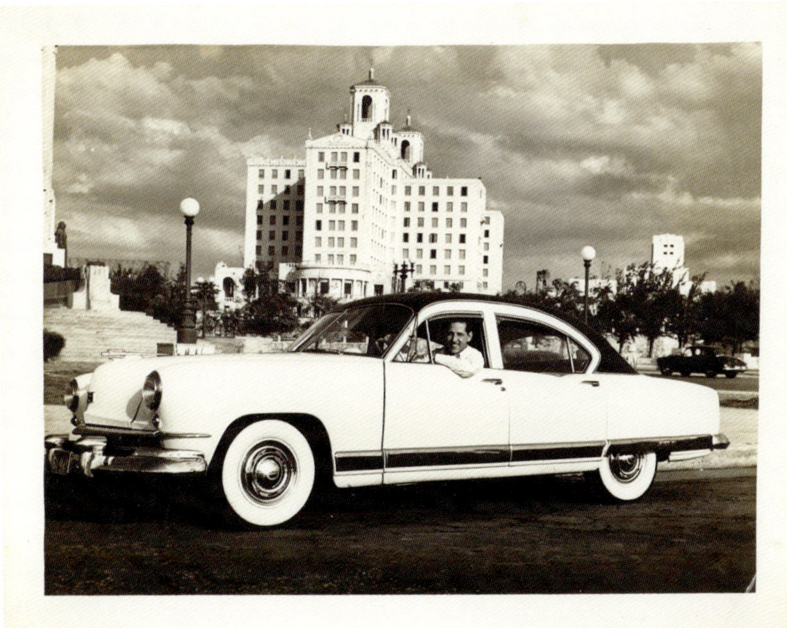

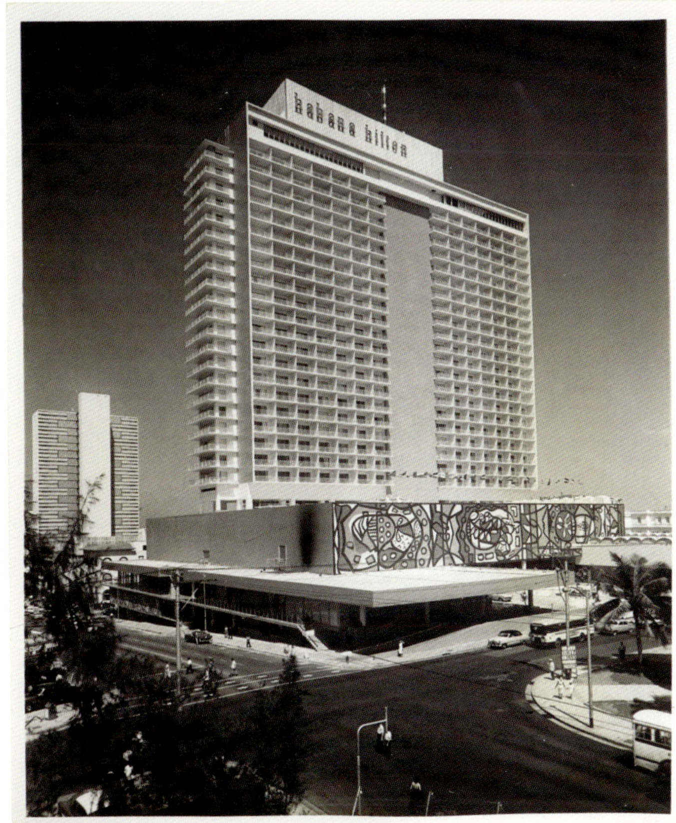

Photographs
Gelatin silver prints

Kaiser Deluxe sedan in front of the Hotel Nacional, c. 1952

Havana Hilton Hotel,
November 17, 1958
Fuente Fotógrafo Comercial,
Havana, photographer

Conrad and Barron Hilton (center and right) **viewing a model of the Havana Hilton Hotel**, c. 1957
Inkjet print

The Wolfsonian–FIU, The Vicki Gold Levi Collection, XC2016.01.1.710, .246, .147

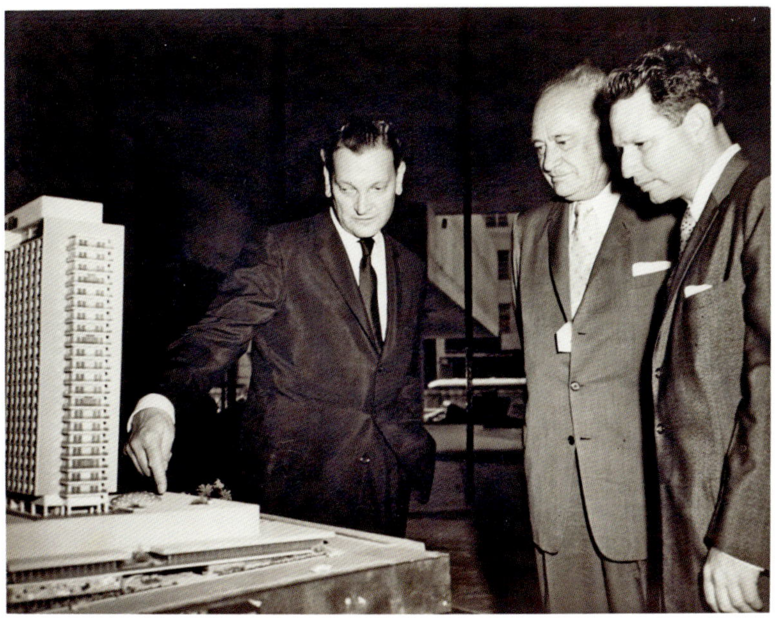

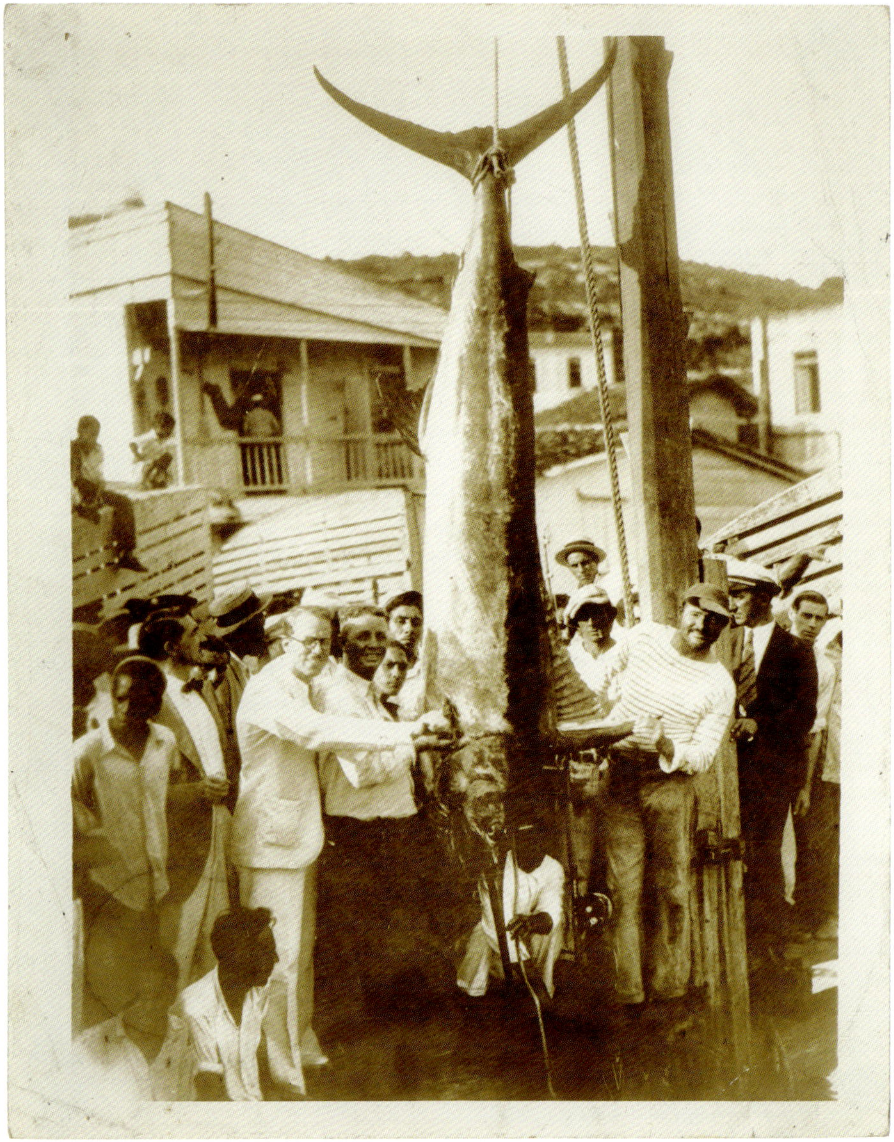

Photograph,
Joseph Kennedy (left) **and Ernest Hemingway** (right) **with a big catch,**
December 7, 1933
International News Photos, Inc., photographer
Gelatin silver print

The Wolfsonian–FIU, The Vicki Gold Levi Collection, XC2016.01.1.12

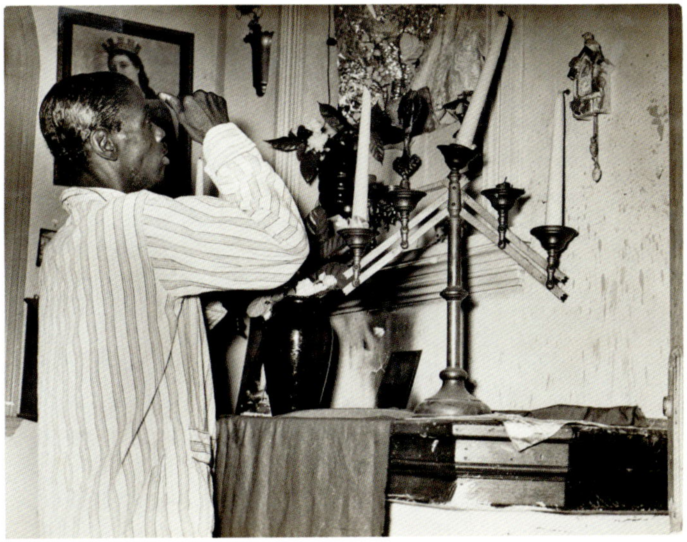

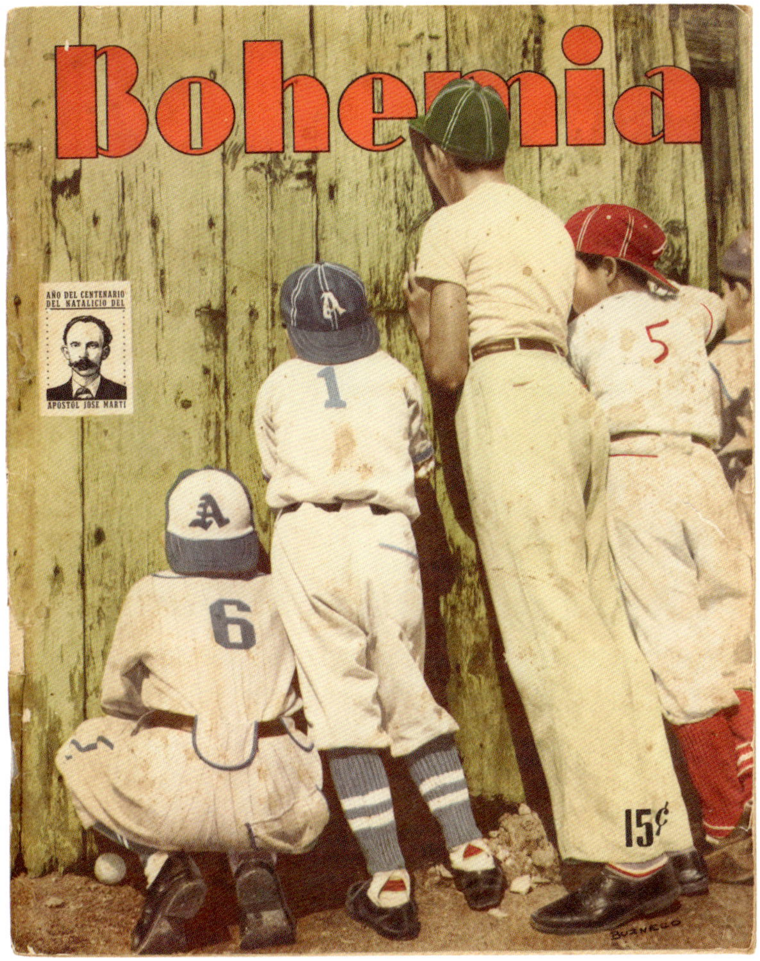

Photograph, **Boxer Eligio Sardiñas Montalvo ("Kid Chocolate") standing before a shrine to Santa Barbara in his home**, c. 1950
United Press Photo, photographer
Gelatin silver print

The Wolfsonian–FIU, The Vicki Gold Levi Collection, XC2016.01.1.274

Periodical, ***Bohemia***, December 13, 1953

The Wolfsonian–FIU, The Vicki Gold Levi Collection, XC2002.11.4.316.26

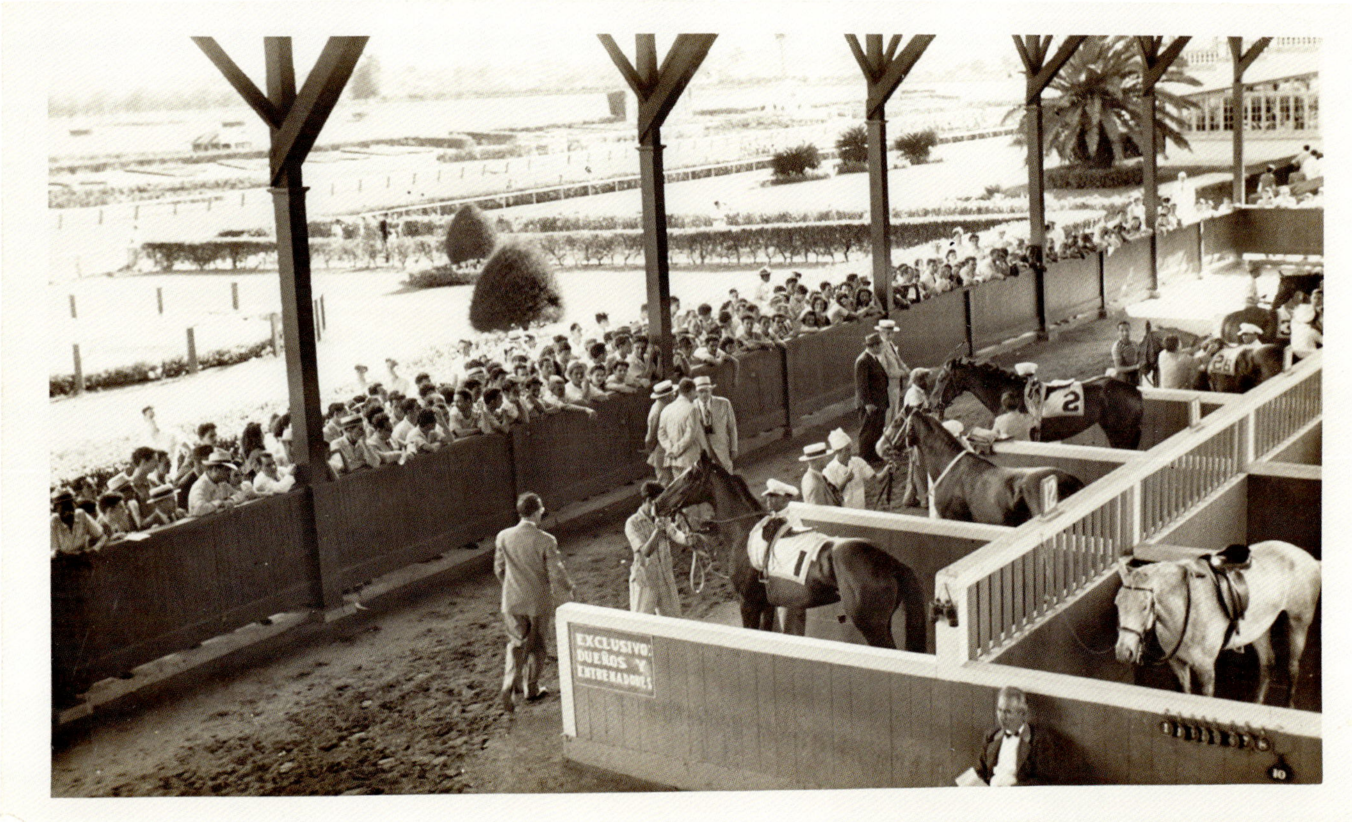

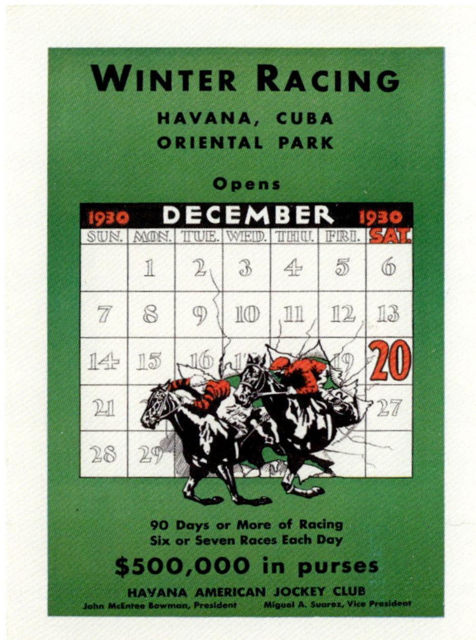

Photograph, **Horse stalls at Oriental Park**, 1944
Gelatin silver print

The Wolfsonian–FIU, The Vicki Gold Levi Collection, XC2016.01.1.942

Flyer, ***Winter Racing, Havana, Cuba, Oriental Park***, 1930

The Wolfsonian–FIU, The Vicki Gold Levi Collection, XC2016.01.1.139

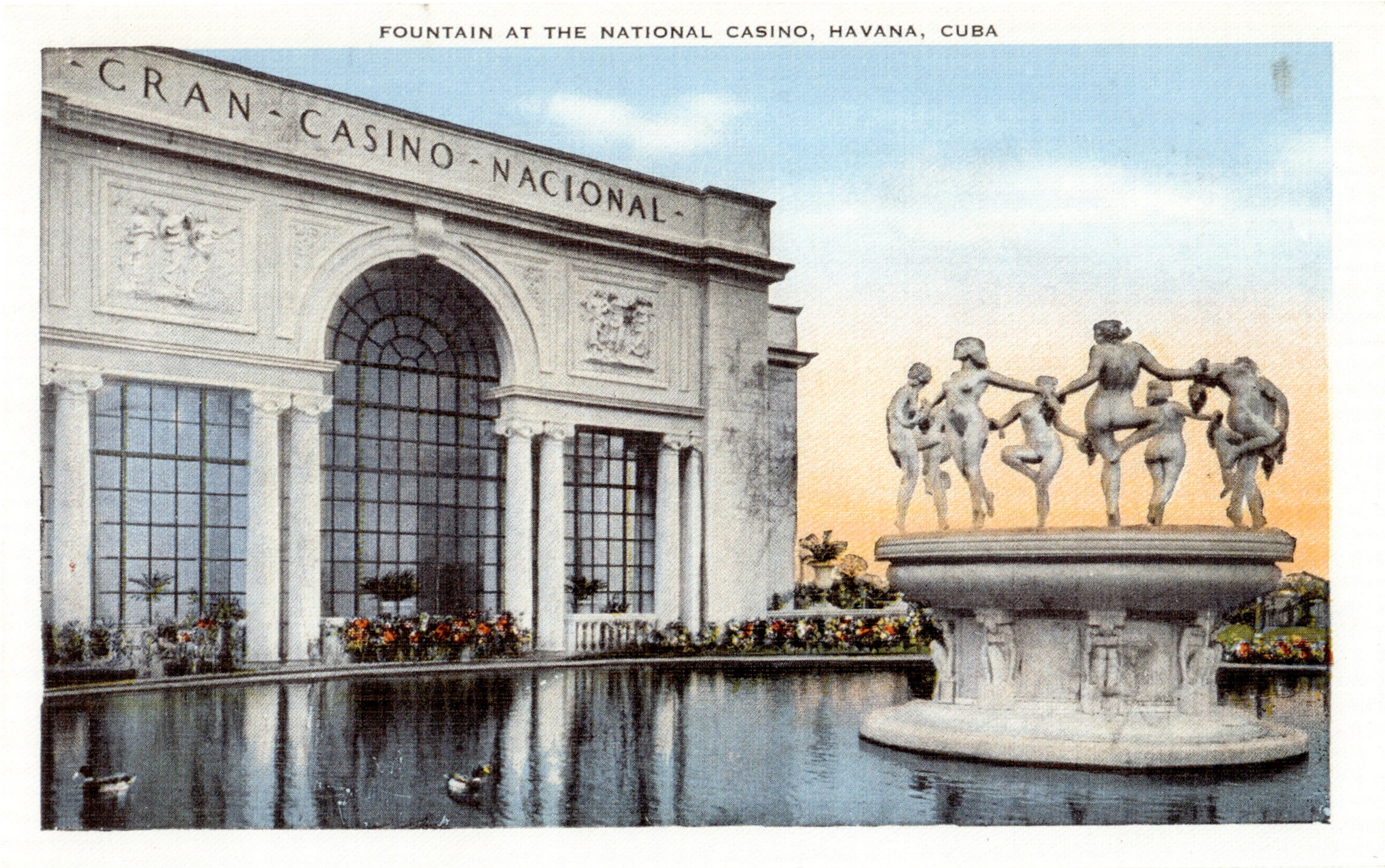

Postcard, ***Fountain at the National Casino, Havana, Cuba***, c. 1950
Roberts & Co., Havana, publisher

La Fuente de las Musas (Fountain of the Muses) was completed in 1920 by sculptor Aldo Gamba (Italian, 1881–after 1944) at the entrance of the Gran Casino Nacional; it was moved to the Tropicana cabaret in 1952.

The Wolfsonian–FIU, Gift of Francis Xavier Luca and Clara Helena Palacio Luca,

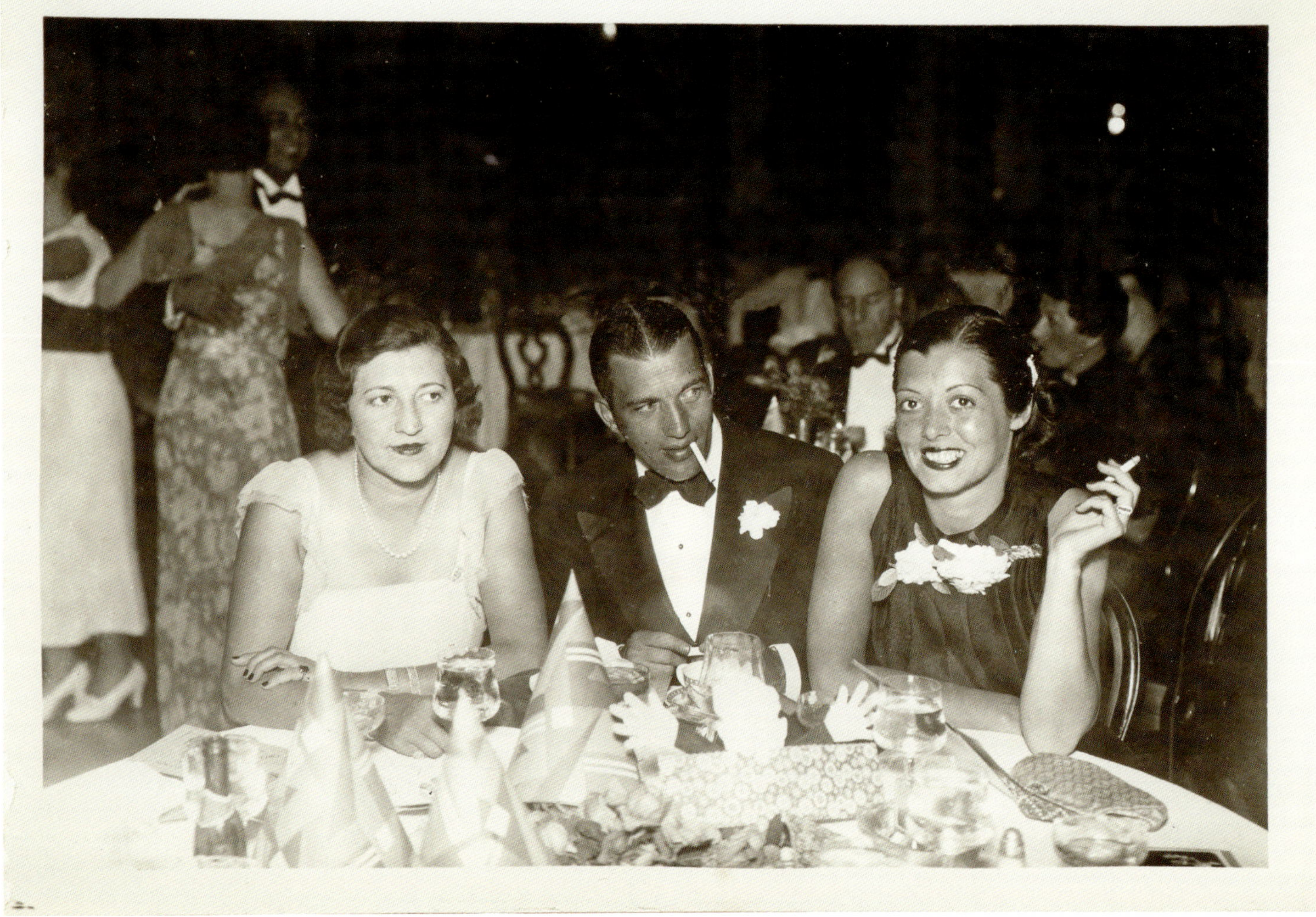

Photograph, **Television personality Ed Sullivan at the Gran Casino Nacional,** c. 1950
Gelatin silver print

The Wolfsonian–FIU, The Vicki Gold Levi Collection, XC2016.01.1.51b

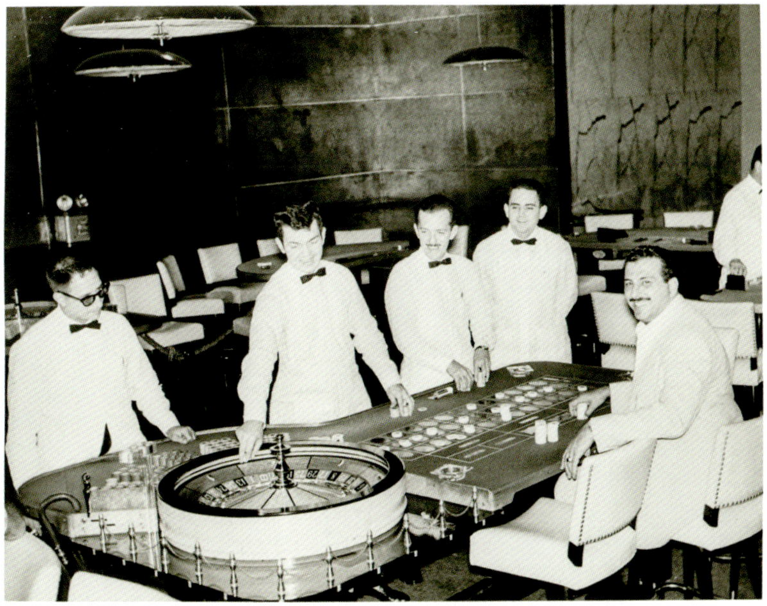

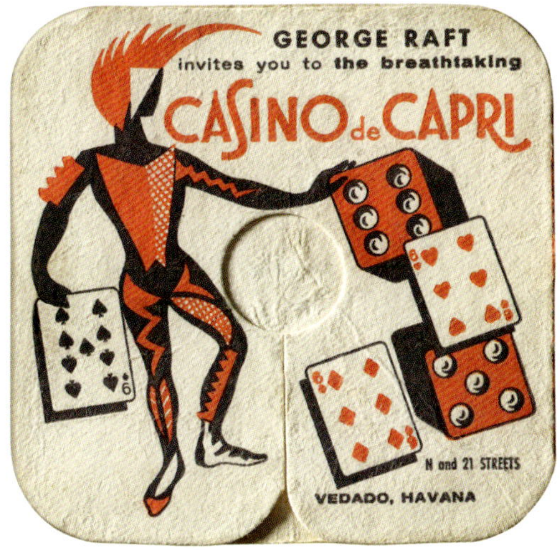

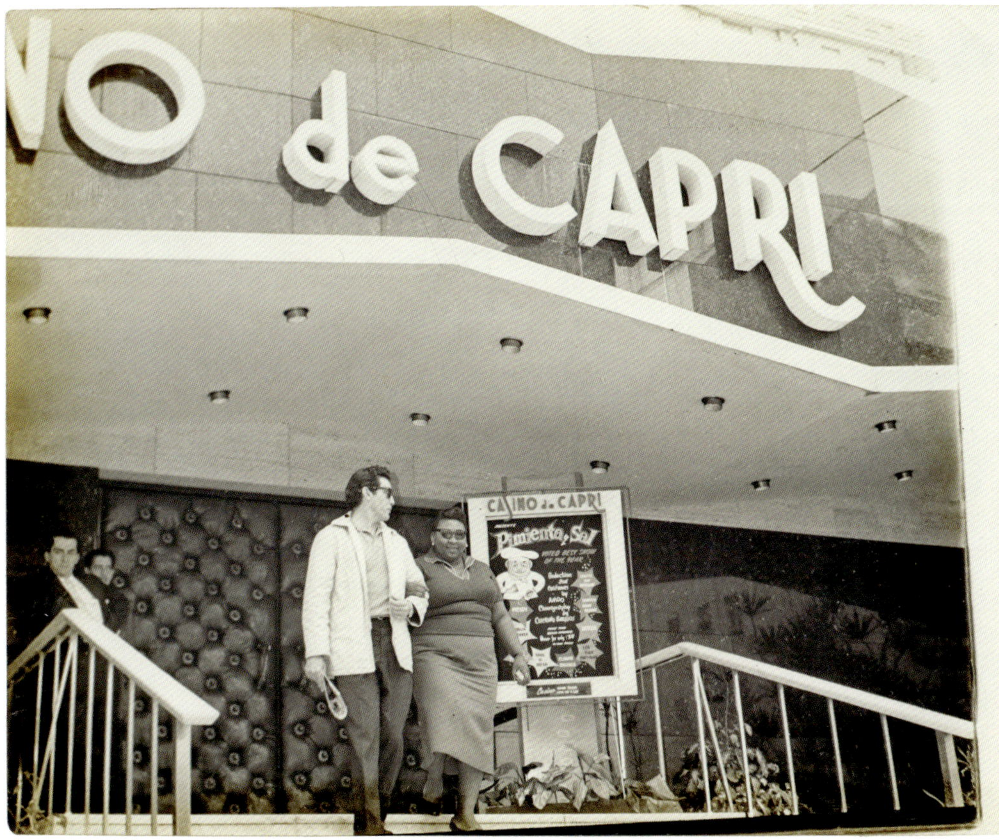

Photograph, **Roulette table at a Havana casino**, c. 1957
Gelatin silver print

The Wolfsonian–FIU, The Vicki Gold Levi Collection, TL2018.13.7

Coaster, ***George Raft Invites You to the Breathtaking Casino de Capri***, c. 1958

The Wolfsonian–FIU, The Vicki Gold Levi Collection, XC2016.01.1.725

Photograph, **Cuban singer Fredesvinda García ("La Freddy"), Casino de Capri entrance**, c. 1957
Gelatin silver print

The Wolfsonian–FIU, The Vicki Gold Levi Collection, XC2016.01.1.844

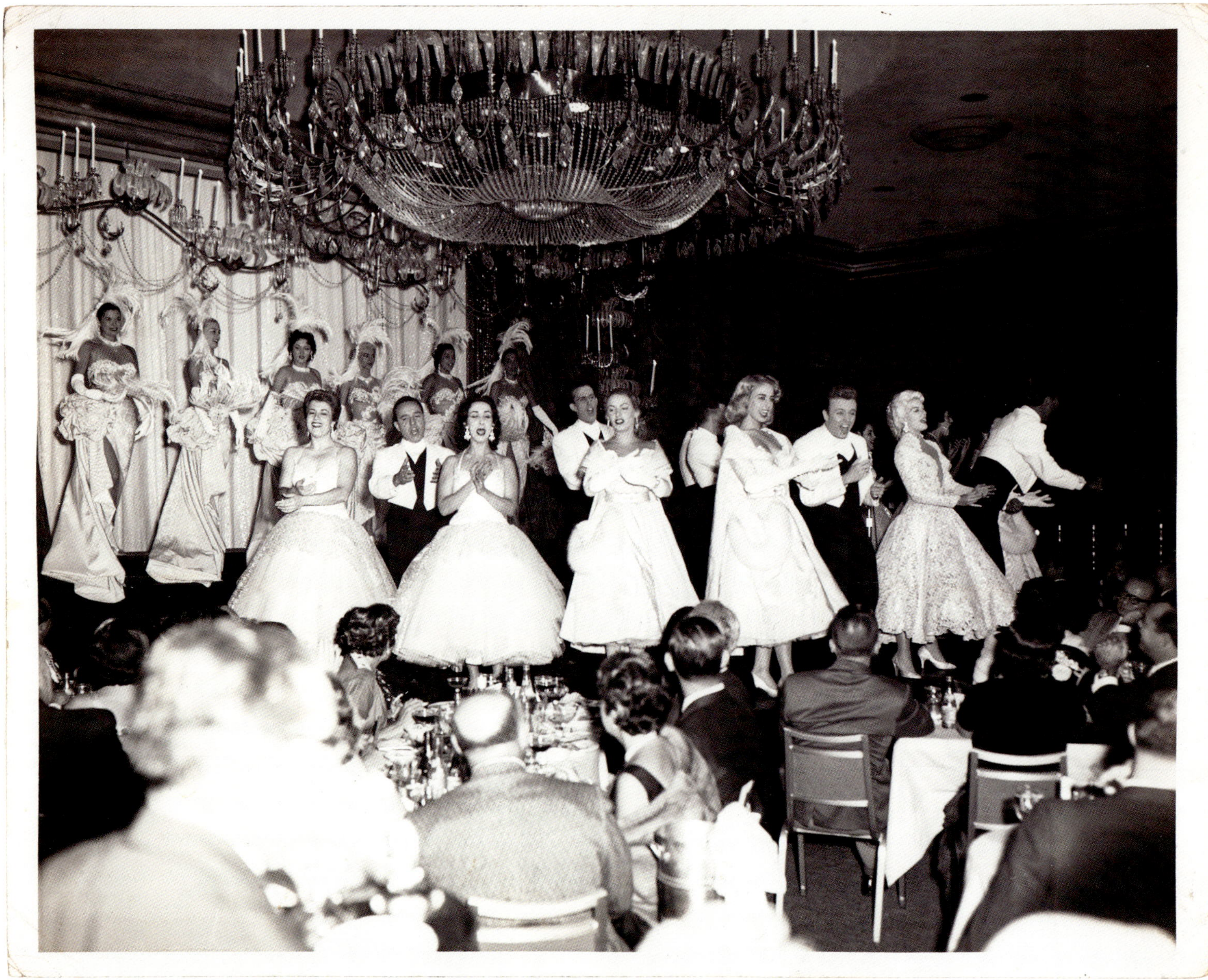

Photograph, **Casino de Capri interior**, c. 1957
Alberto Korda (Cuban, 1928–2001), photographer
Gelatin silver print

The Wolfsonian–FIU, The Vicki Gold Levi Collection, XC2016.01.1.798.1

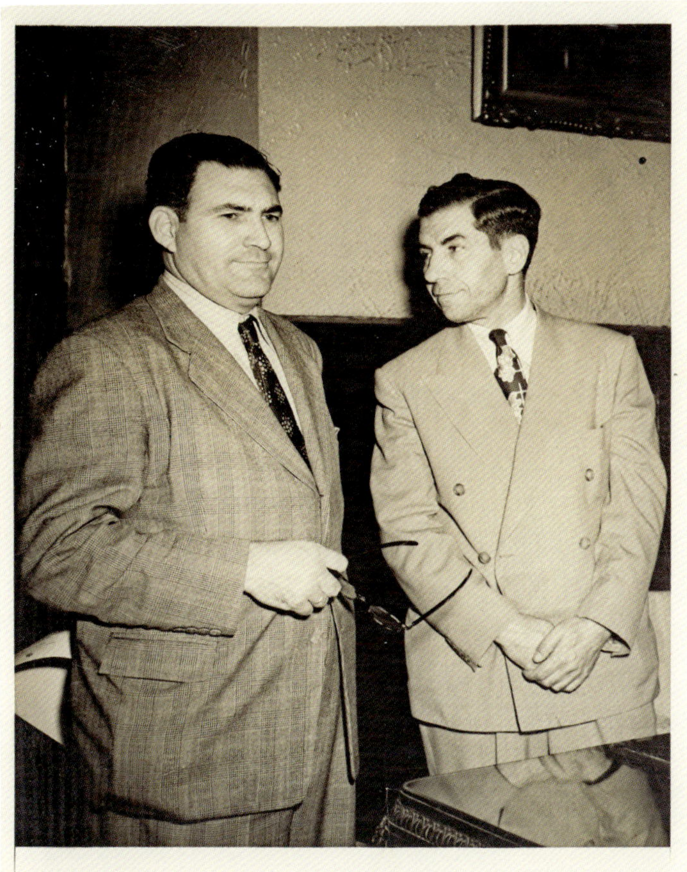

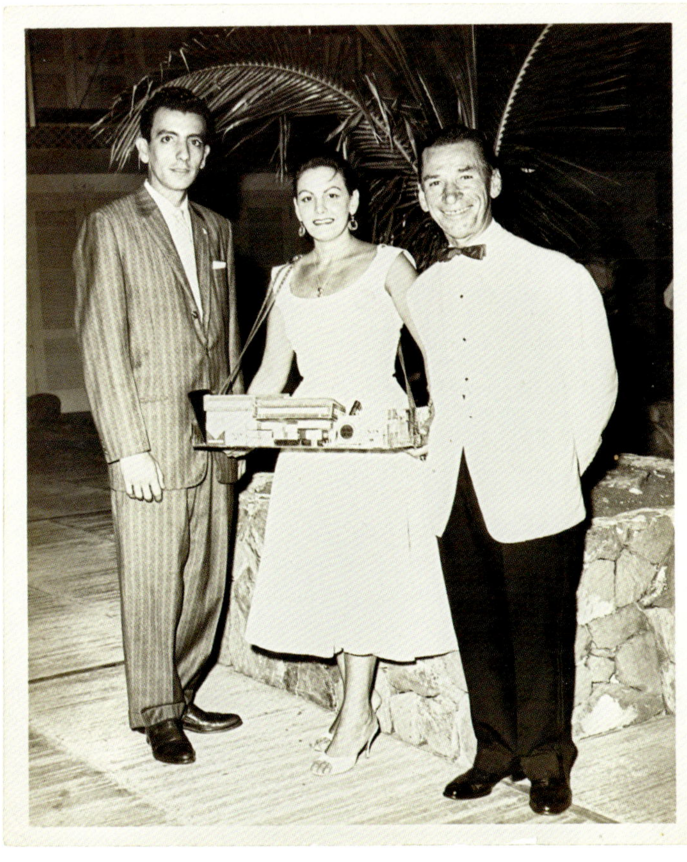

Photographs
Gelatin silver prints

Lucky Luciano (right) **under arrest in Havana and pending deportation**, February 23, 1947

Meyer Lansky (right) **at the opening of the Hotel Riviera**, December 1957

The Wolfsonian–FIU, The Vicki Gold Levi Collection, XC2016.01.1.778, .1218

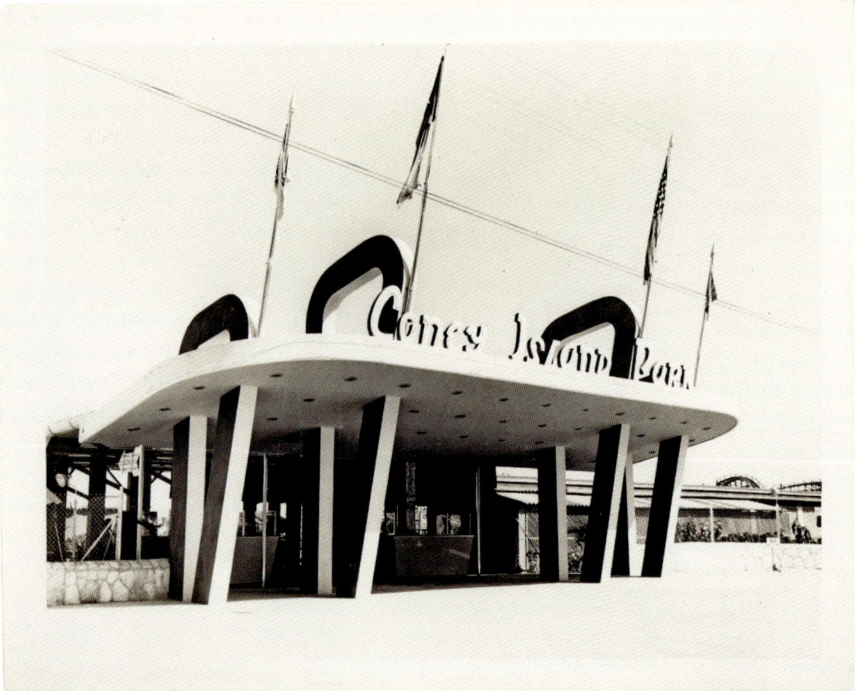

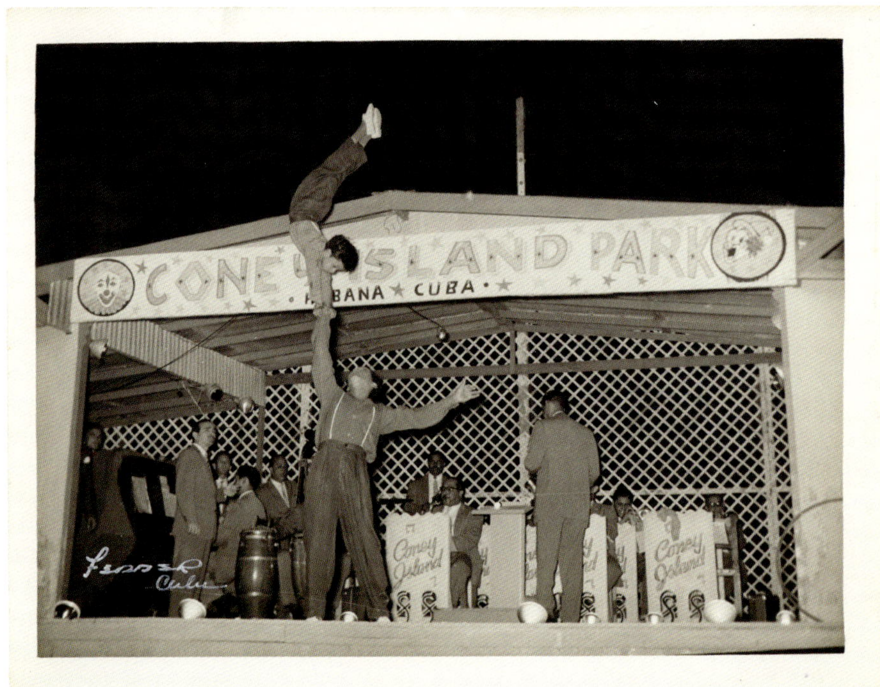

Photographs
Gelatin silver prints

Entrance to Coney Island Park, c. 1955

Acrobats at Coney Island Park, c. 1955

The Wolfsonian–FIU, The Vicki Gold Levi Collection, XC2016.01.1.159, .72

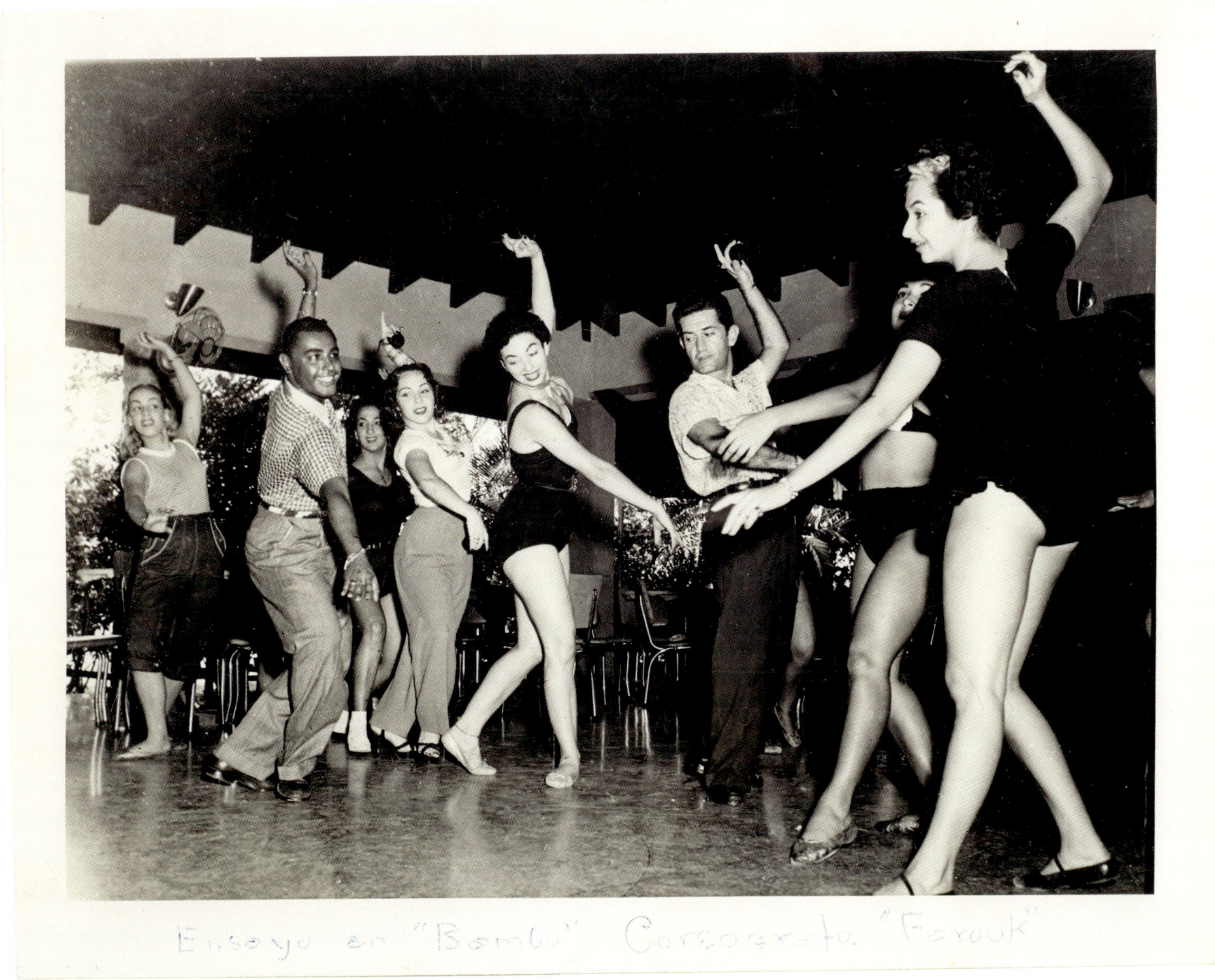

Photograph, **Choreographer "Farouk" working with dancers at El Bambú**, c. 1955
Gelatin silver print

The Wolfsonian–FIU, The Vicki Gold Levi Collection, XC2016.01.1.879

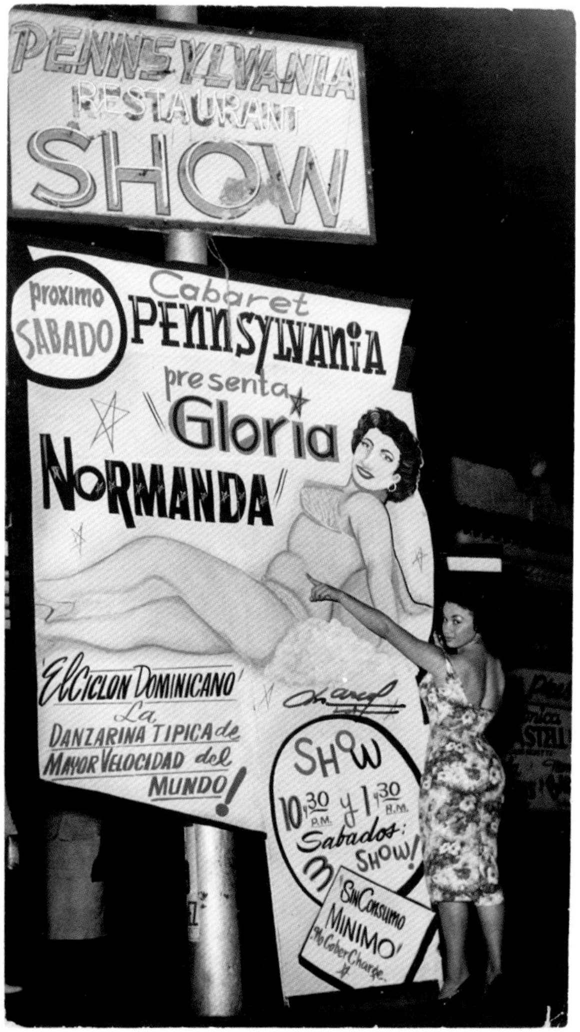

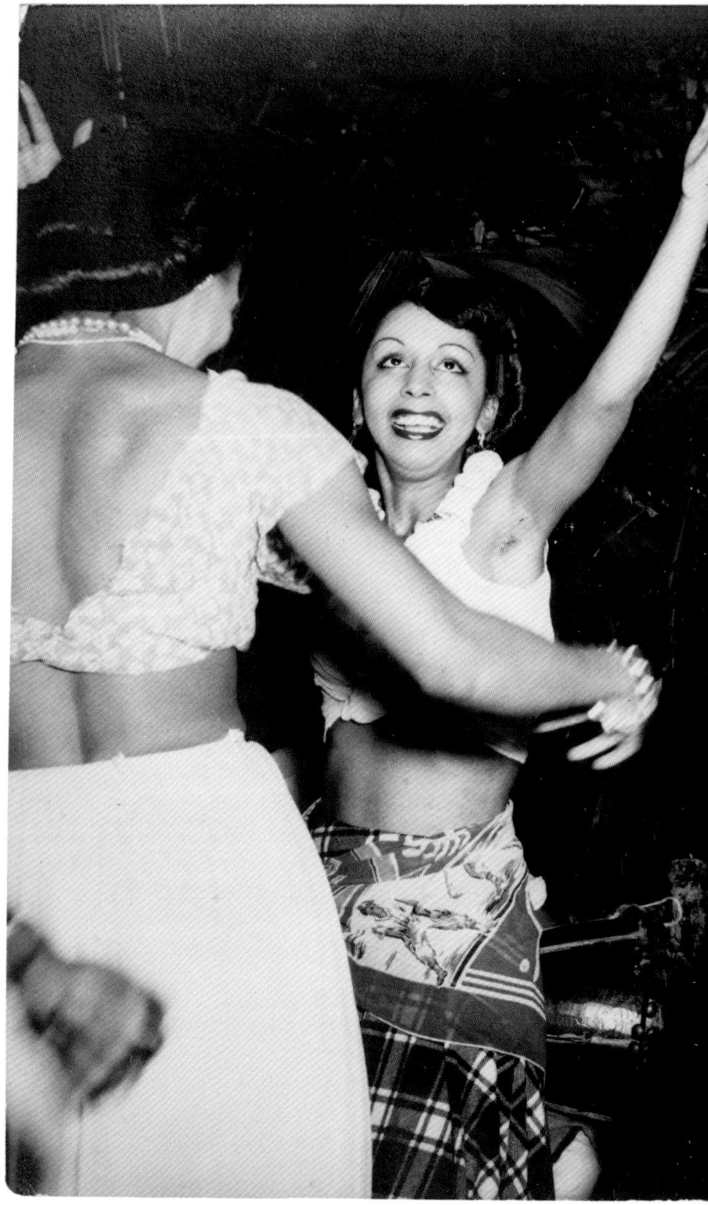

Photographs
Gelatin silver prints

Gloria Normanda ("El Ciclon Dominicano"), **pointing to her sign at the Pennsylvania**, c. 1957

The Wolfsonian–FIU, The Vicki Gold Levi Collection, XC2016.01.1.31

Dancers, c. 1955

Vicki Gold Levi private collection, TL2018.13.3

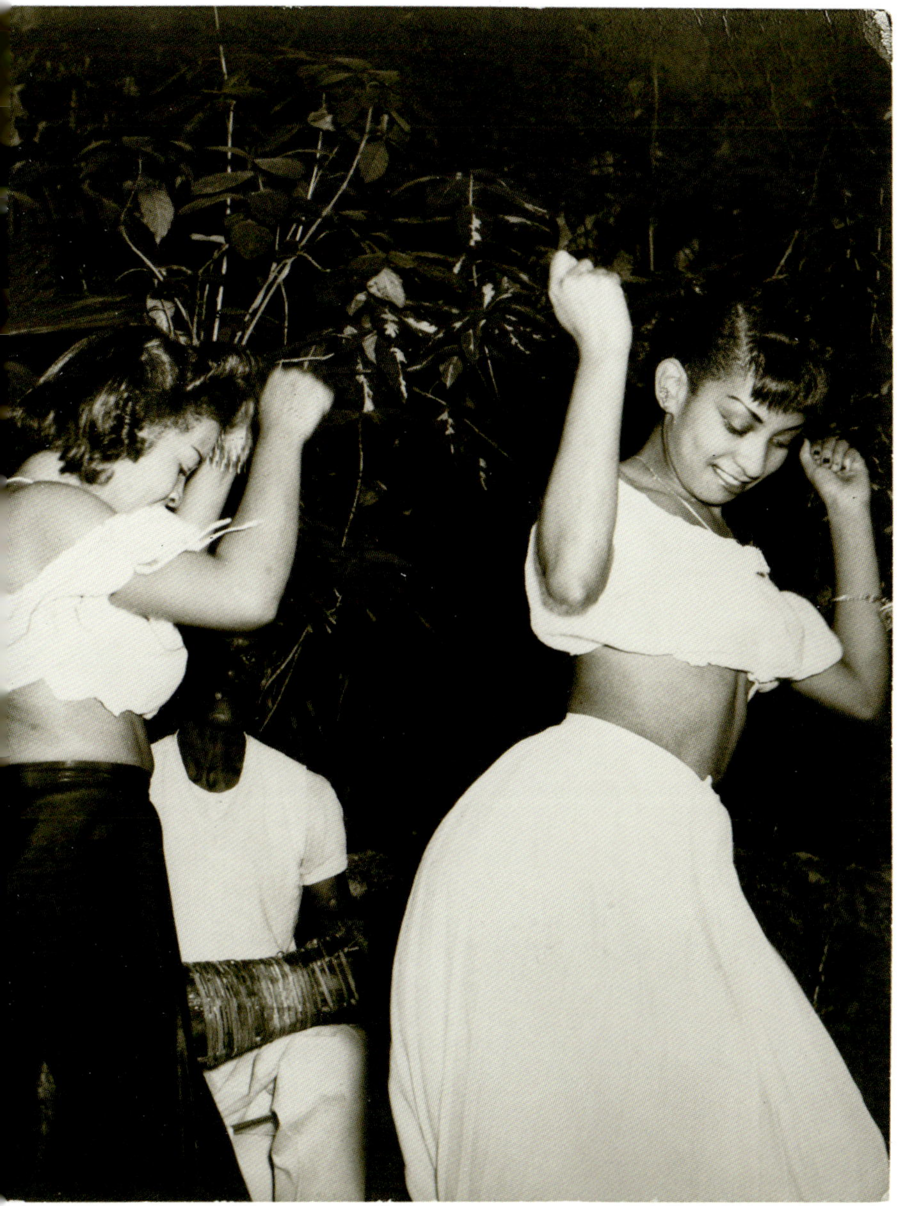

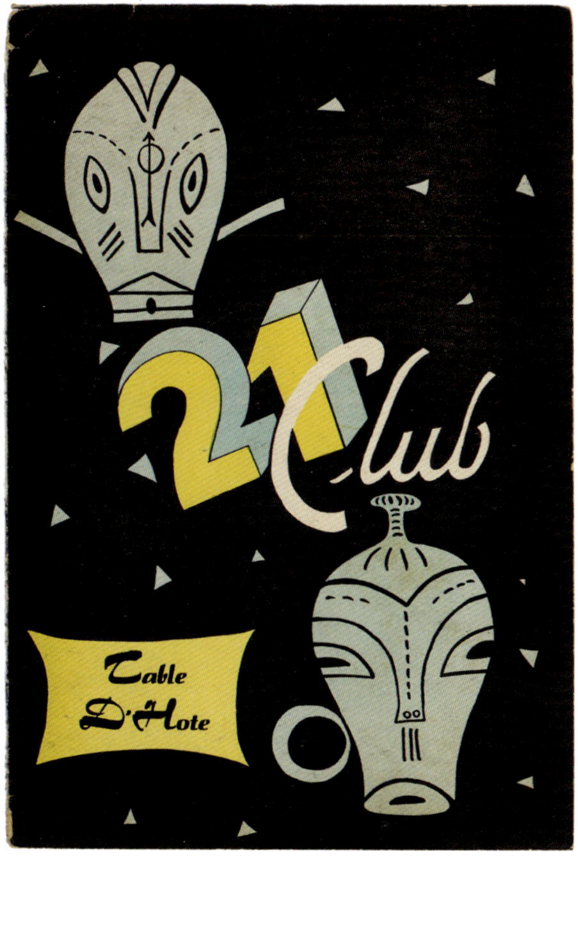

Photograph folder, ***Club 21: Table D'Hote***, c. 1955

The Wolfsonian–FIU, The Vicki Gold Levi Collection, XC2016.01.1.732

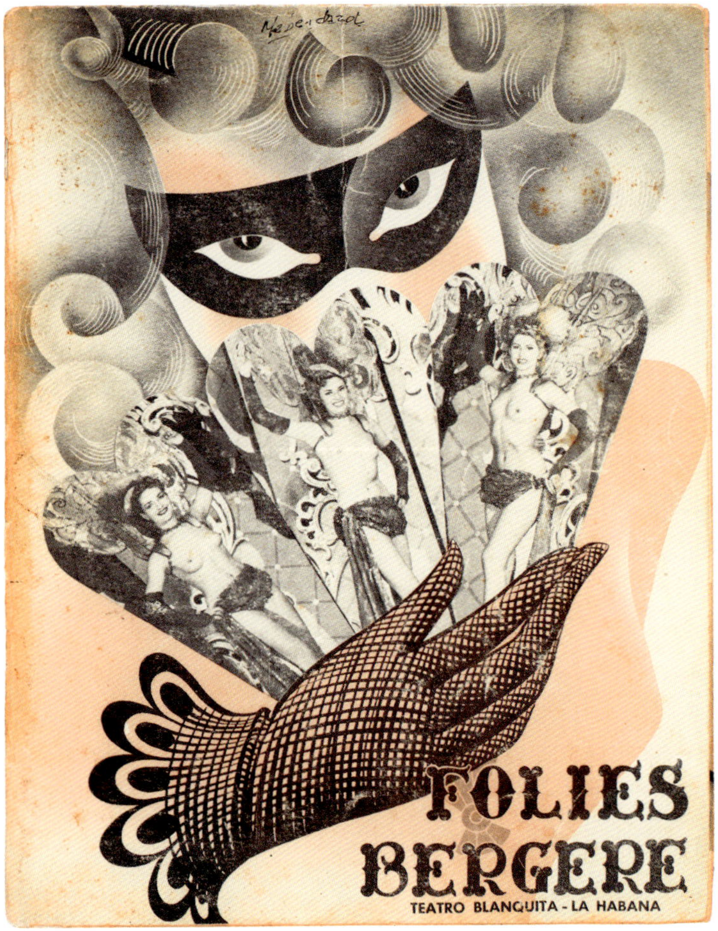

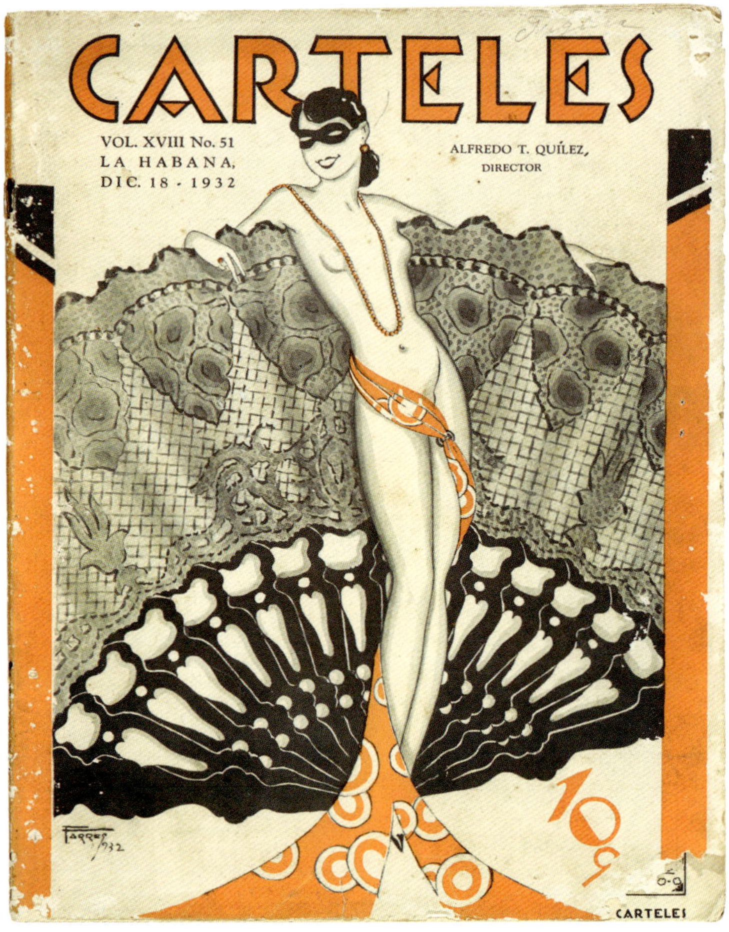

Program, ***Folies Bergere: Teatro Blanquita, La Habana***, c. 1955

The Wolfsonian–FIU, The Vicki Gold Levi Collection, XC2002.11.4.227

Periodical, ***Carteles***, December 18, 1932
Osvaldo Farrés (Cuban, 1902–1985), cover illustrator

The Wolfsonian–FIU, The Vicki Gold Levi Collection, XC2016.01.1.1338

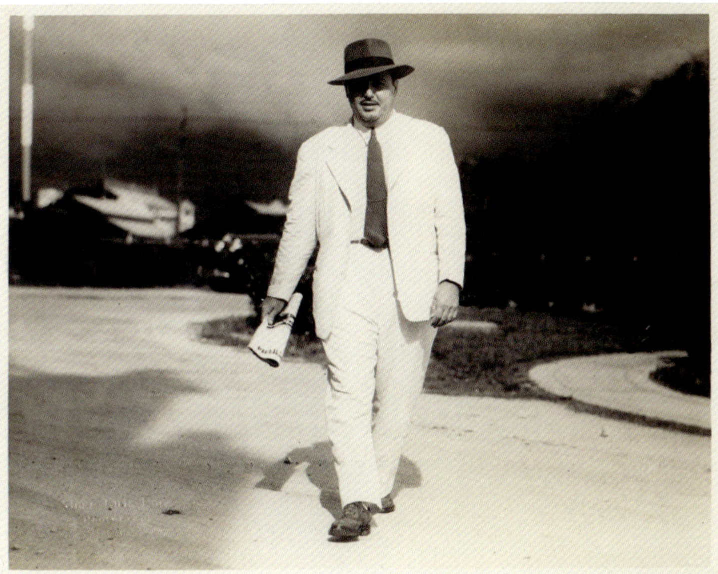

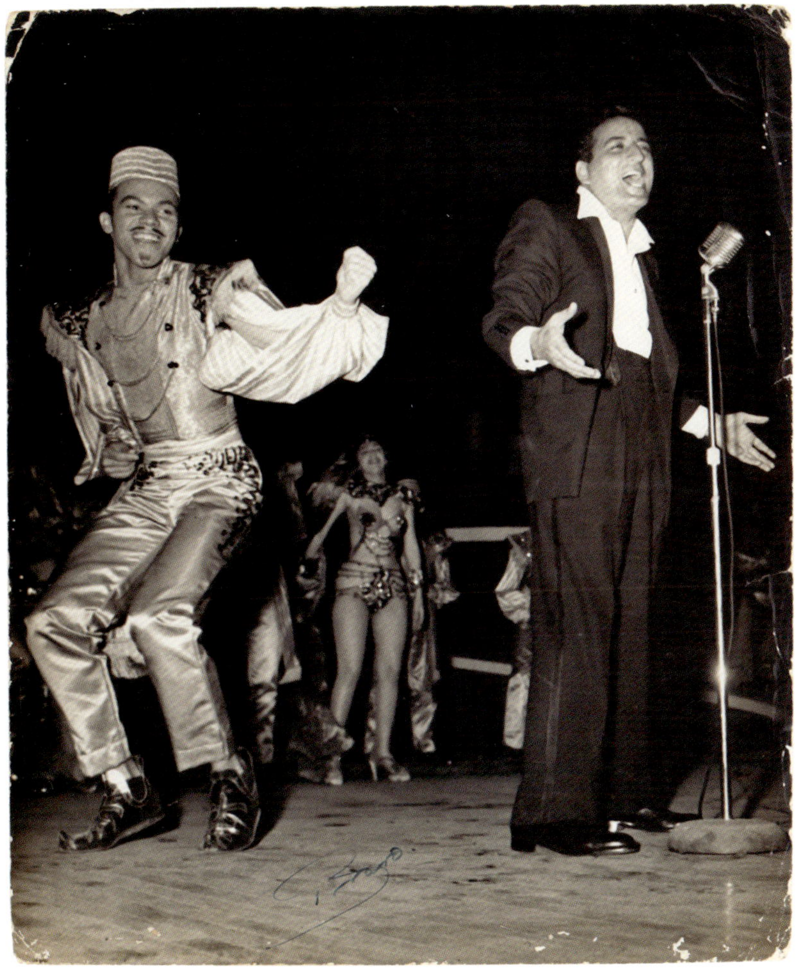

Photographs
Gelatin silver prints

Indolencio Pertierra, owner of Montmartre, 1941
José Luis López, photographer

Singer Tony Bennett (right) **and Tomaí Morales at Montmartre**, 1957
Rey y Bravo, photographer

The Wolfsonian–FIU, The Vicki Gold Levi Collection, XC2016.01.1.188, .779

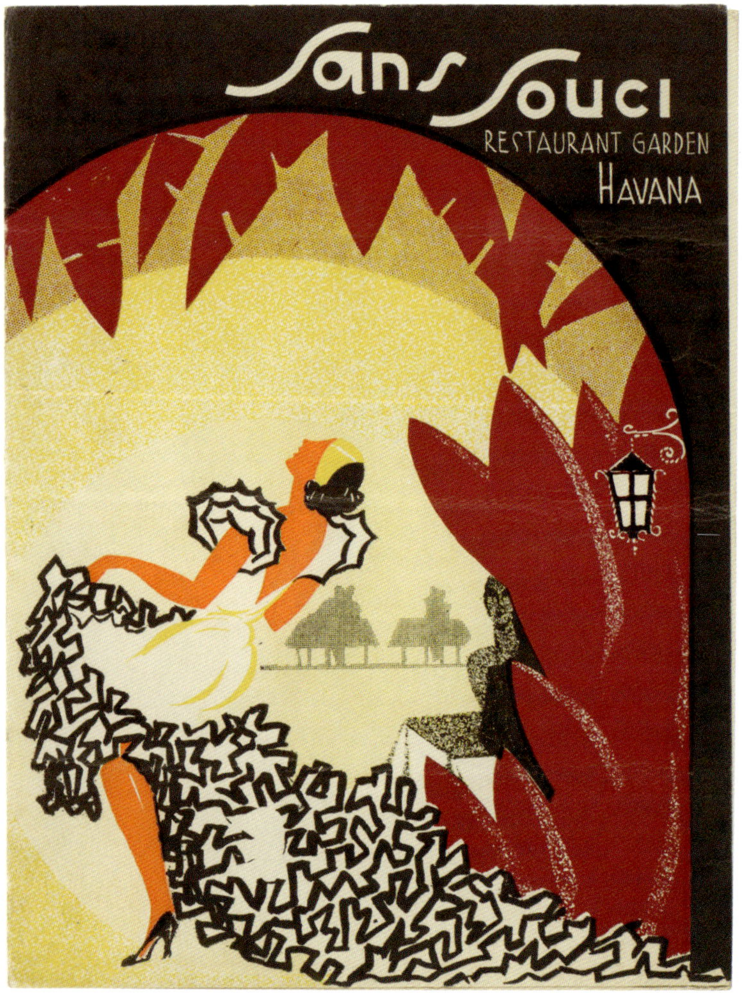

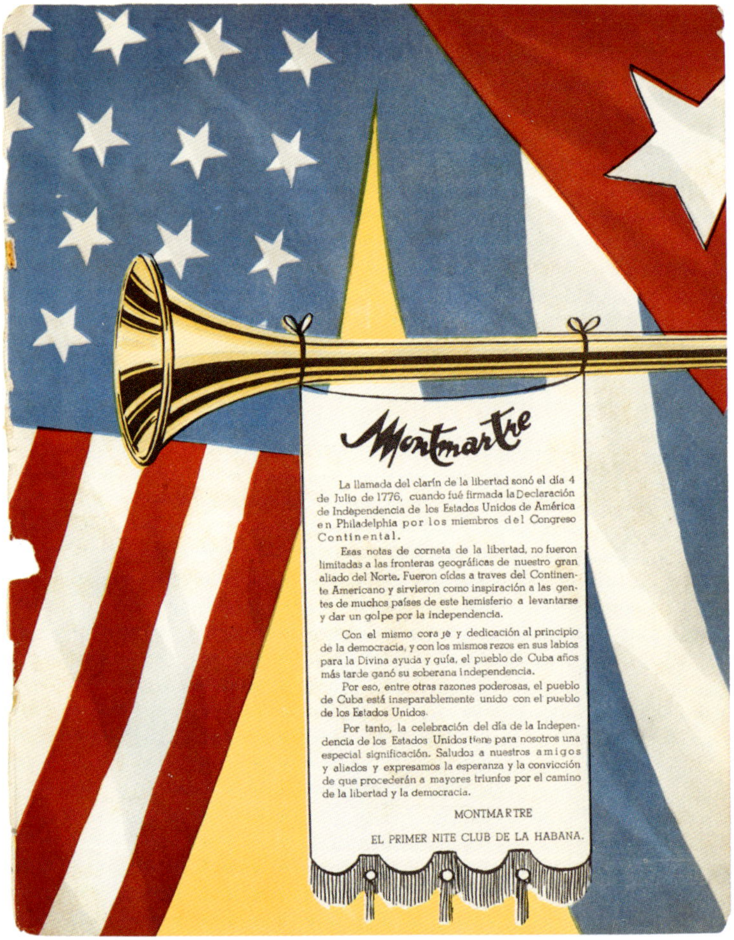

Menu, *Sans Souci Restaurant Garden, Havana*, c. 1950

The Wolfsonian–FIU, The Vicki Gold Levi Collection, XC2002.11.4.130

Advertisement, *Montmartre*, c. 1955

The Wolfsonian–FIU, The Vicki Gold Levi Collection, XC2016.01.1.791.2

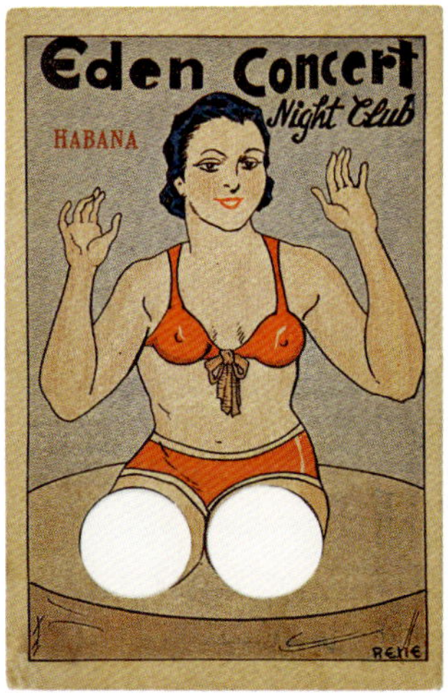

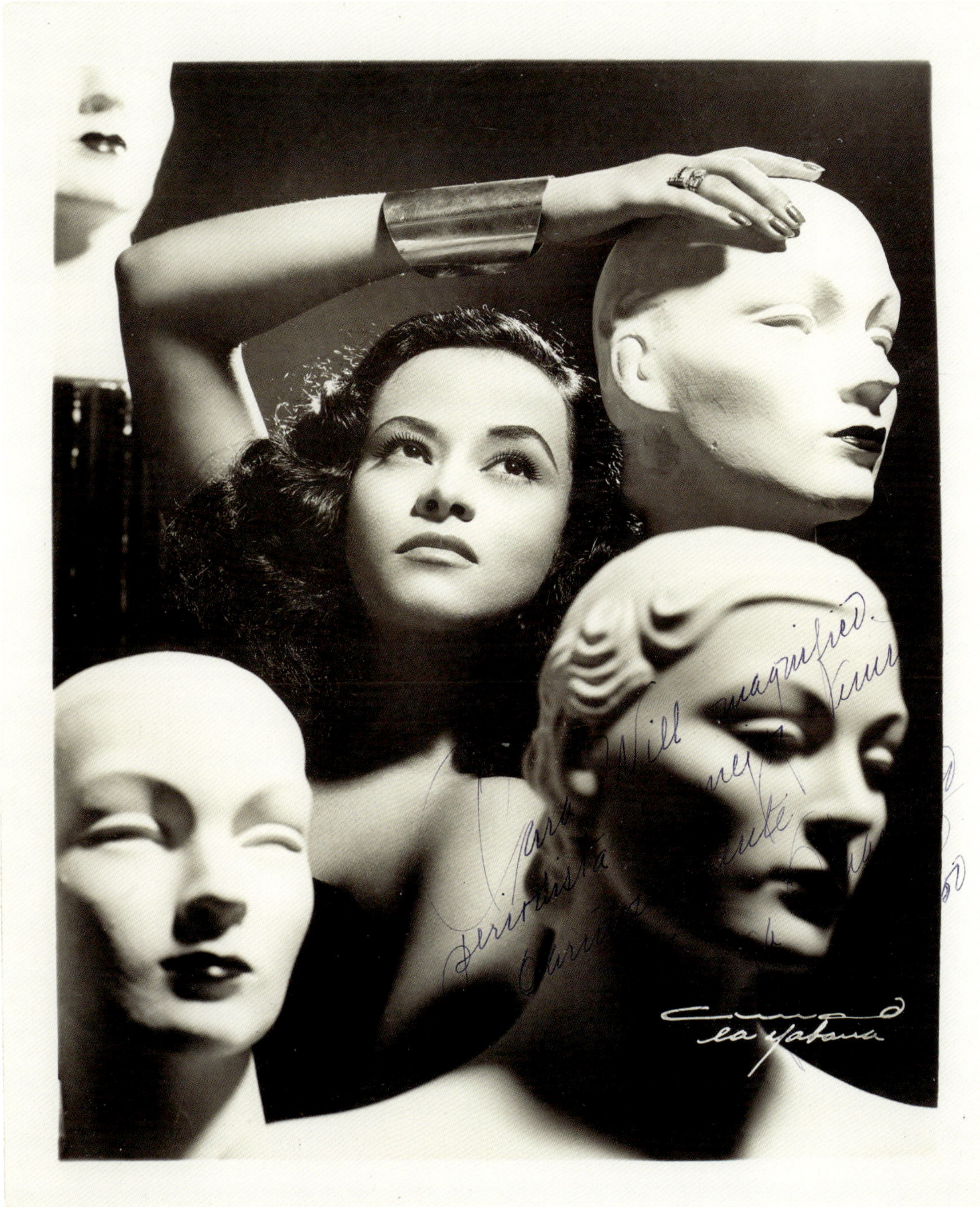

Postcard, ***Eden Concert Night Club, Habana***, c. 1935

This whimsical souvenir allowed the purchaser to insert a finger in each hole to make the entertainer's "legs" dance.

The Wolfsonian–FIU, The Vicki Gold Levi Collection, XC2016.01.1.729

Photograph, **Dancer Olga Chaviano**, c. 1955
Armand (Armenak Arzrouni; b. Ottoman Empire, 1901–1963), **photographer**
Gelatin silver print

A star at Sans Souci, Olga Chaviano was also purported to be the lover of the casino's mob boss, Norman Rothman.

The Wolfsonian–FIU, The Vicki Gold Levi Collection, XC2016.01.1.87

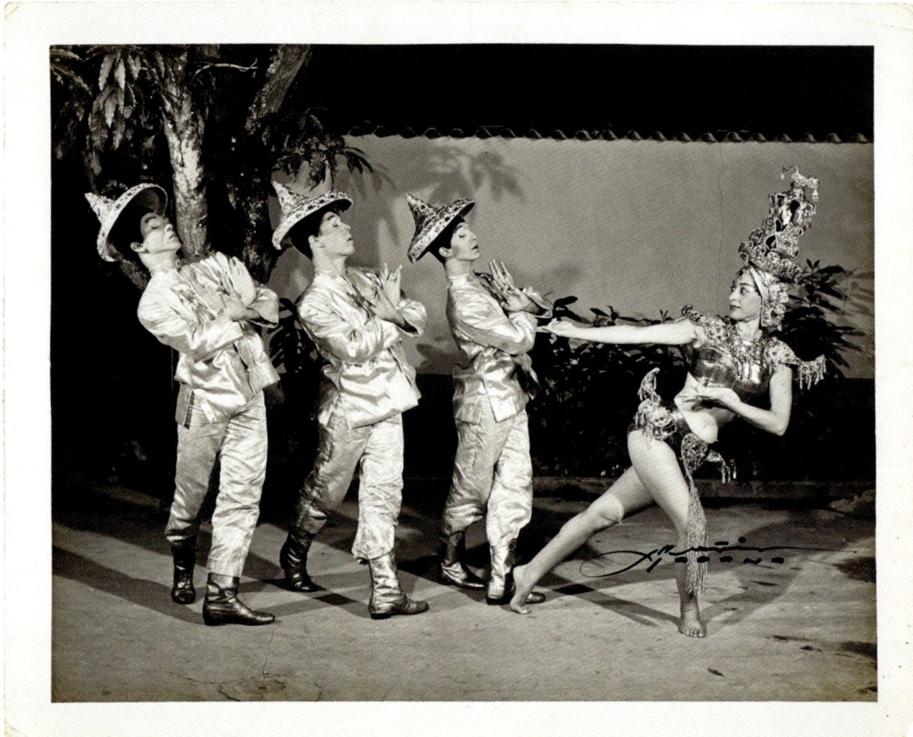

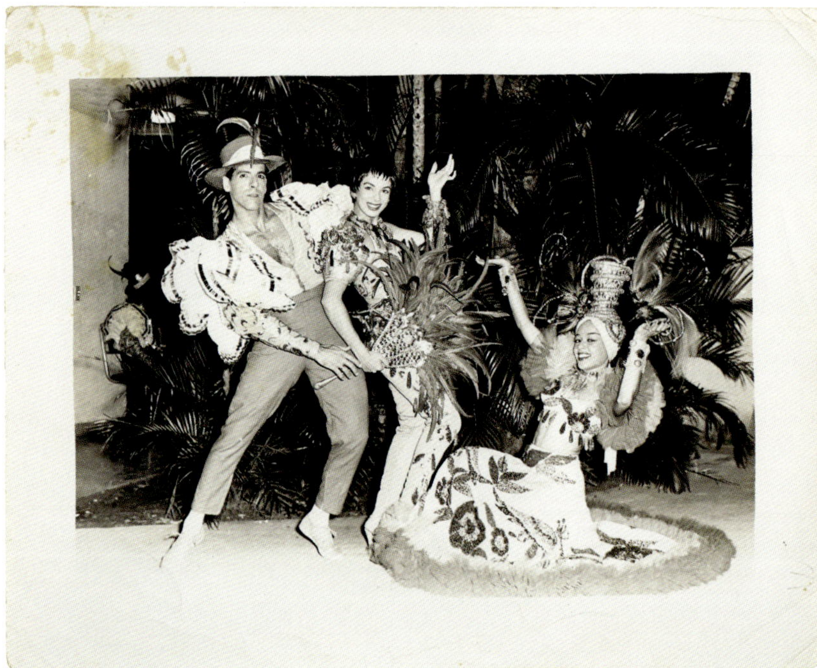

Photographs
Gelatin silver prints

Tropicana performers in Asian-style costumes, November 16, 1957
Vicente Muñiz (Cuban, 1917–2007), Havana, photographer

Juan de la Portilla, Gladys Robau, and Tropicana performer (left to right), c. 1955

The Wolfsonian–FIU, The Vicki Gold Levi Collection, XC2016.01.1.1176, .1172

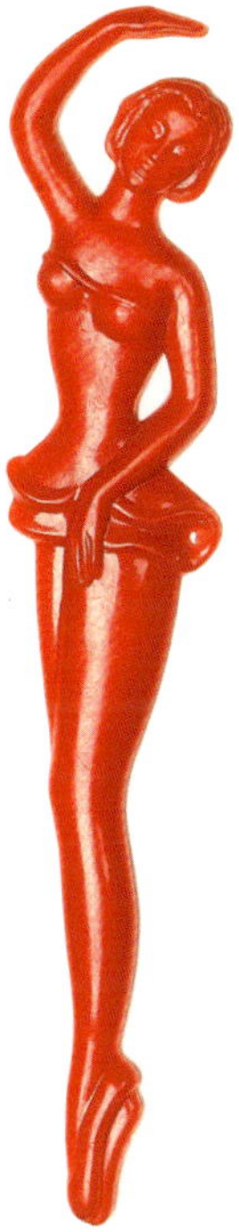

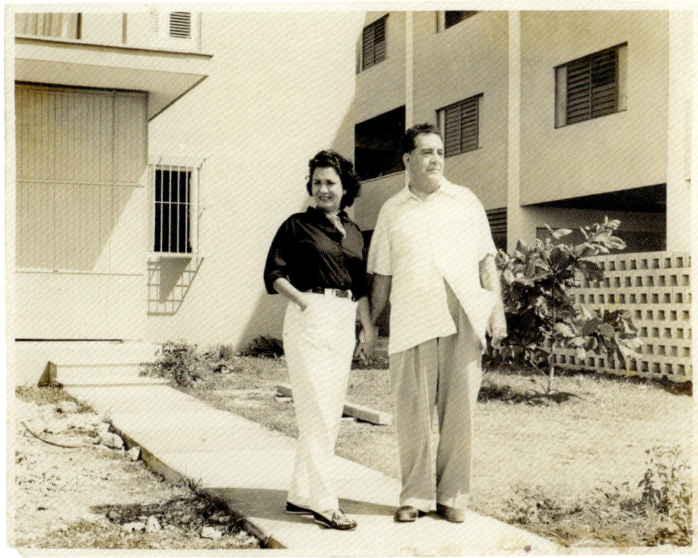

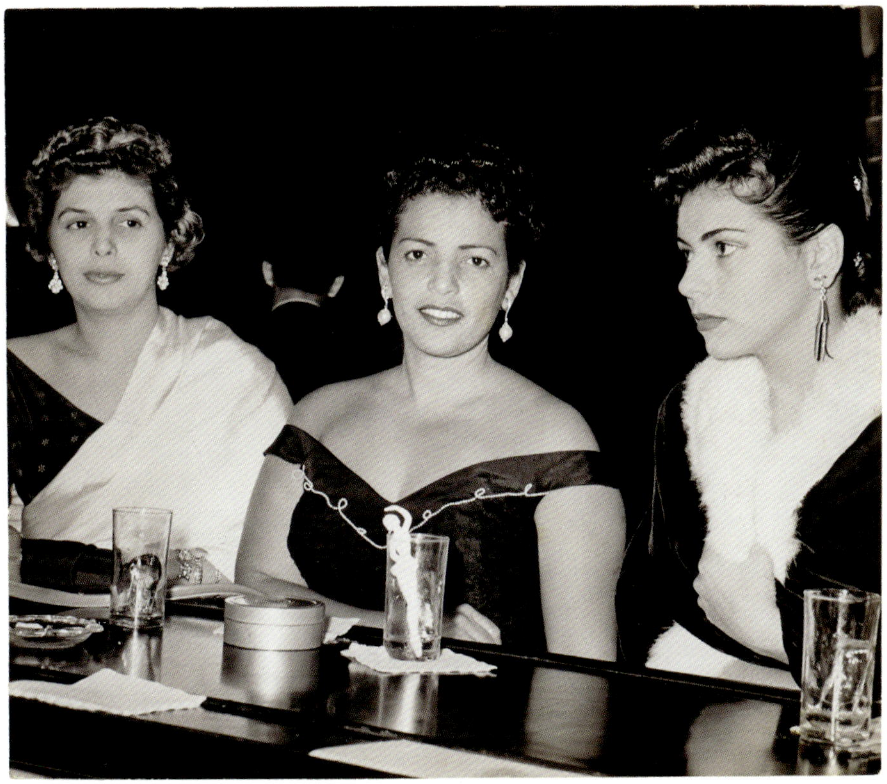

Tropicana ballerina cocktail swizzle stick, c. 1956

Vicki Gold Levi private collection, TL2018.15.25

Photographs
Gelatin silver prints

Martín and Ofelia Fox, 1957
Tropicana owner Martín Fox married Ofelia Suarez in Arcos de Cristal on October 5, 1952. The couple's lives revolved around the nightclub, which they hosted seven nights a week.

Women at Tropicana, c. 1956

The Wolfsonian–FIU, The Vicki Gold Levi Collection, XC2016.01.1.780, .1177

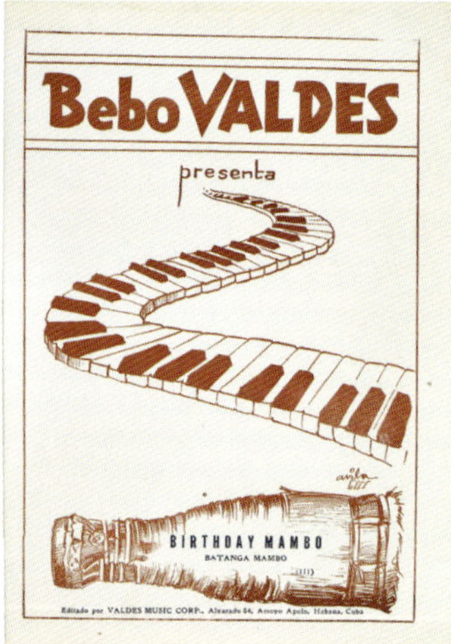

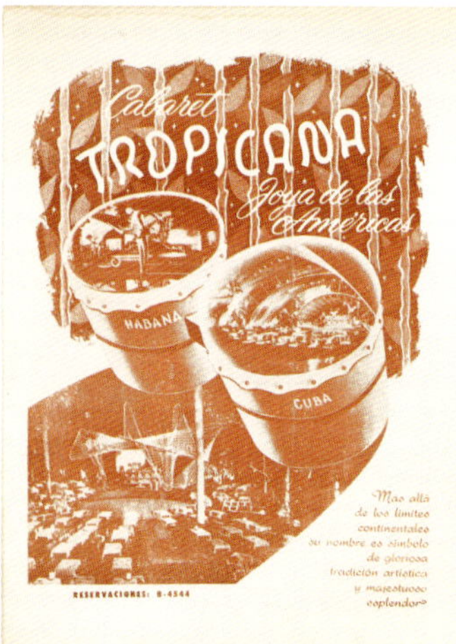

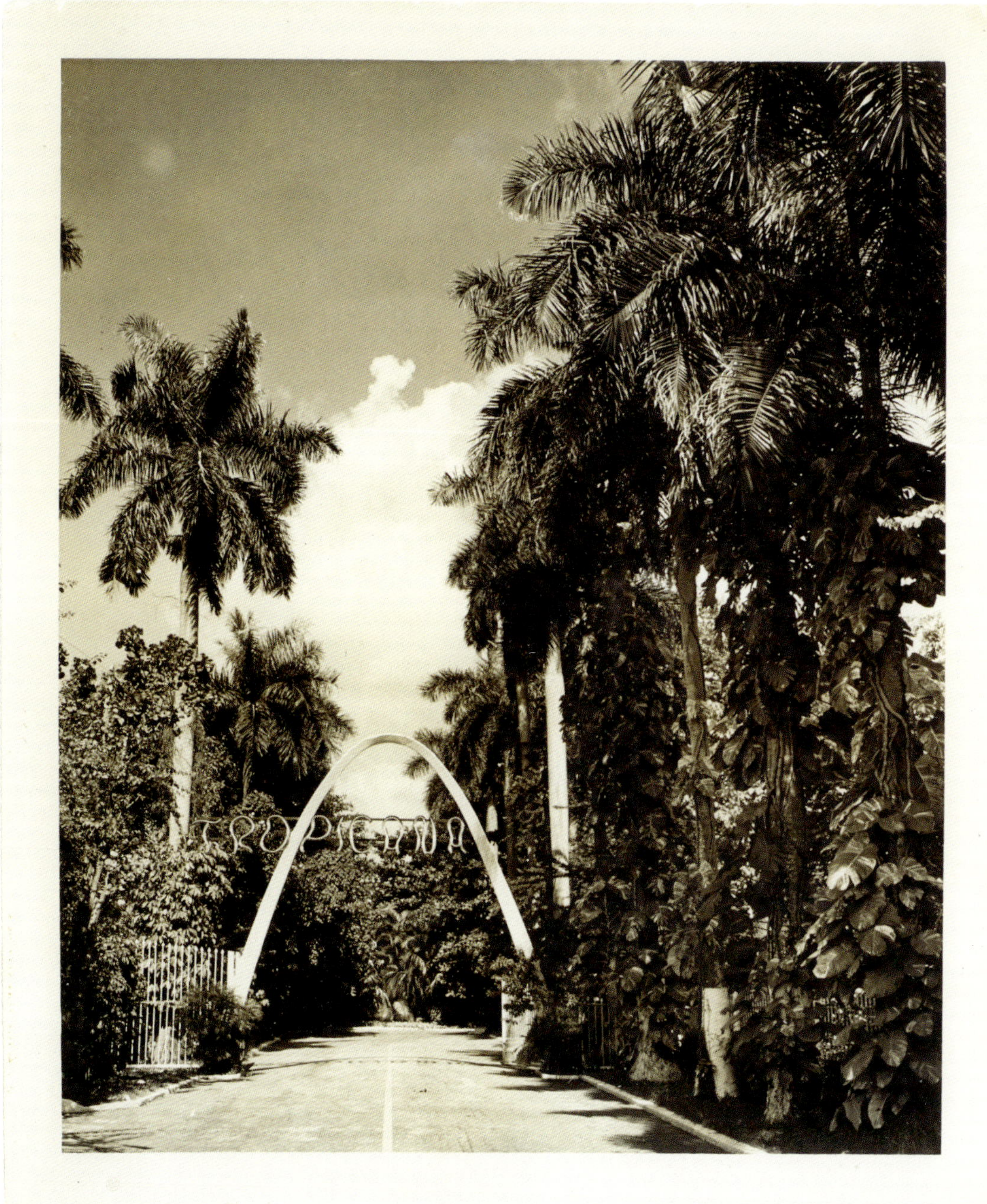

Announcement, ***Bebo Valdés presenta Birthday Mambo, Batanga Mambo***, c. 1955
Valdes Music Corp., Havana, publisher

The Wolfsonian–FIU, The Vicki Gold Levi Collection, XC2016.01.1.923

Photograph, **Tropicana entrance**, c. 1958
Vicente Muñiz (Cuban, 1917–2007), photographer
Gelatin silver print

The Wolfsonian–FIU, The Vicki Gold Levi Collection, XC2016.01.1.88

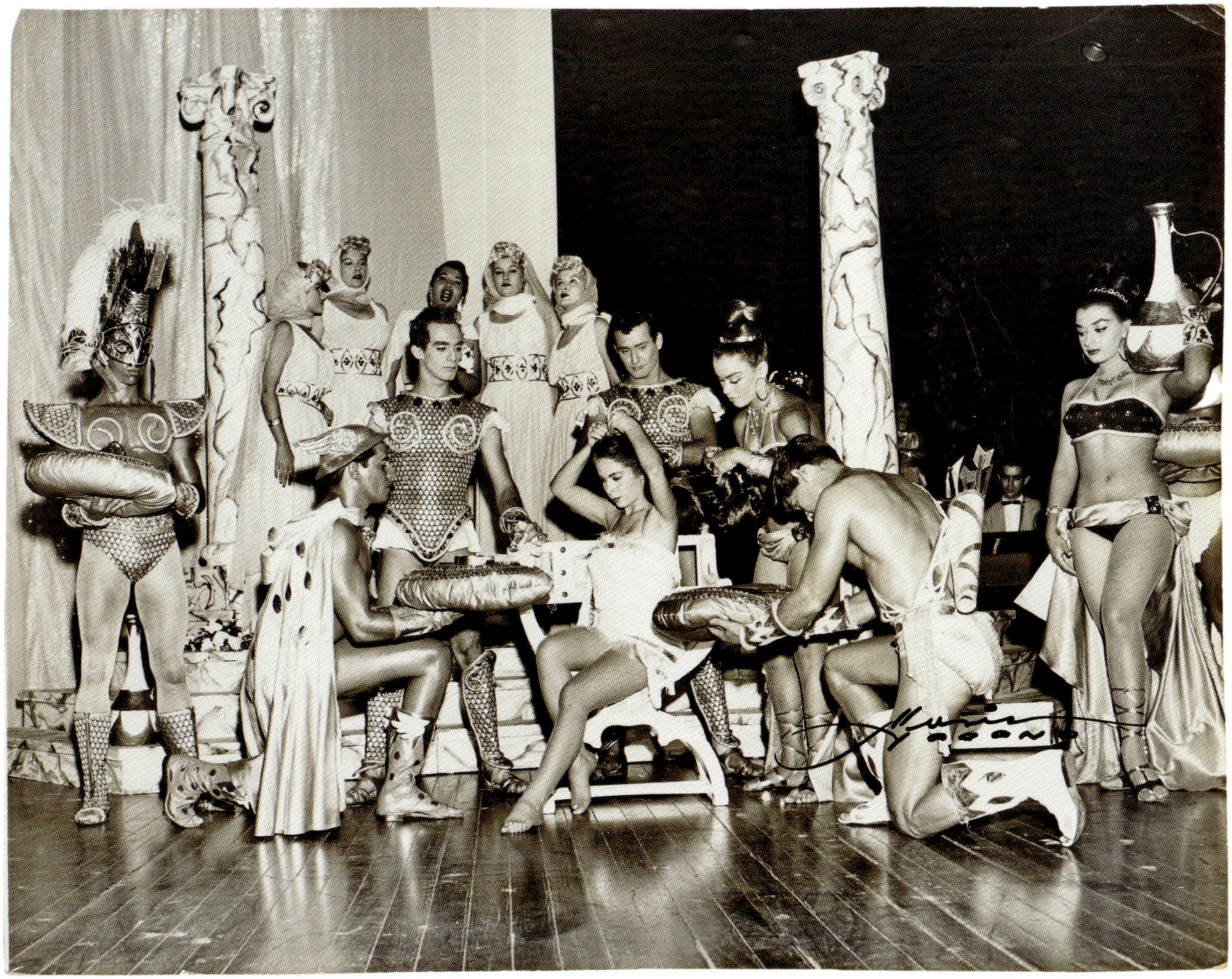

Photograph, **Diosas de carne (Goddesses of the Flesh)**, 1958
Gelatin silver print

This production, choreographed by Rodney and based on the women of Greek literature and mythology, paid tribute to female sexuality.

The Wolfsonian–FIU, The Vicki Gold Levi Collection, XC2016.01.1.1169

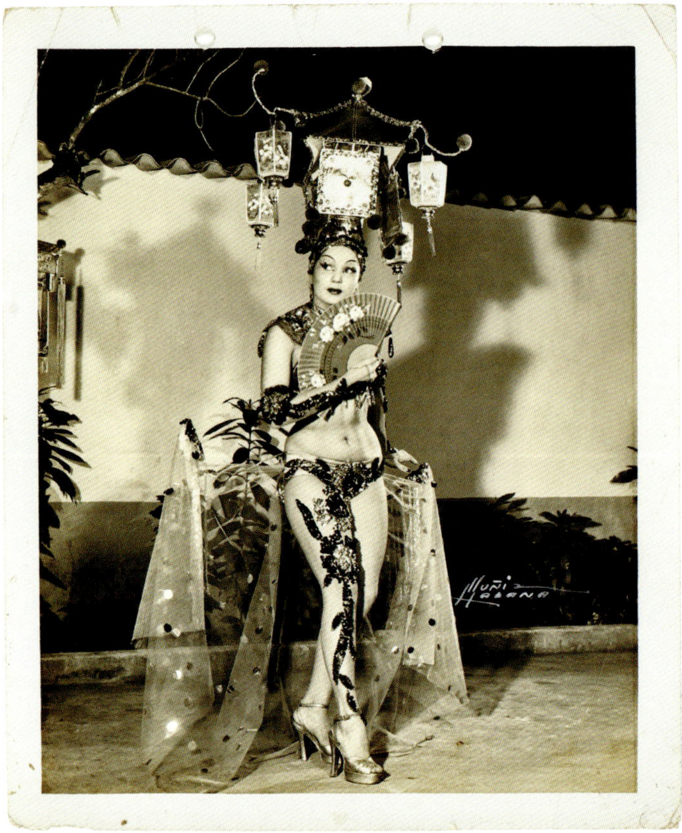

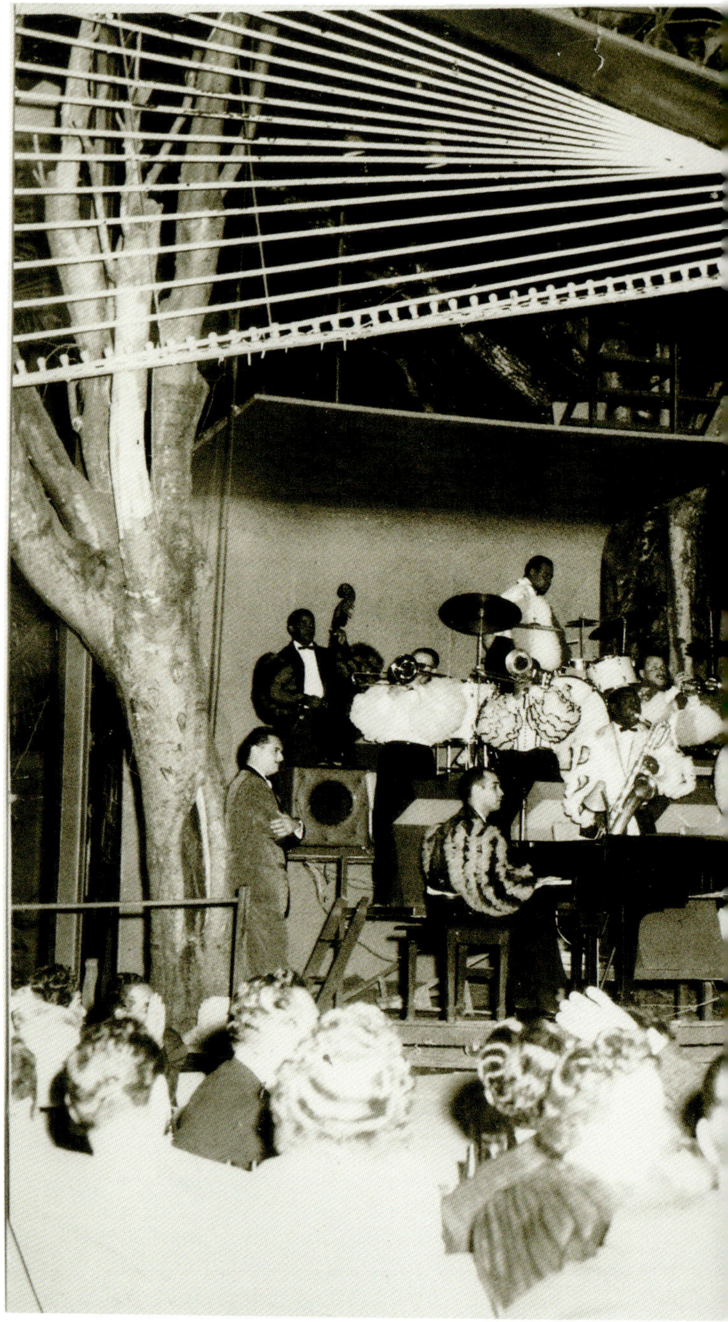

Photographs

Dancer at Tropicana, 1955
Vicente Muñiz (Cuban, 1917–2007),
Havana, photographer
Gelatin silver print

Tropicana, c. 1958
Inkjet print

Tropicana choreographer Rodney with showgirls, c. 1954
Gelatin silver print

Vicki Gold Levi private collection,
TL2018.13.1, .6, .5

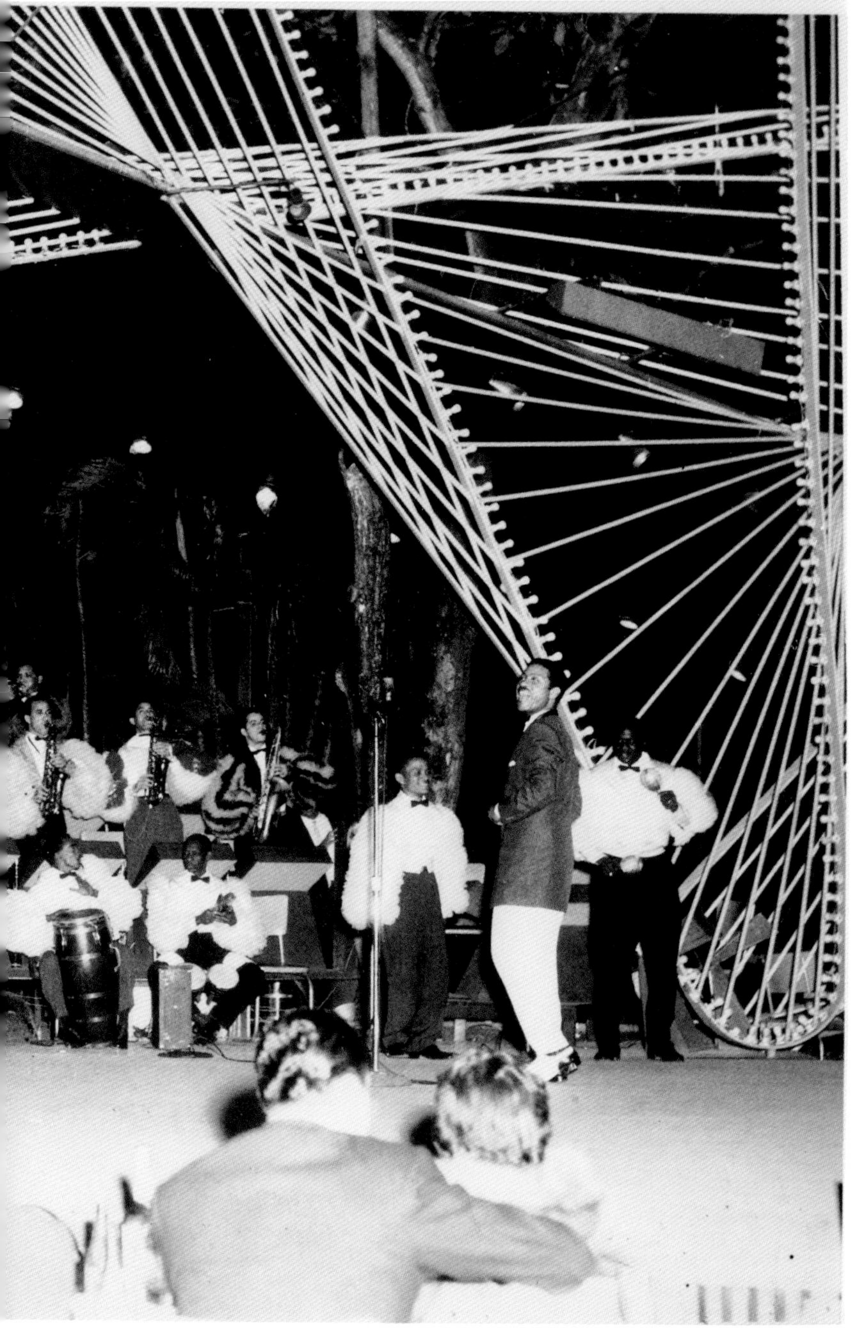

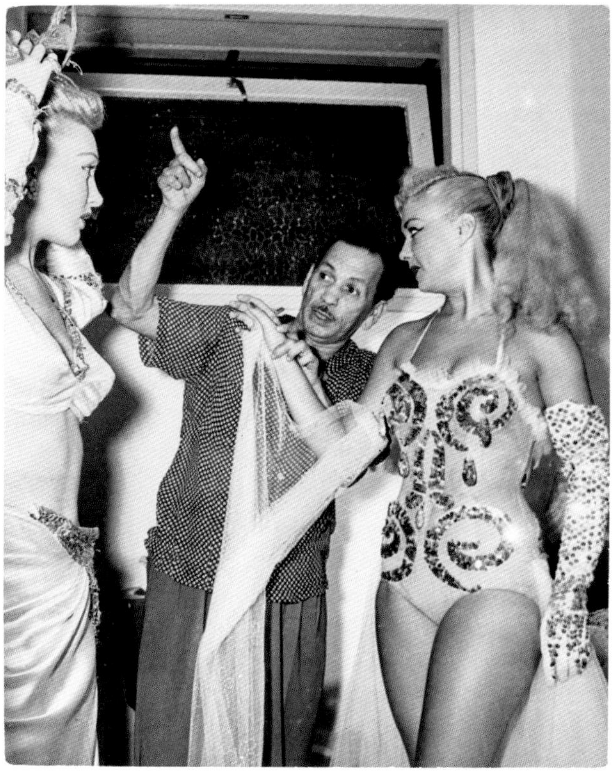

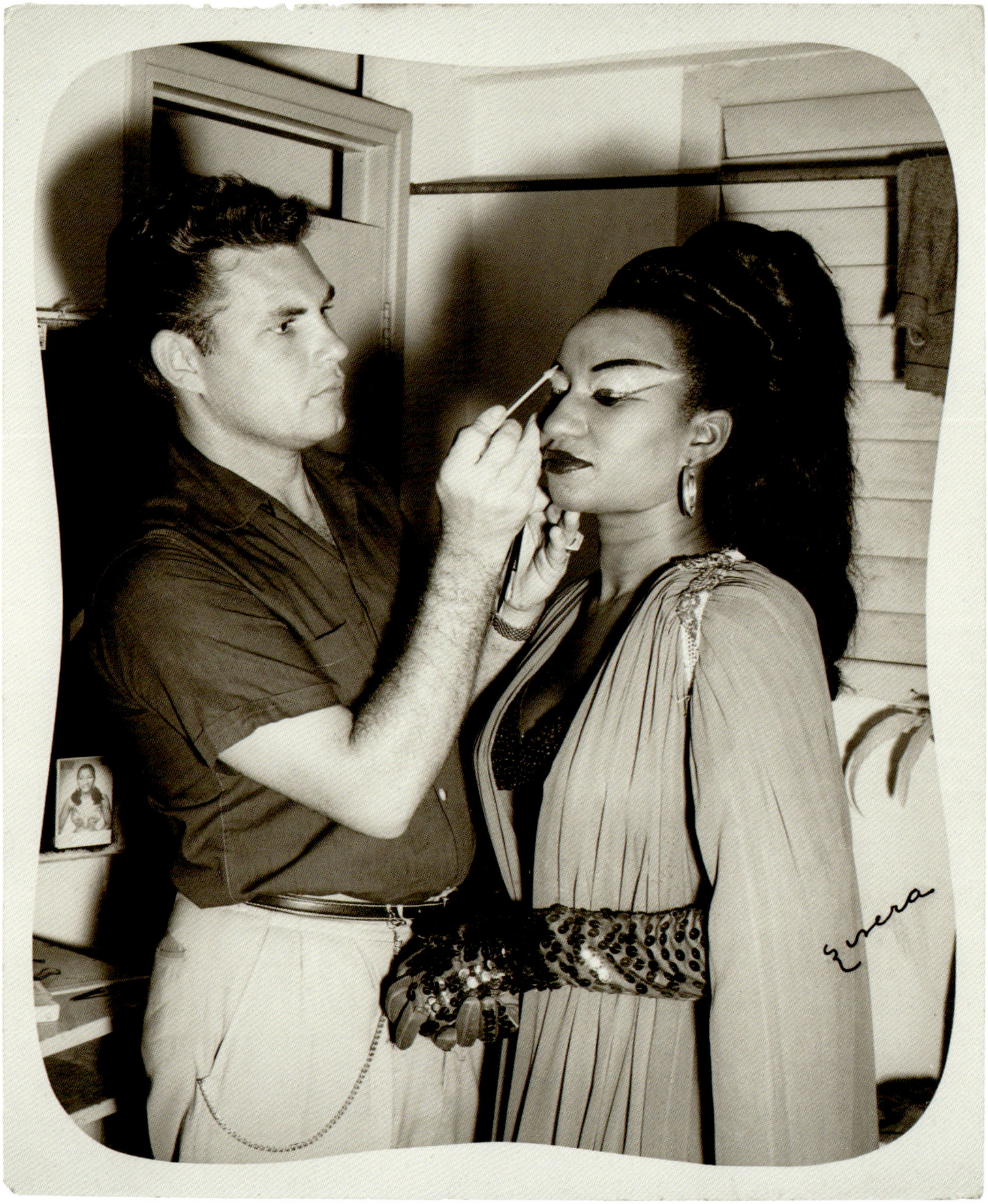

Photograph, **Celia Cruz with makeup artist at Tropicana**, c. 1958
Gelatin silver print

Vicki Gold Levi private collection, TL2018.13.4

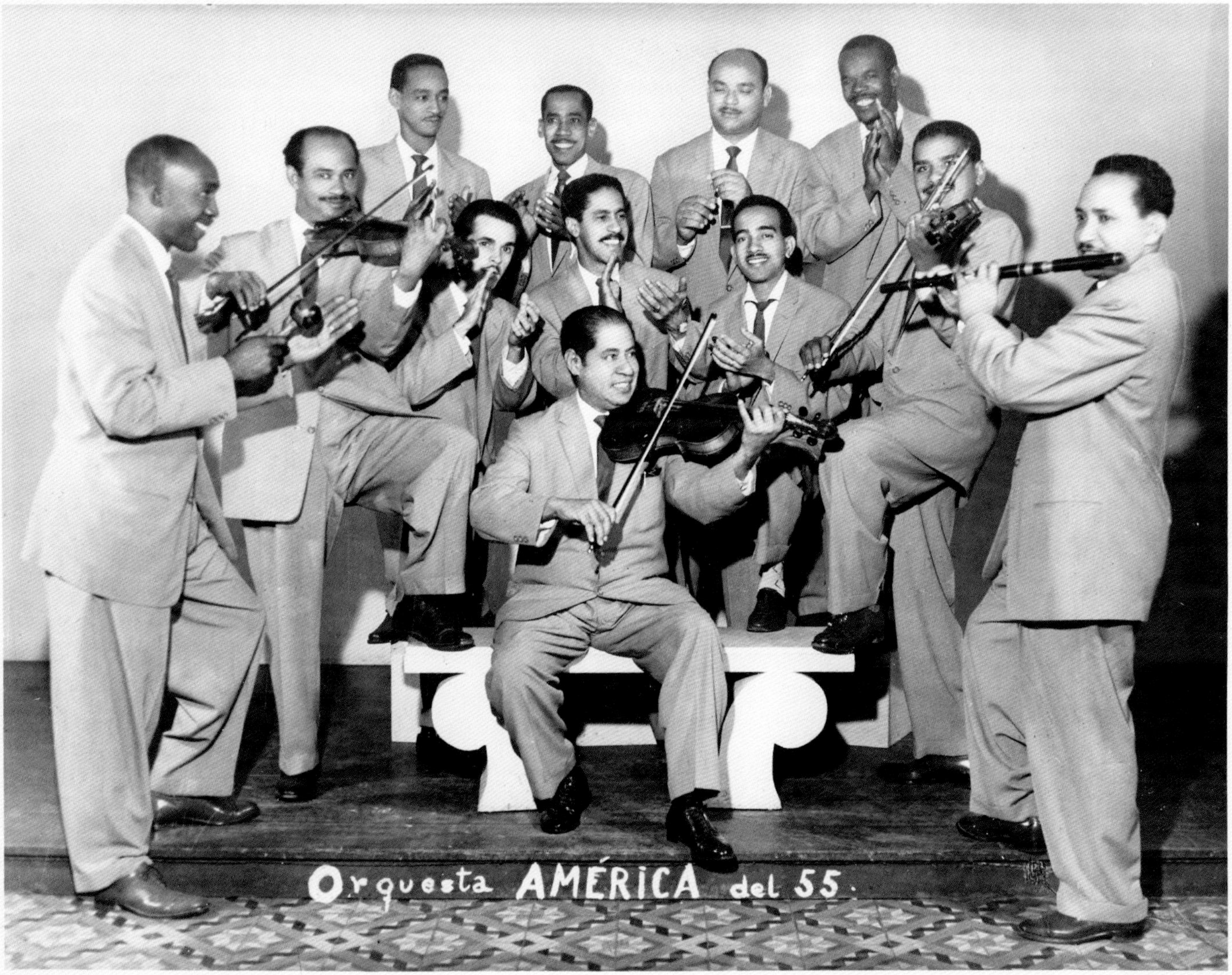

Photograph, **Musician Enrique Jorrín and the Orquesta América**, c. 1955
Gelatin silver print

The Wolfsonian–FIU, The Vicki Gold Levi Collection, XC2016.01.1.632

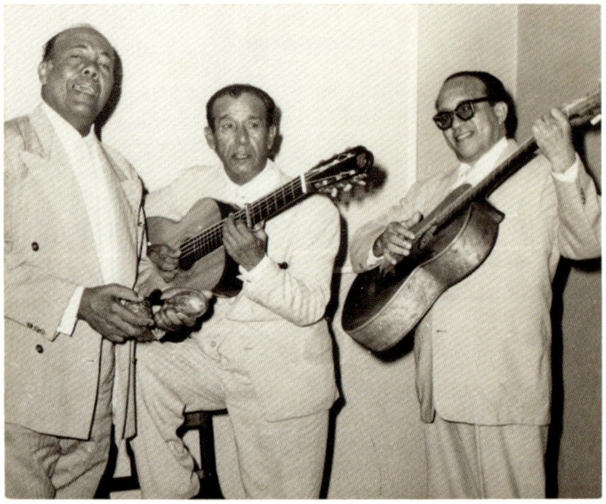

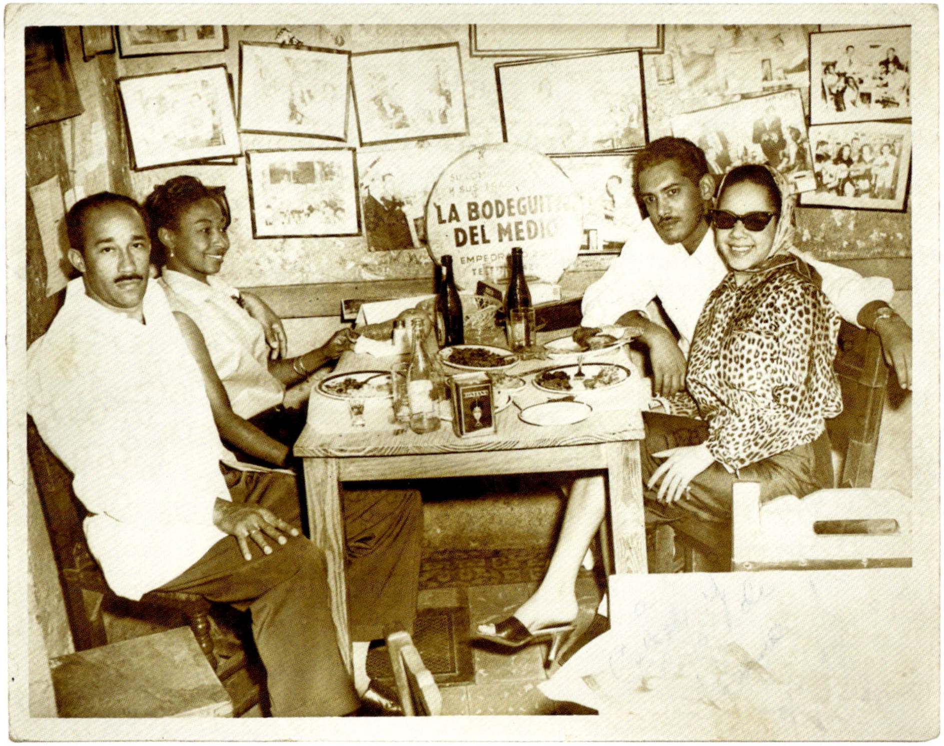

Photographs
Gelatin silver prints

Trio Matamoros: Siro Rodríguez, Miguel Matamoros, and Rafael Cueto (left to right), c. 1950

Singer in Orquesta Sensación, a friend, singer Pacho Alonso, and the "queen of bolero" Celeste Mendoza (left to right) **at La Bodeguita del Medio,** c. 1950

The Wolfsonian–FIU, The Vicki Gold Levi Collection, XC2016.01.1.172, .874

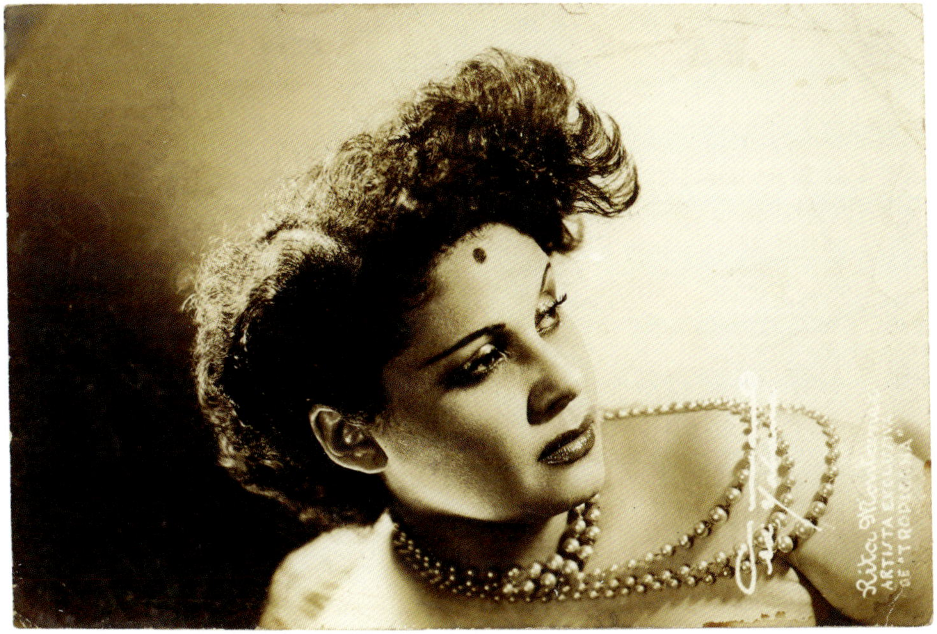

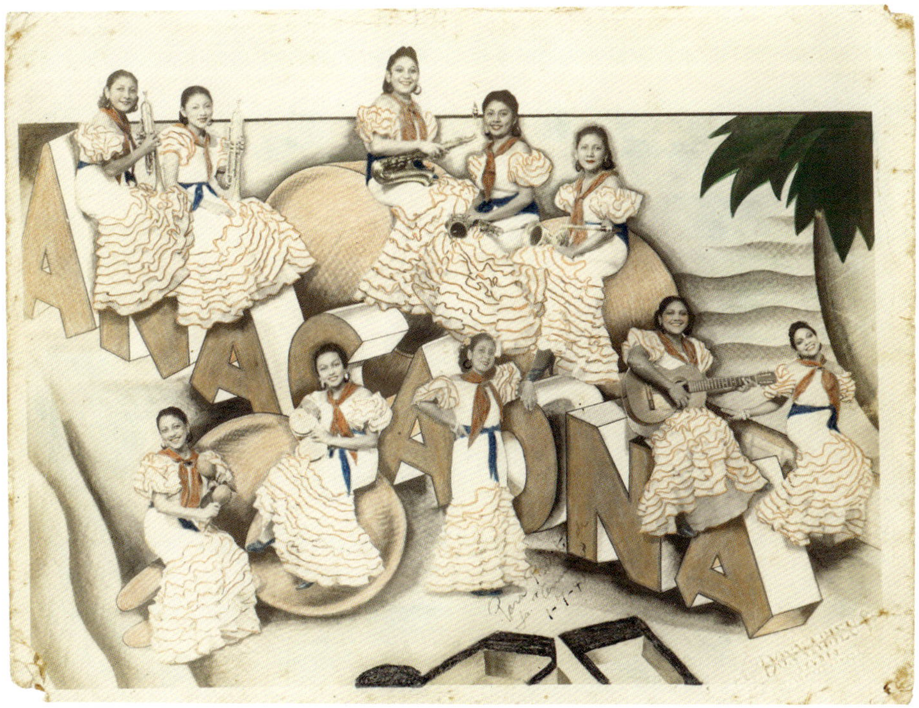

Photographs
Gelatin silver prints

Singer Rita Montaner, c. 1940

All-female band Anacaona,
January 7, 1940
Donnadieu Studio,
photographer

The Wolfsonian–FIU, The Vicki Gold Levi Collection, XC2016.01.1.611, .85

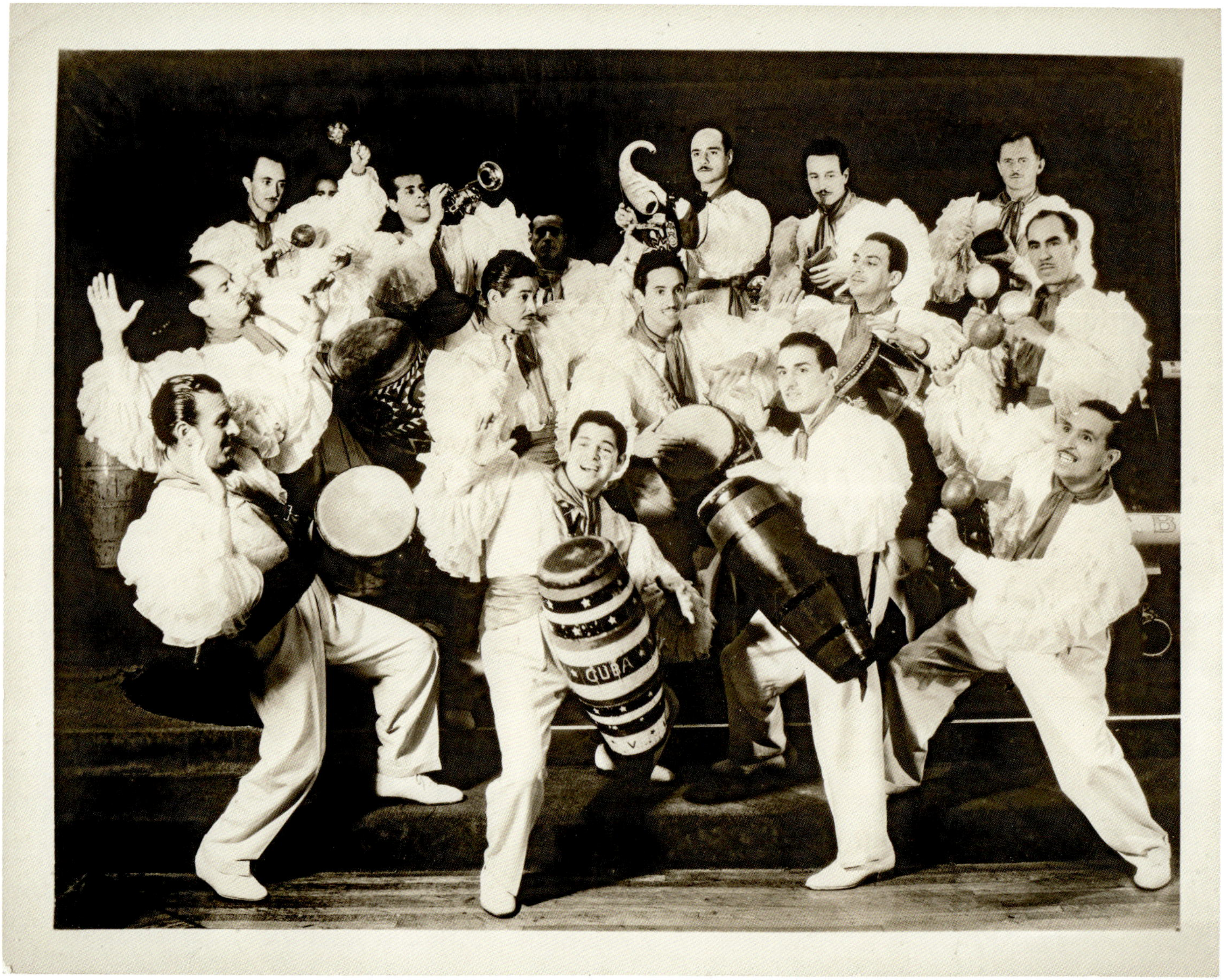

Photograph, **Lecuona Boys**,
c. 1957
Gelatin silver print

Vicki Gold Levi private collection,
TL2018.13.2

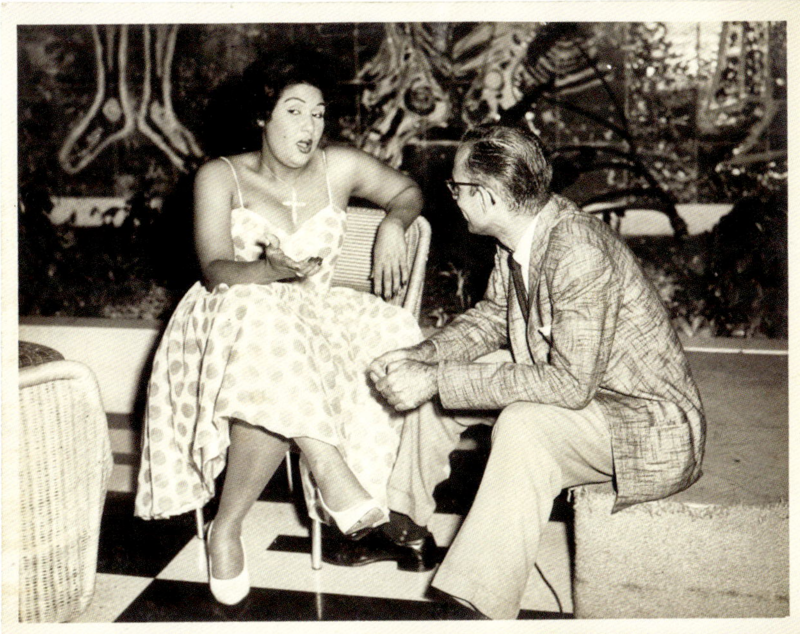

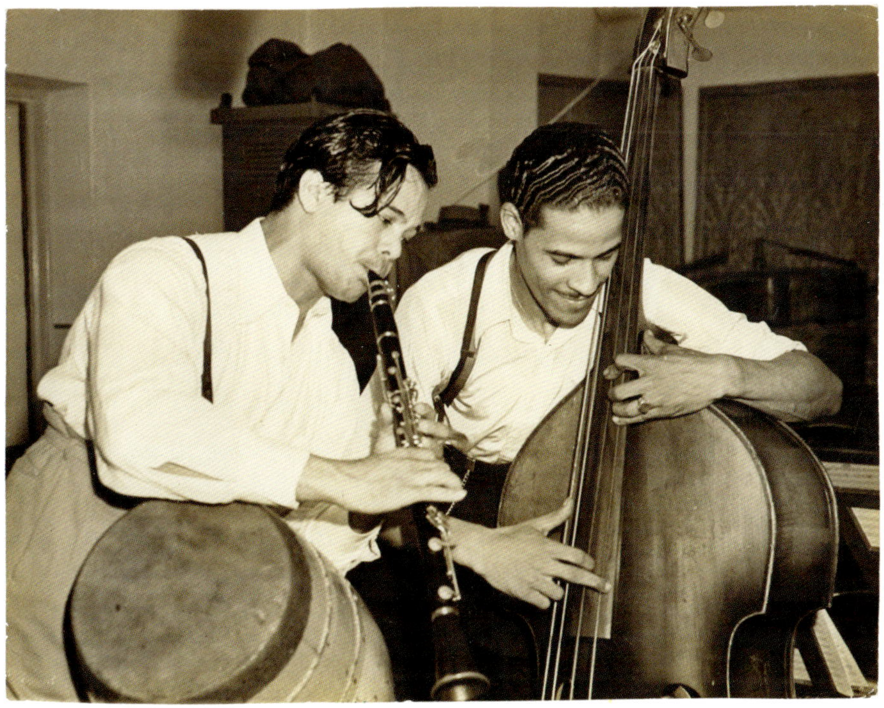

Photographs
Gelatin silver prints

Singer Olga Guillot being interviewed for a Cuban television show, c. 1955

Singer and musician Miguelito Valdés ("Mr. Babalú," left), 1942

The Wolfsonian–FIU, The Vicki Gold Levi Collection, XC2016.01.1.116, .46

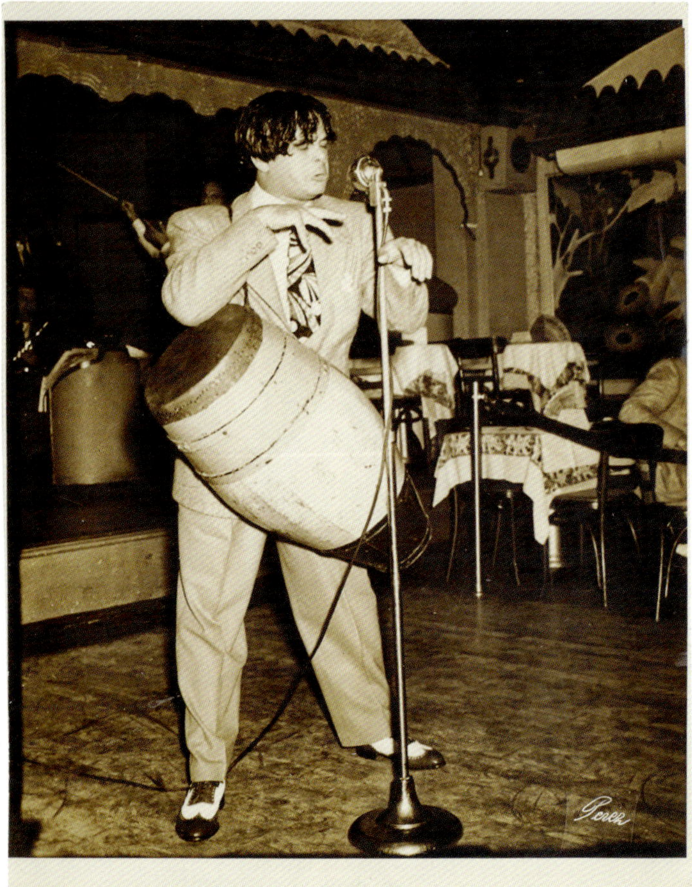

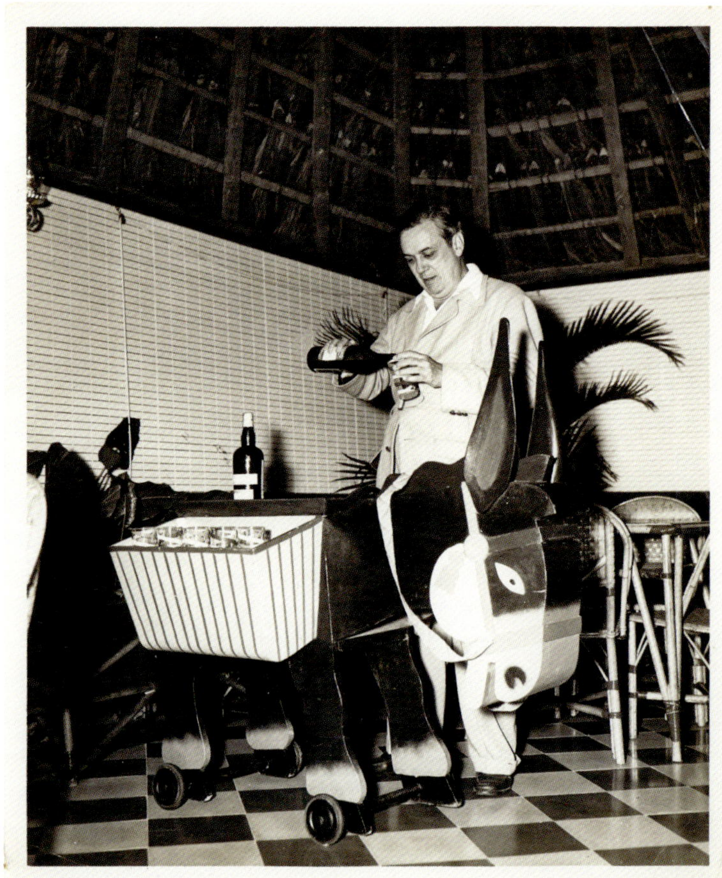

Photographs
Gelatin silver prints

Singer and musician Miguelito Valdés ("Mr. Babalú"), c. 1950

Cuban composer Ernesto Lecuona, c. 1950

The Wolfsonian–FIU, The Vicki Gold Levi Collection, XC2016.01.1.843, .33

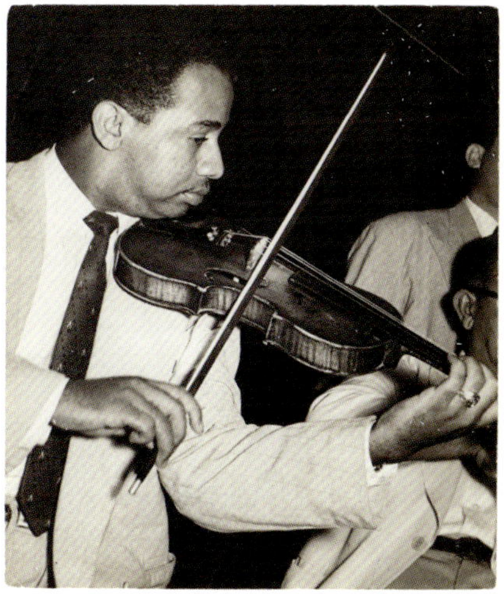

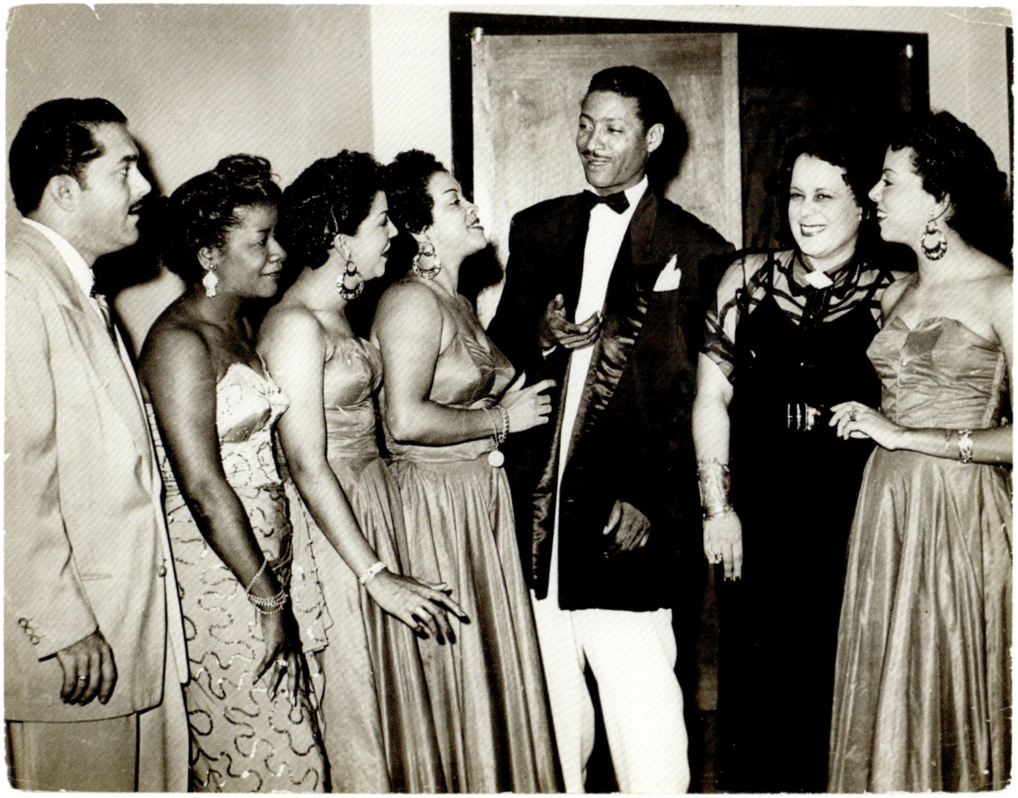

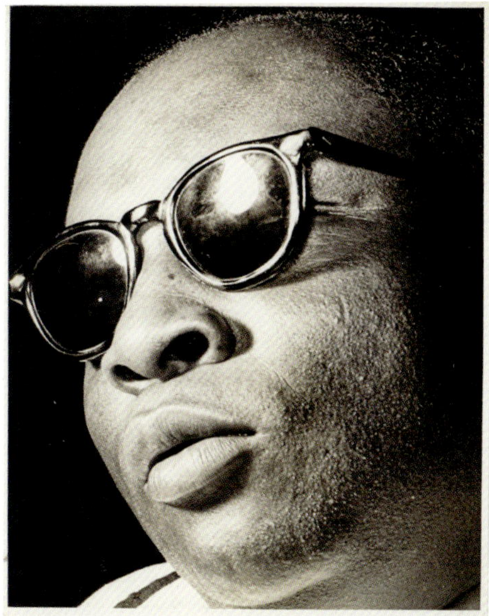

Photographs
Gelatin silver prints

Violinist, composer, and inventor of the cha-cha-cha Enrique Jorrín, June 1953

Singer Benny Moré (center) **and pianist and composer Isolina Carrillo** (second from left) **with members of her Conjunto Siboney performing for a Radio Progreso broadcast**, March 26, 1954
Osvaldo Alburquerque, photographer

Musician, composer, and band leader Arsenio Rodríguez, c. 1950

The Wolfsonian–FIU, The Vicki Gold Levi Collection, XC2016.01.1.607, .525, .612

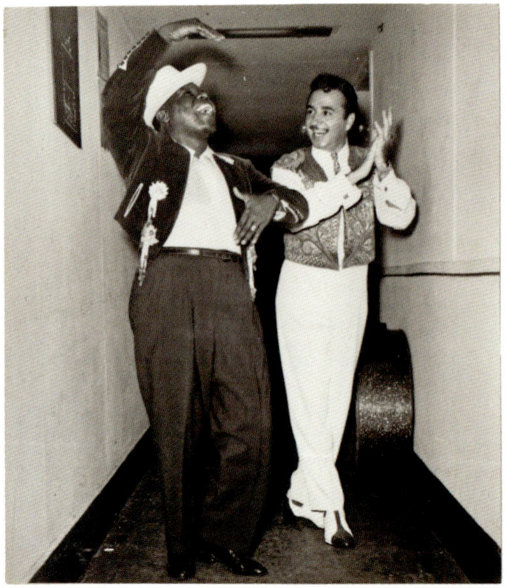

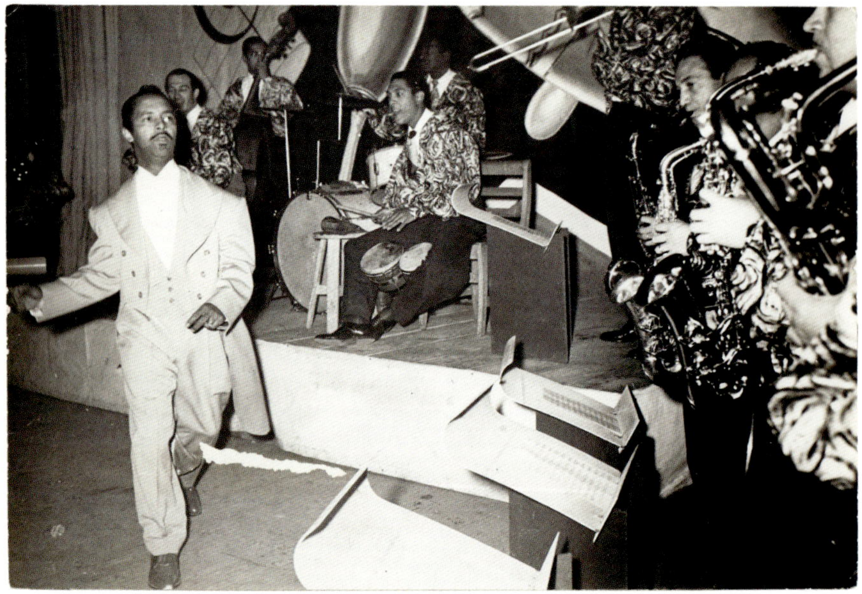

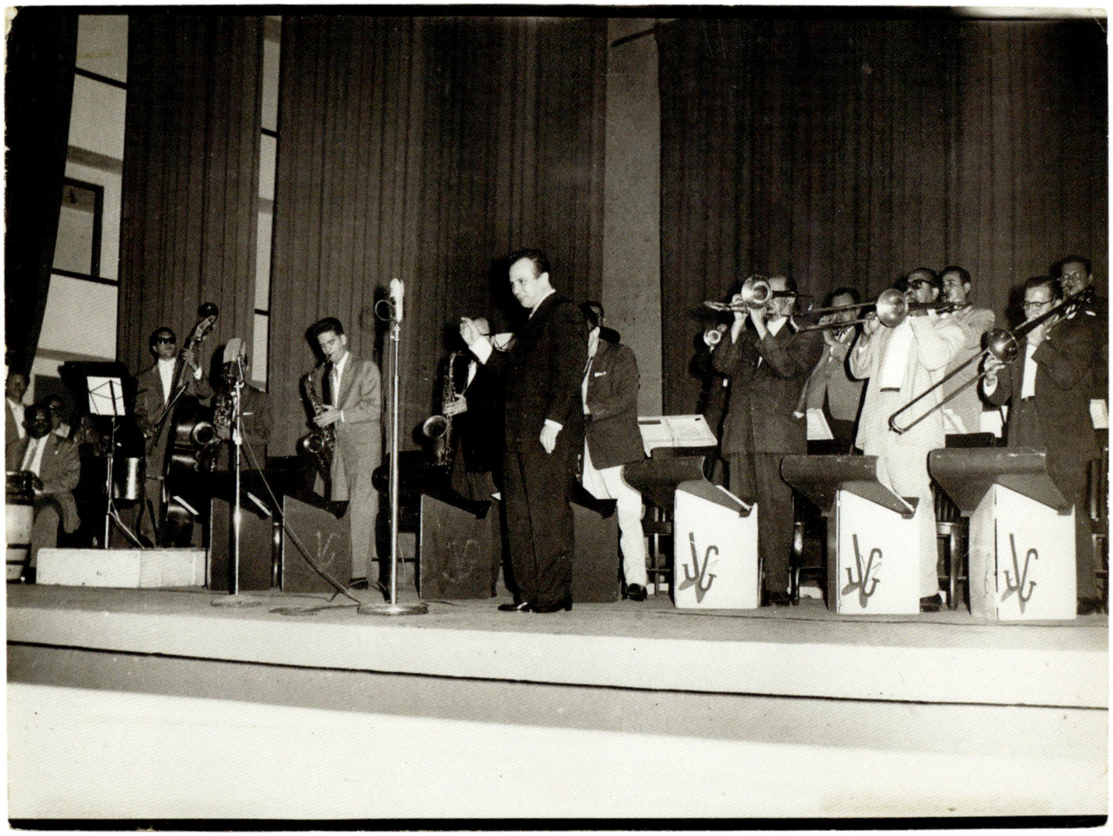

Photographs
Gelatin silver prints

Singer, pianist, and songwriter Ignacio Jacinto Villa Fernández ("Bola de Nieve" or "Snowball," left) **and one of Los Churumbeles de España**, c. 1950

Band leader and popularizer of the mambo Pérez Prado, December 31, 1950

Composer, arranger, and conductor Arturo ("Chico") **O'Farrill with Julio Gutiérrez's orchestra**, c. 1955

The Wolfsonian–FIU, The Vicki Gold Levi Collection, XC2016.01.1.461, .613, .609

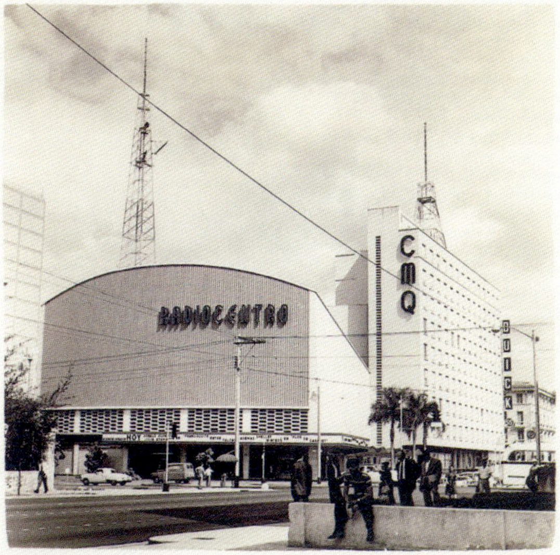

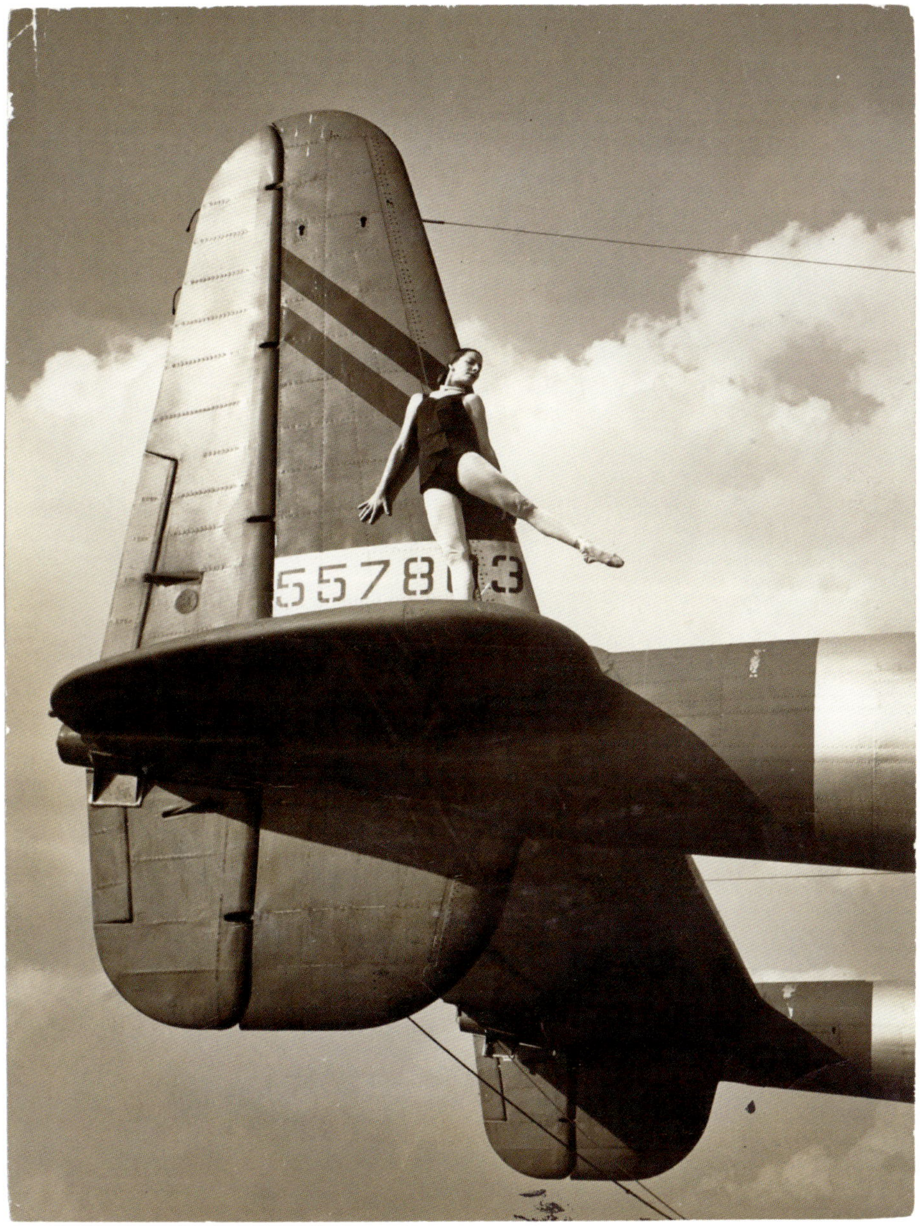

Photographs
Gelatin silver prints

CMQ Radiocentro, c. 1955

Ballerina Alicia Alonso on the wing of a C-28 during the American National Ballet Theatre visit to Frankfurt, Germany, 1959

The Wolfsonian–FIU, The Vicki Gold Levi Collection, XC2016.01.1.639, .446

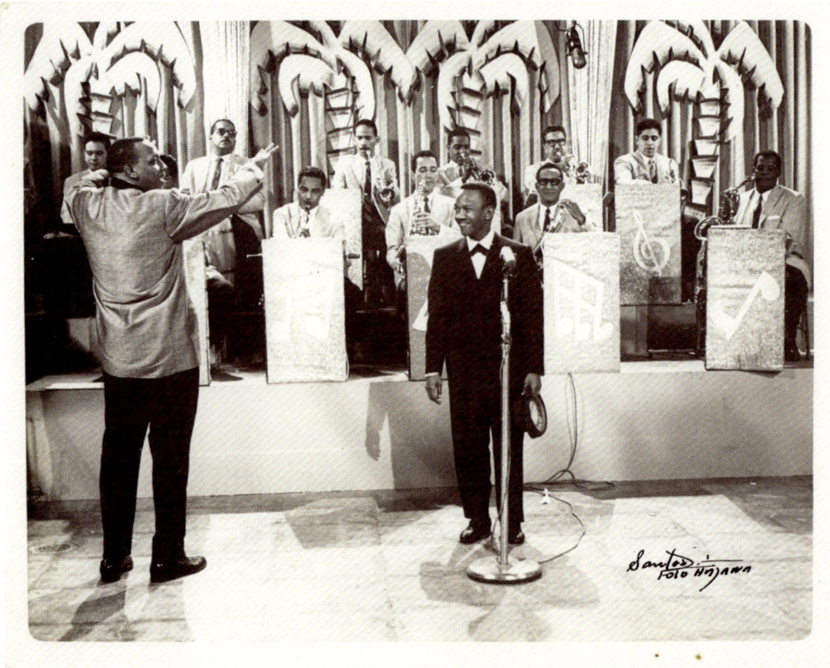

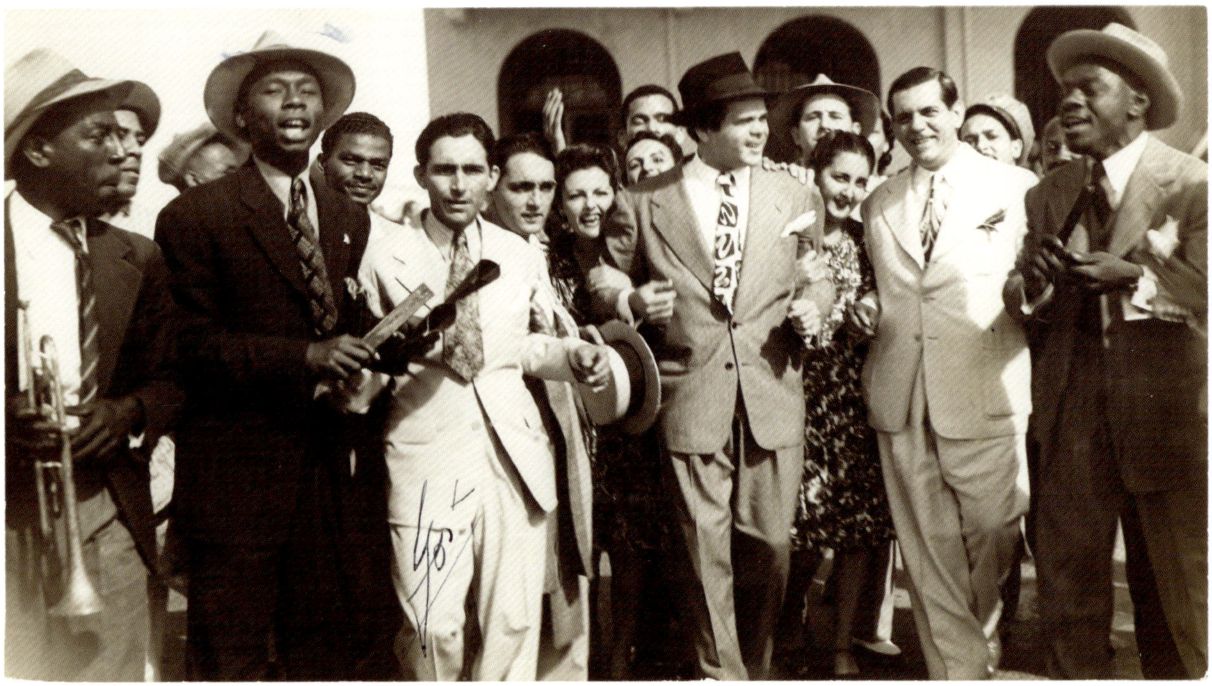

Photographs
Gelatin silver prints

Bandleader, composer, and pianist Bebo Valdés (left) **and singer Rolando Laserie** (center), c. 1950
Santos, photographer

Silvestre Mendez (left), **musician Miguelito Valdés** (center), **and percussionist and composer Chano Pozo** (far right), c. 1948

The Wolfsonian–FIU, The Vicki Gold Levi Collection, XC2016.01.1.606, .47

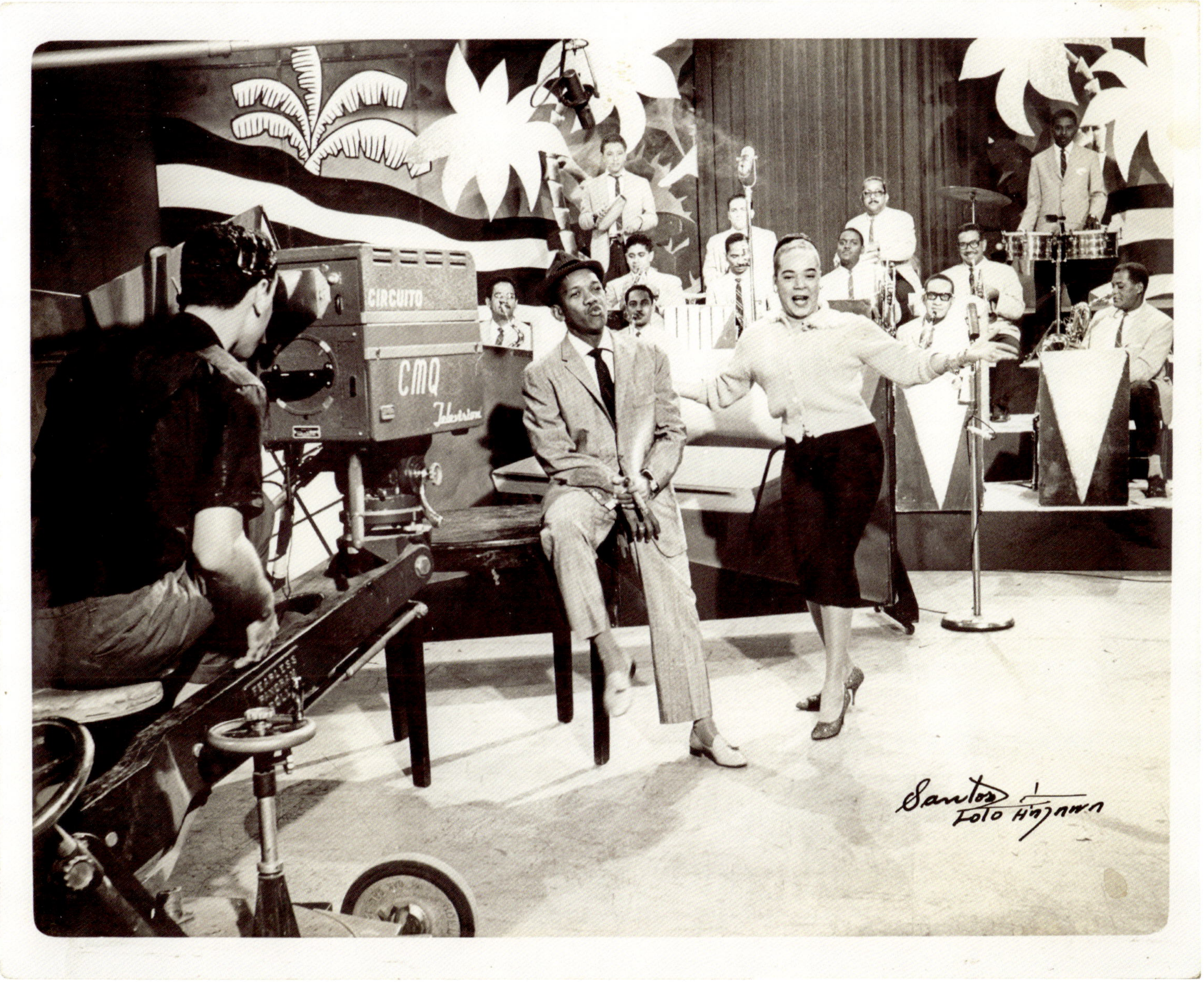

Photograph, **Singers Rolando Laserie and Celeste Mendoza at CMQ Radiocentro**, c. 1952
Santos, photographer
Gelatin silver print

The Wolfsonian–FIU, The Vicki Gold Levi Collection, XC2016.01.1.26

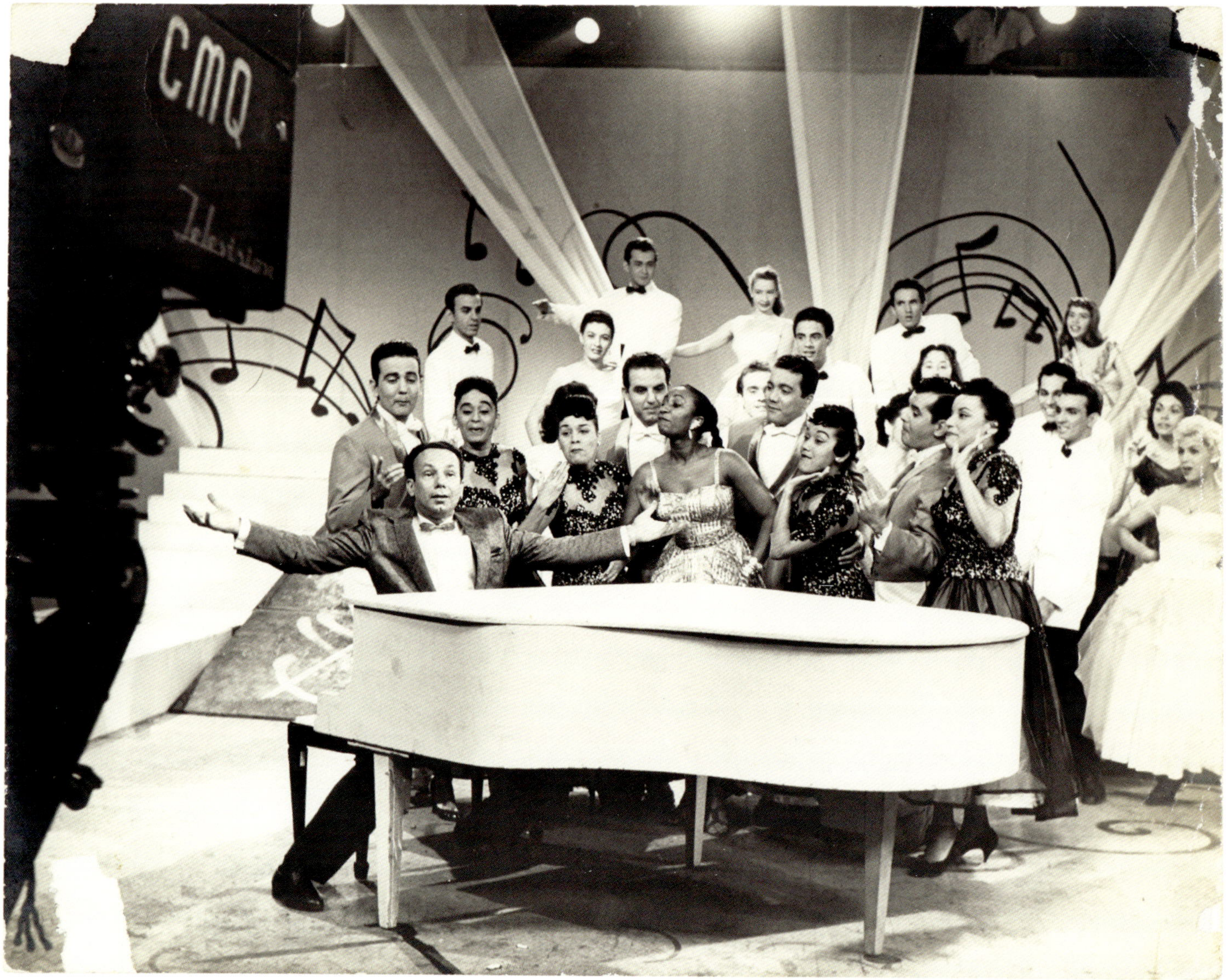

Photograph, **CMQ studios performance with singers Omara Portuondo, Celia Cruz, Moriana Secada, and Elena Burke** (left to right), c. 1955
Gelatin silver print

The Wolfsonian–FIU, The Vicki Gold Levi Collection, XC2016.01.1.25

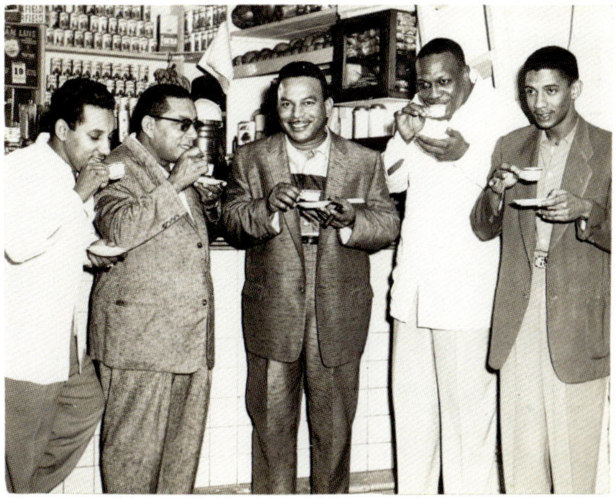

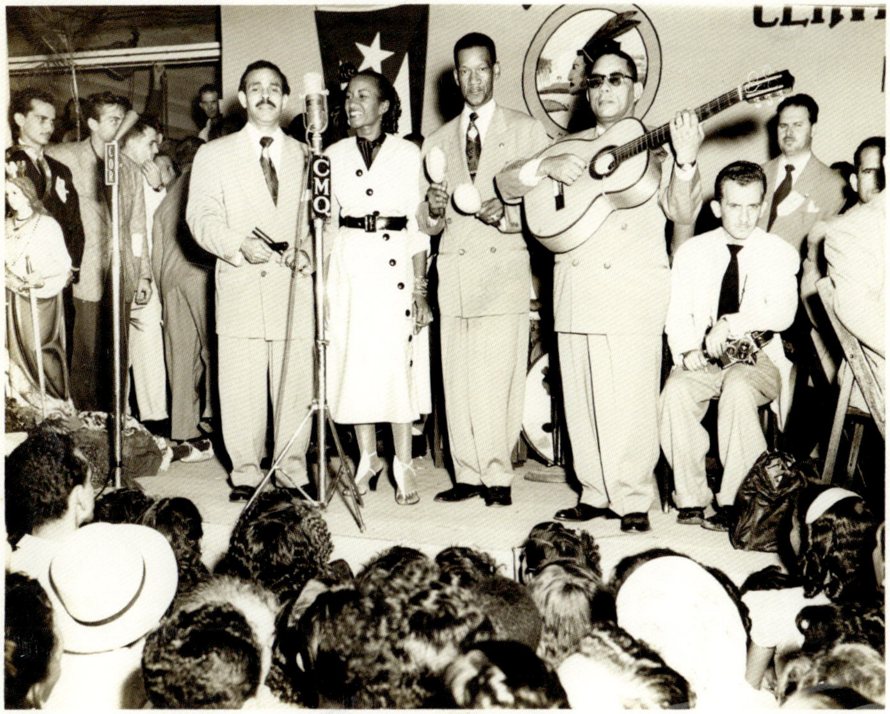

Photographs
Gelatin silver prints

Singer Vicentico Valdés (center) **meeting in Havana to record with La Sonora Matancera, led by Rogelio Martínez** (second from left), **arranger Bebo Valdés** (second from right), **and composer Javier Vázquez** (far right), December 1958

Singer Celia Cruz and La Sonora Matancera, c. 1955

The Wolfsonian–FIU, The Vicki Gold Levi Collection, XC2016.01.1.608, .27

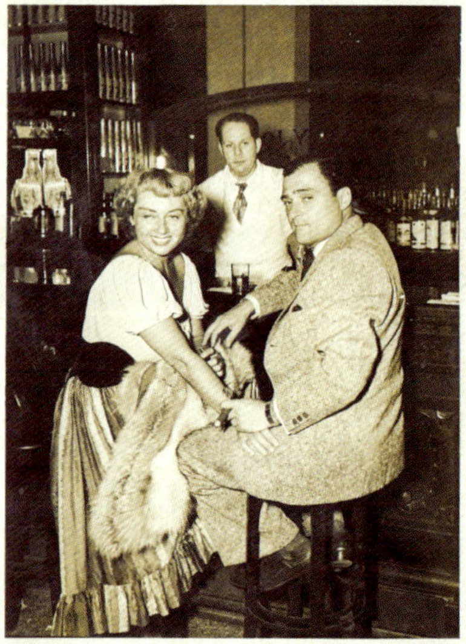

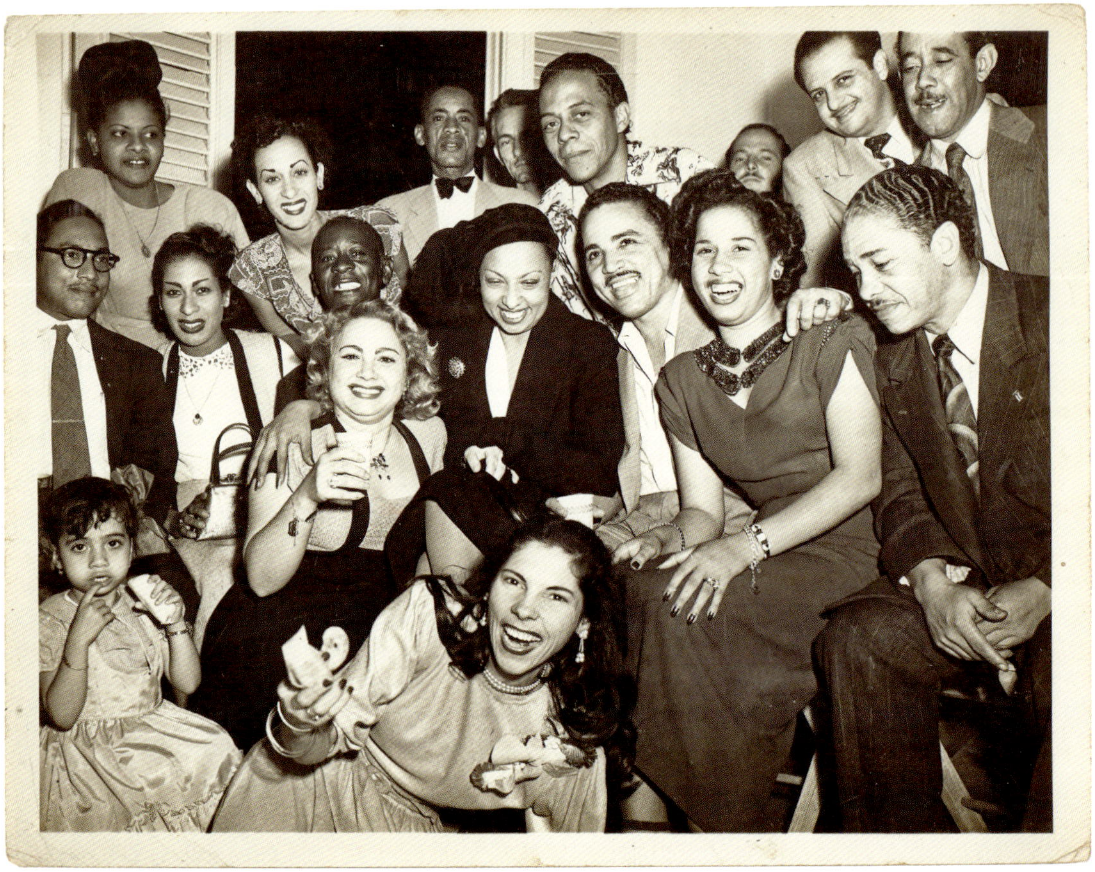

Photographs
Gelatin silver prints

Actress and star of *Havana Widows* (1933) Joan Blondell and her husband, actor and producer Michael Todd at Sloppy Joe's Bar, c. 1948

Josephine Baker (center) **next to pianist Felo Bergaza in the Tropicana dressing room,** c. 1950

The Wolfsonian–FIU, The Vicki Gold Levi Collection, XC2016.01.1.1154, .455

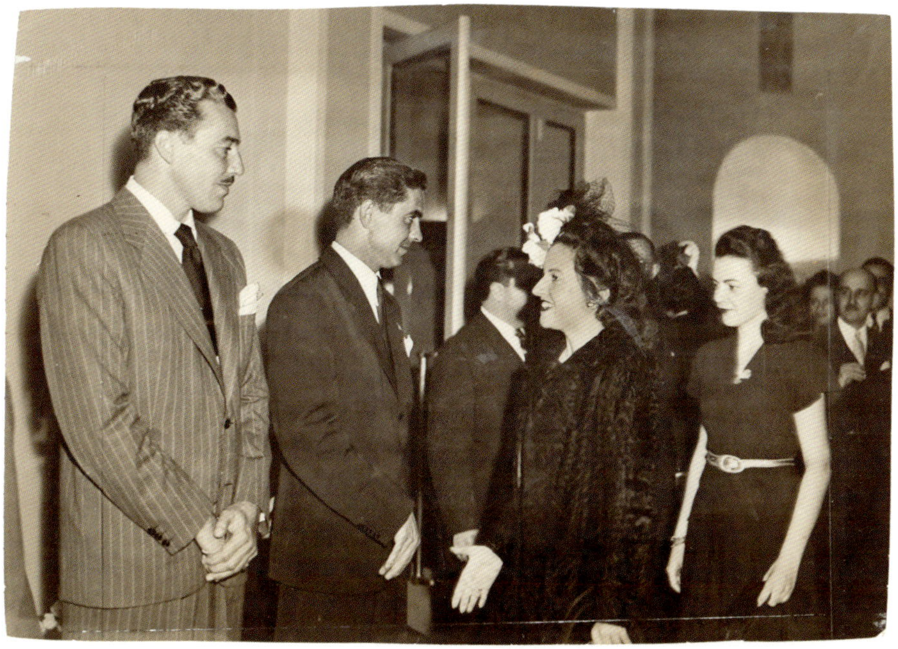

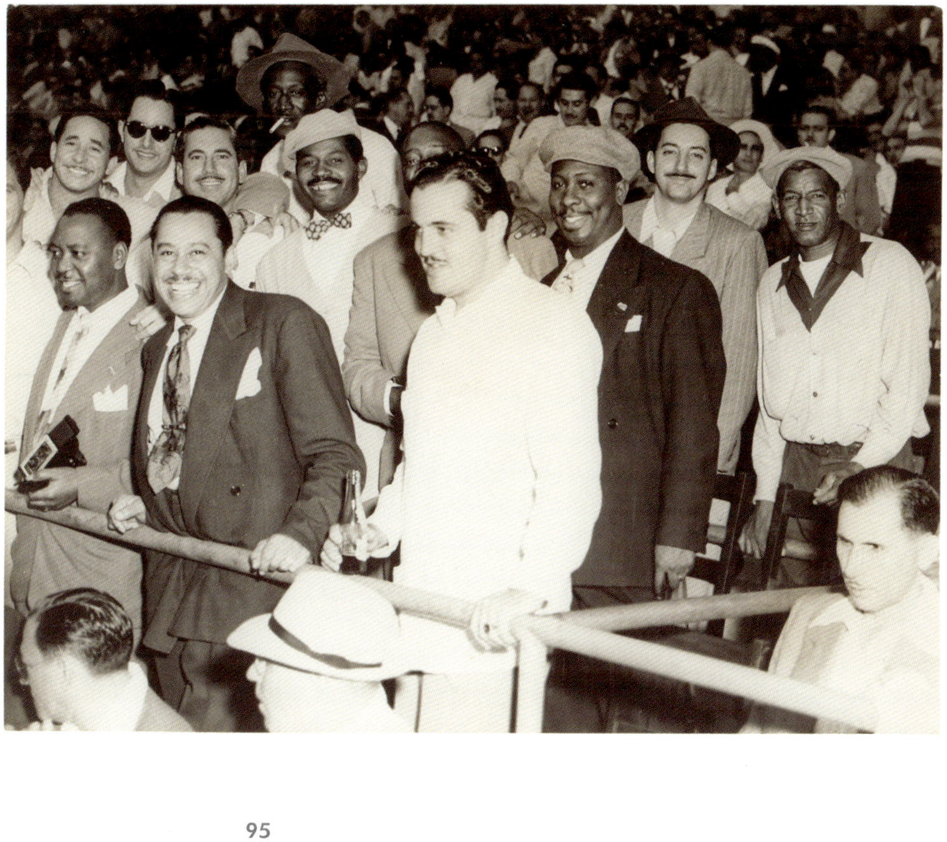

Photographs
Gelatin silver prints

Actors Cesar Romero and Tyrone Power (from left) **at the Hotel Plaza,** September 1940
M. Casales, photographer

Singer Cab Calloway (second from left) **with Mario Agüero** (center) **and the conjunto musicians at a baseball game,** c. 1950

The Wolfsonian–FIU, The Vicki Gold Levi Collection, XC2016.01.1.193, .194

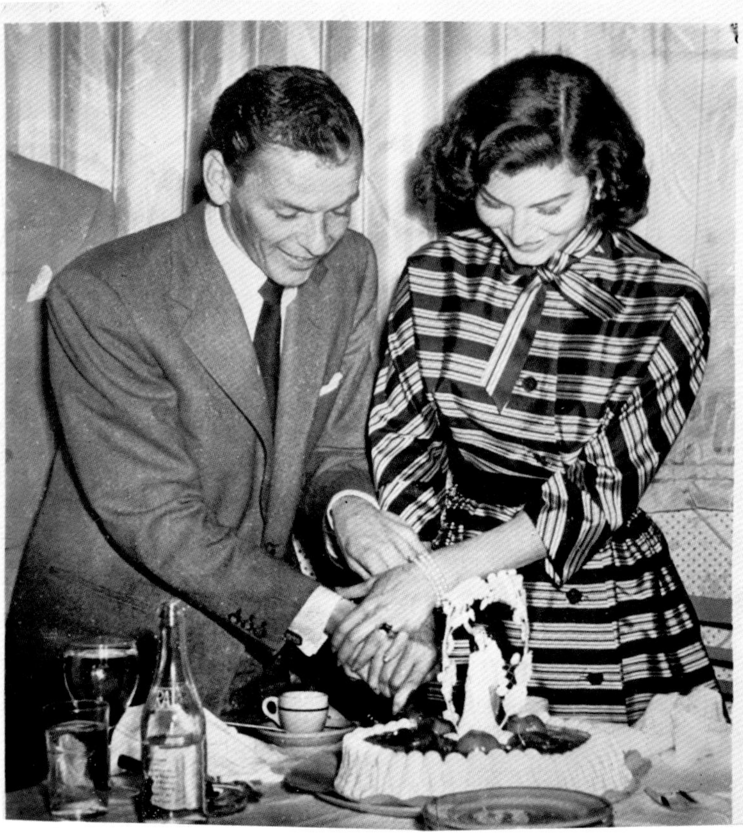

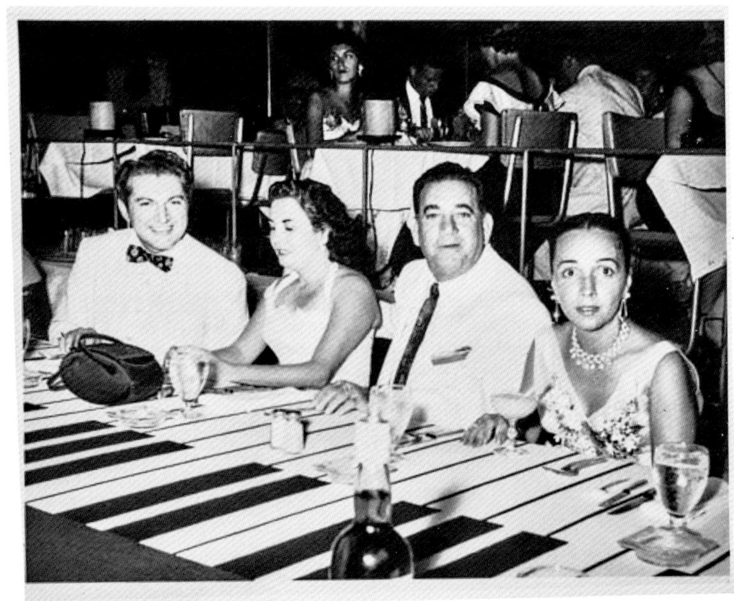

Photograph, **Singer Frank Sinatra and actress Ava Gardner honeymooning in Havana**, November 9, 1951
Gelatin silver print

The Wolfsonian–FIU, The Vicki Gold Levi Collection, XC2016.01.1.1219

Photograph, **Pianist and singer Liberace** (far left) **with Tropicana owners Ophelia and Martín Fox**, August 22, 1956
Inkjet print

Vicki Gold Levi private collection, TL2018.15.27

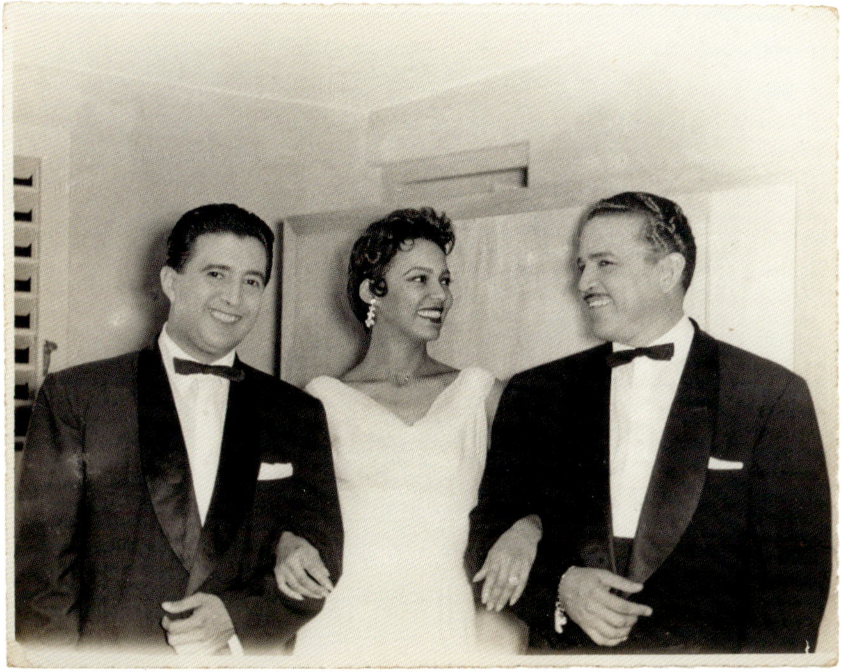

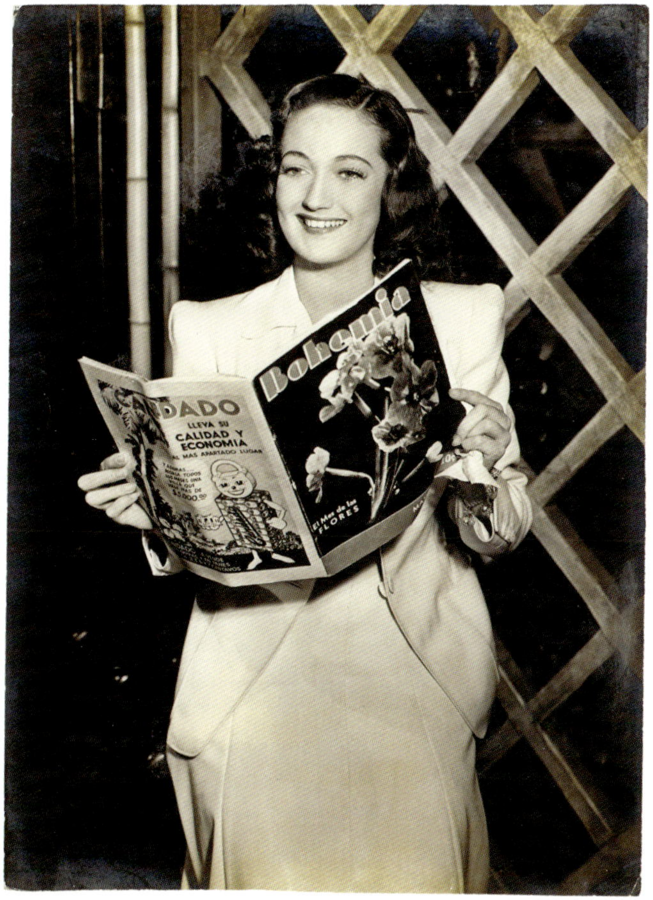

Photographs
Gelatin silver prints

Actress, singer, and dancer Dorothy Dandridge in Cuba following the debut of *Carmen Jones*, 1954

Actress and singer Dorothy Lamour reading *Bohemia,* c. 1940

The Wolfsonian–FIU, The Vicki Gold Levi Collection, XC2016.01.1.195, .235

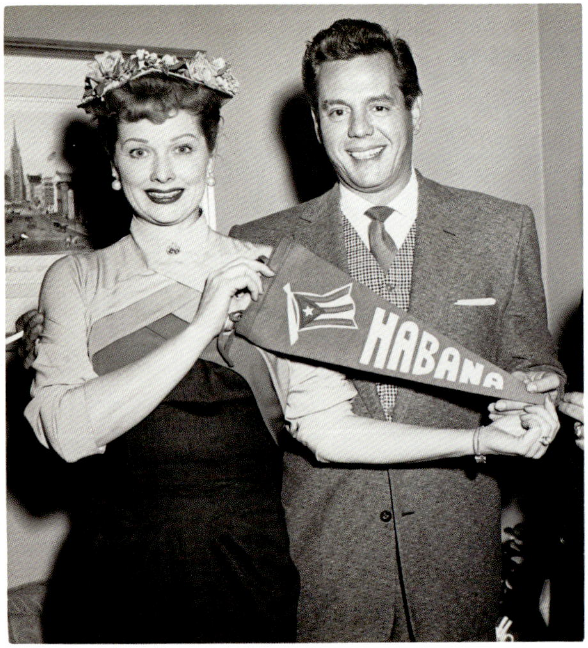

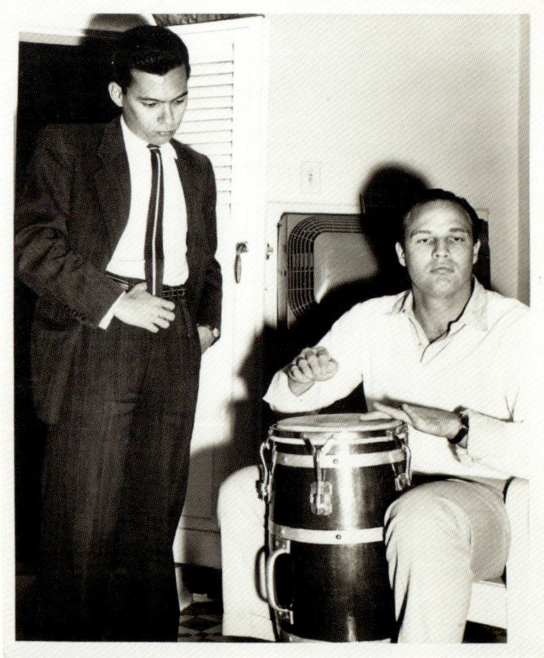

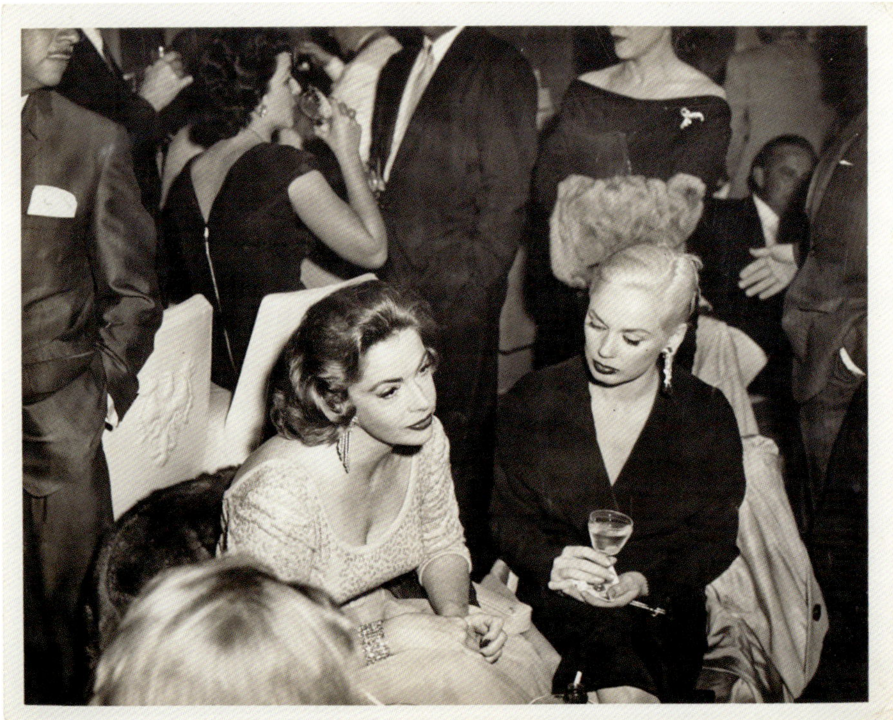

Photographs
Gelatin silver prints

Actress Lucille Ball with musician and actor Desi Arnaz, April 11, 1954

Cuban author Guillermo Cabrera Infante and American actor Marlon Brando, 1956

Actress Jayne Meadows (left) **with actress and model Mamie Van Doren at the Hotel Riviera,** December 10, 1957

The Wolfsonian–FIU, The Vicki Gold Levi Collection, XC2016.01.1.1347, .1217, .199

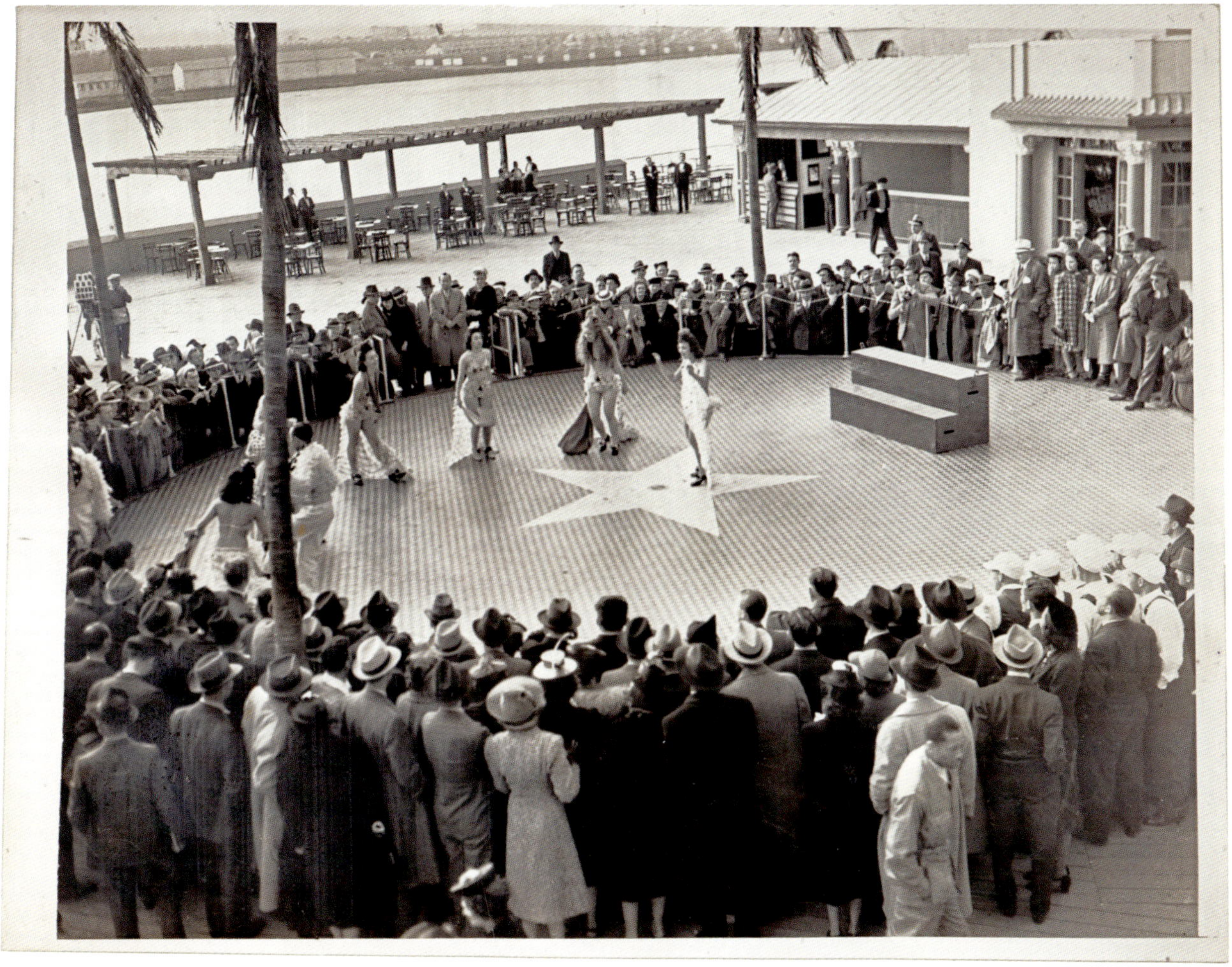

Photograph, **Dancers at the Cuban Village, opening of New York World's Fair,**
April 30, 1939
Acme, New York, photographer
Gelatin silver print

The Wolfsonian–FIU, Gift of Francis Xavier Luca and Clara Helena Palacio Luca, XC2016.10.2.3

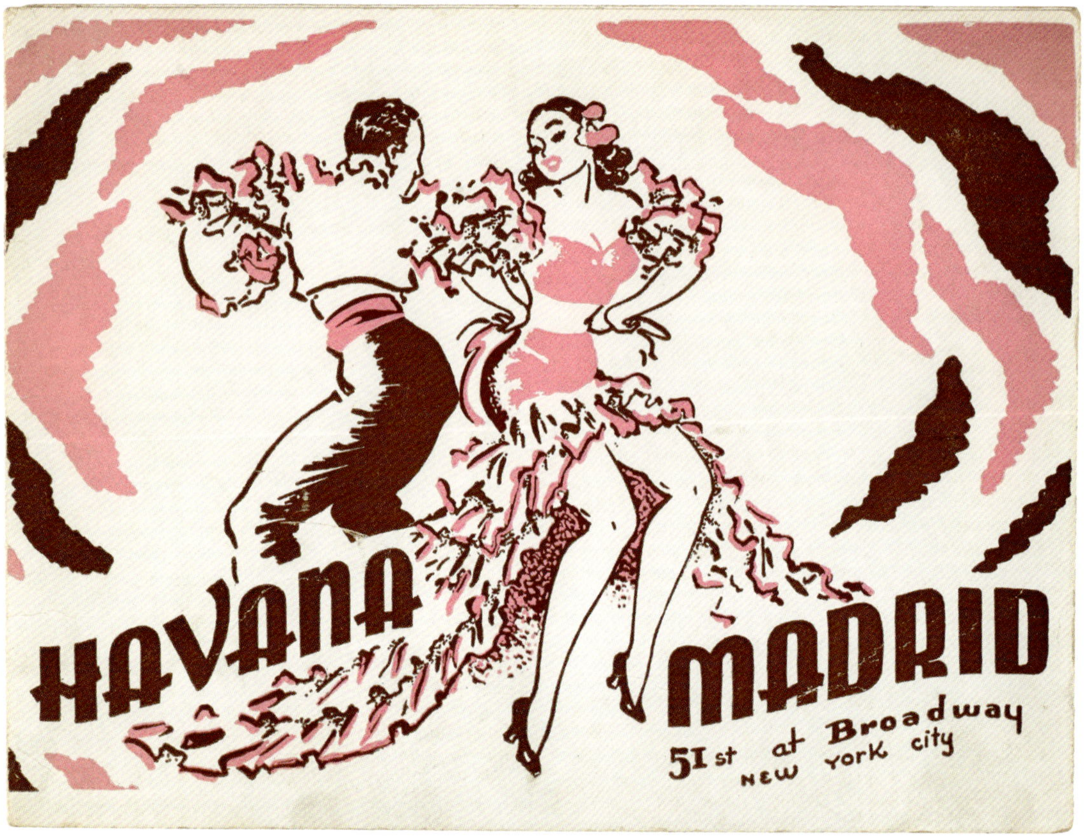

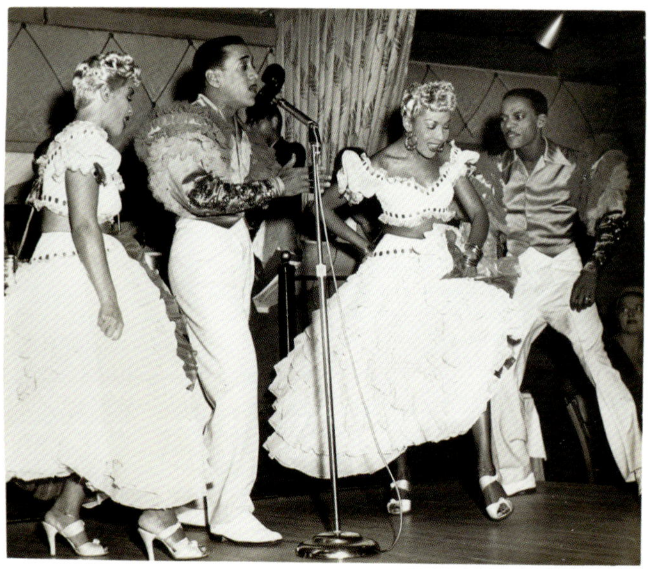

Photograph folder, ***Havana Madrid***, c. 1943

The Wolfsonian–FIU, The Vicki Gold Levi Collection, XC2016.01.1.768

Photograph, **Elba, Sirelda, Ebano, and Leyte** (left to right) **of the Cuarteto Facundo performing at the Chateau Madrid, New York**, 1953
Osvaldo Salas, photographer
Gelatin silver print

The Wolfsonian–FIU, The Vicki Gold Levi Collection, XC2016.01.1.260

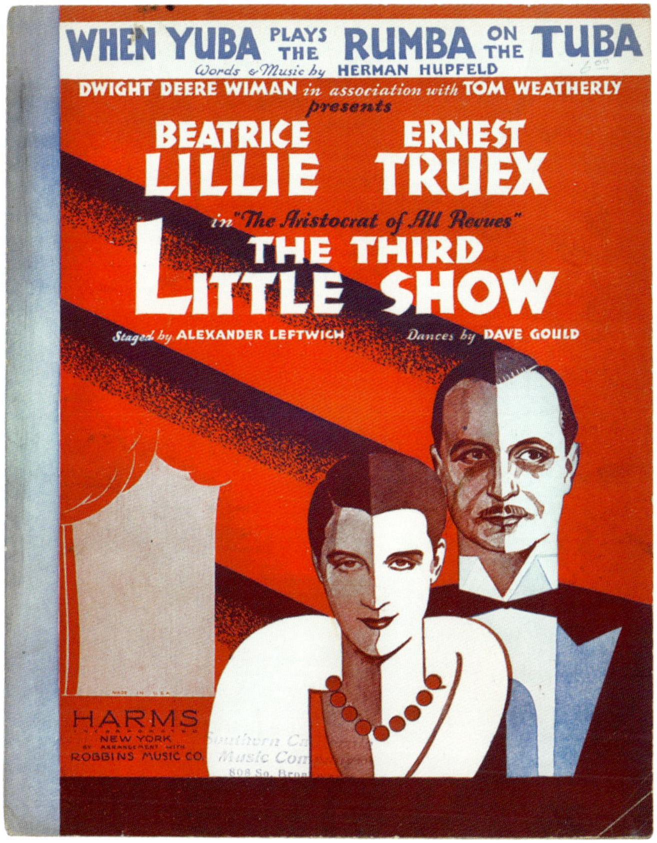

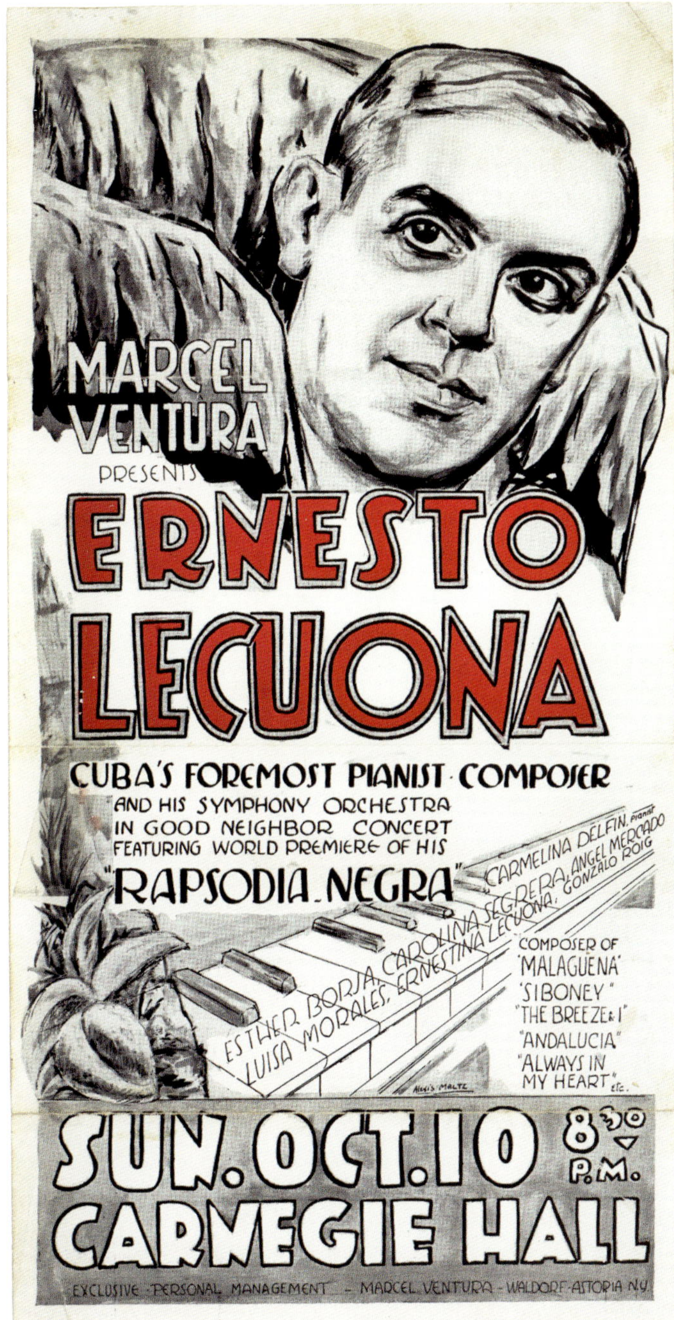

Sheet music cover, ***When Yuba Plays the Rumba on the Tuba***, 1931
Herman Hupfeld, composer and lyricist
Harms, Inc., New York, by arrangement with Robbins Music Co., publisher

The Wolfsonian–FIU, The Vicki Gold Levi Collection, XC2016.01.1.1001

Announcement, ***Marcel Ventura Presents Ernesto Lecuona, Cuba's Foremost Pianist Composer***, 1948

The Wolfsonian–FIU, The Vicki Gold Levi Collection, XC2016.01.1.1010

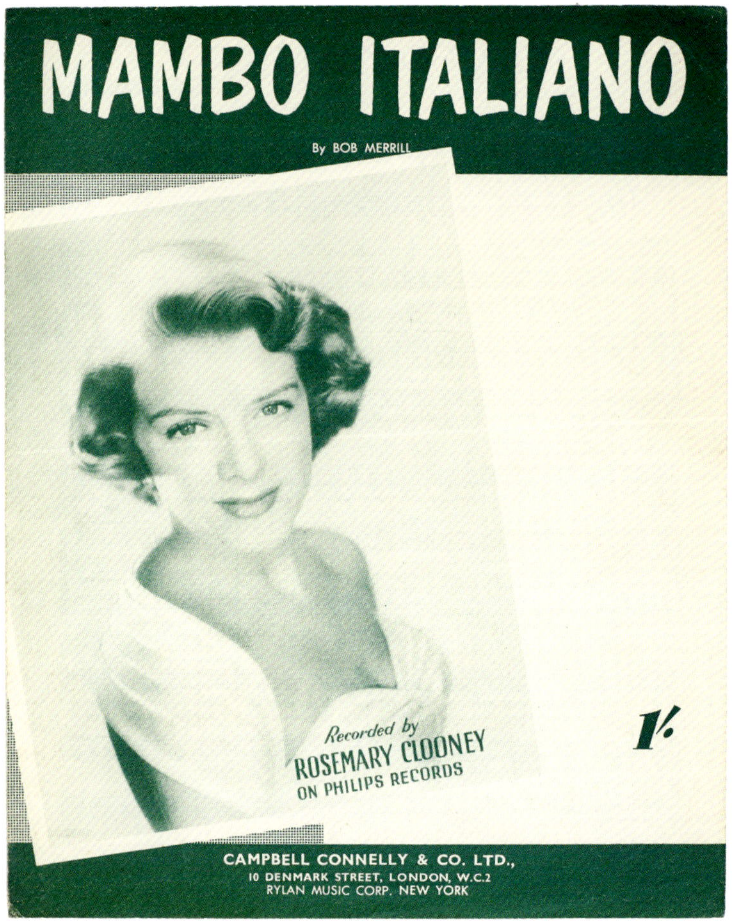

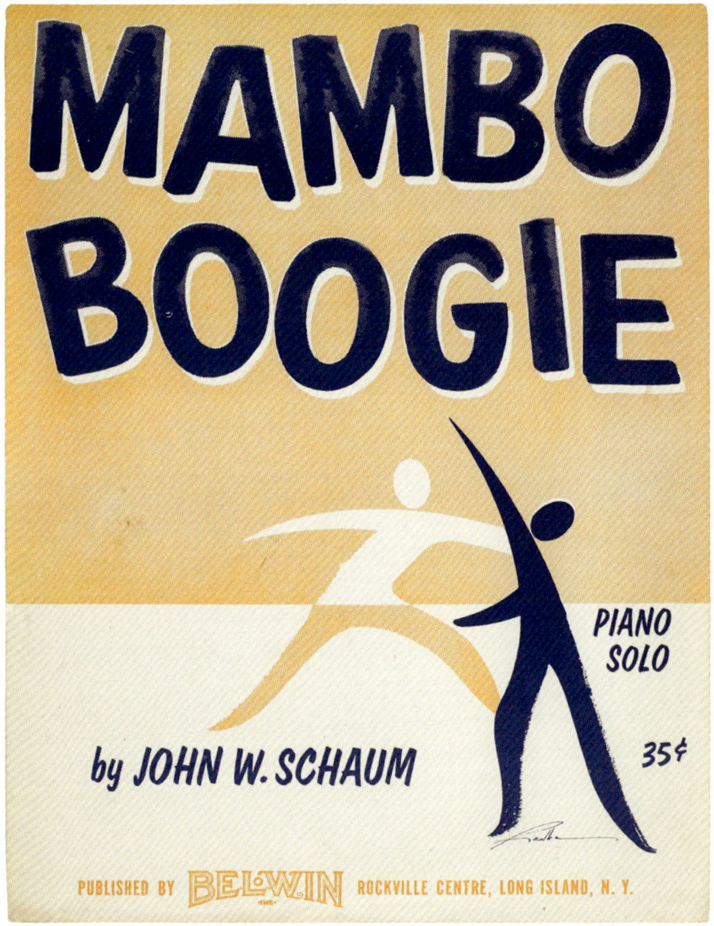

Sheet music covers

Mambo Italiano, 1954
Bob Merrill, composer and lyricist
Rylan Music Corp., New York, and Campbell, Connelly & Co., Ltd., London, publishers

Mambo Boogie, 1955
John W. Schaum (American, 1905–1988), composer
Belwin, Long Island, New York, publisher

The Wolfsonian–FIU, The Vicki Gold Levi Collection, XC2016.01.1.1229, .1231

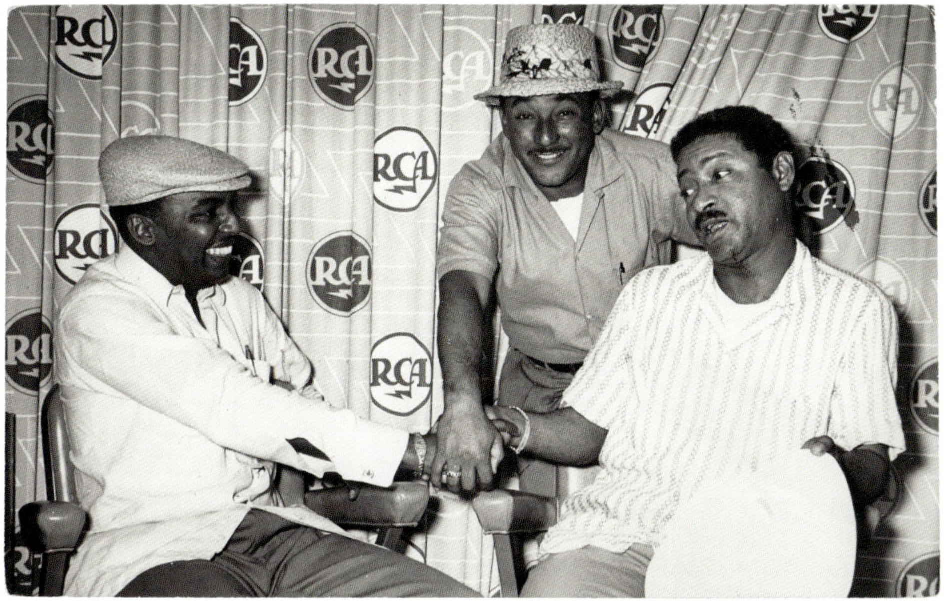

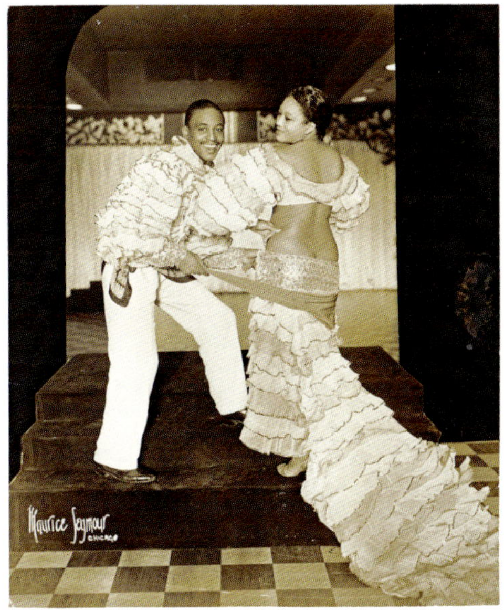

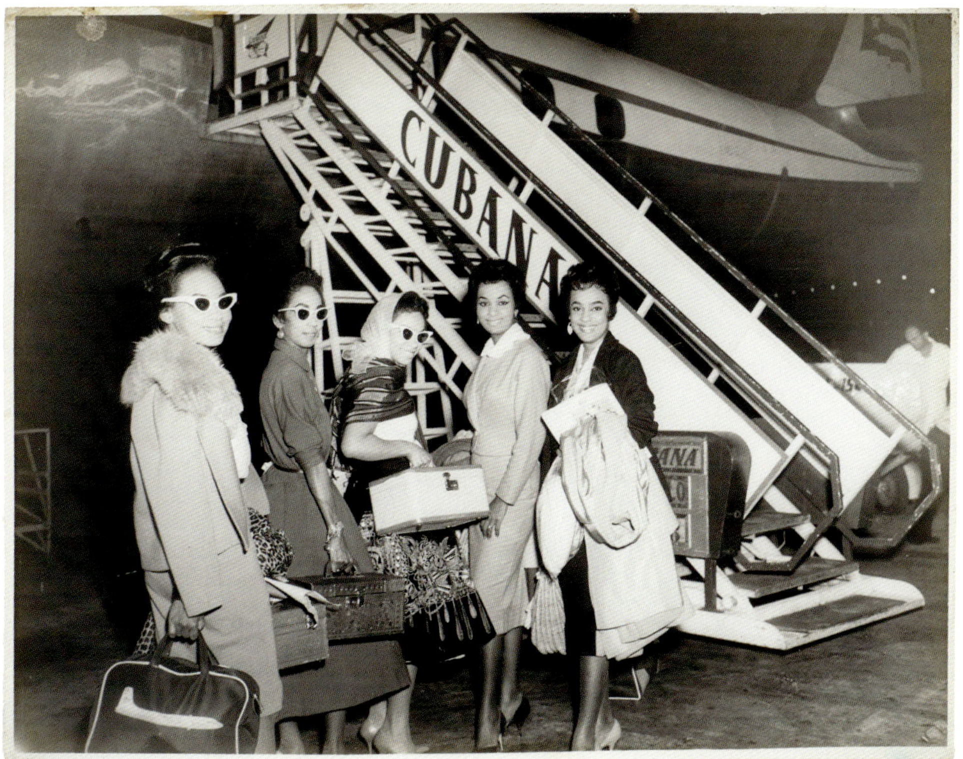

Photographs
Gelatin silver prints

Violinist and leader of the Orquesta Aragón Rafael Lay, drummer Orestes Varona, and singer Benny Moré (left to right) **at the RCA-Victor recording studios**, c. 1950

René and Estela (René Rivero Guillén and Ramona Ajón), **rumba dancers at Cuba Pavilion, Chicago World's Fair**, c. 1933
Maurice Seymour, Chicago, photographer

Las Hermanas Benítez boarding a plane, c. 1955

The Wolfsonian–FIU, The Vicki Gold Levi Collection, XC2016.01.1.37, .716, .254

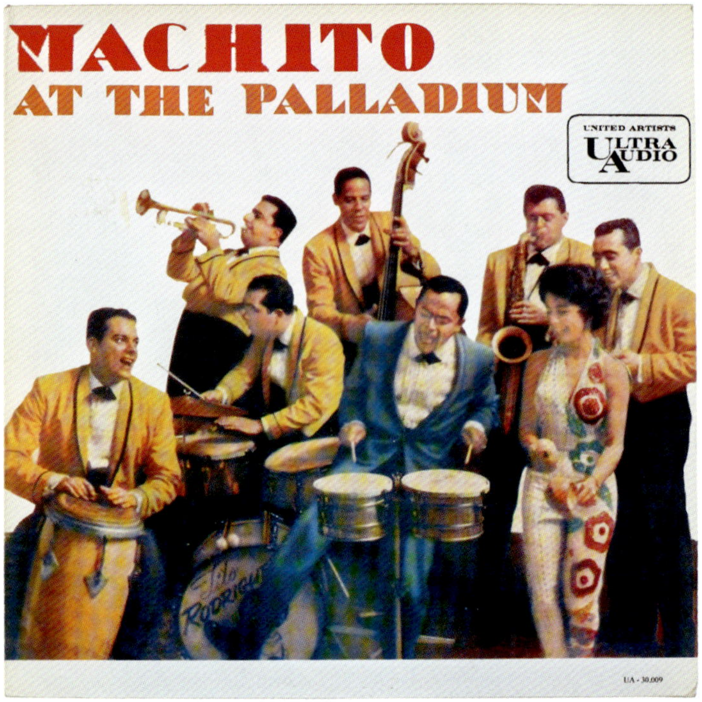

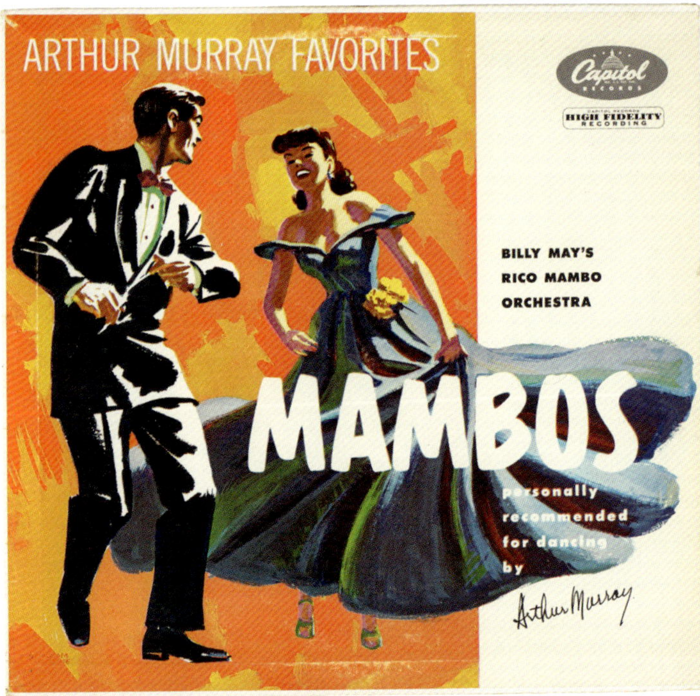

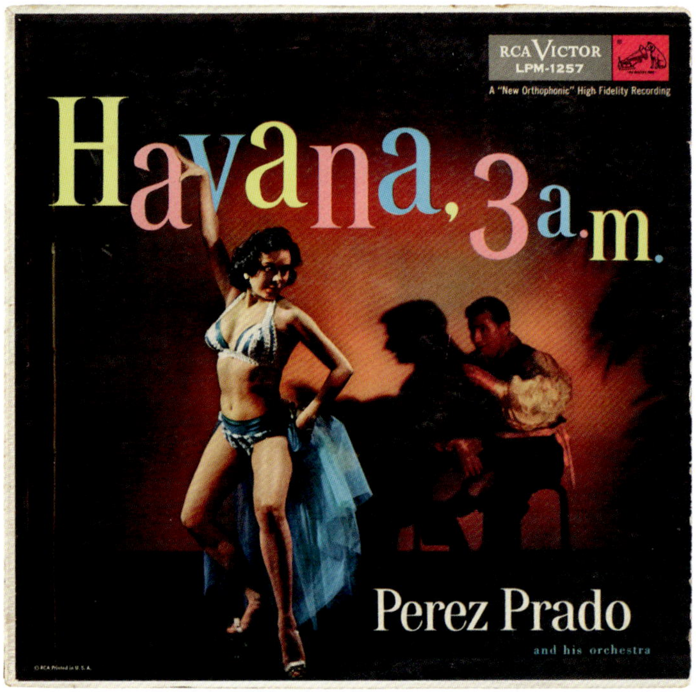

Album covers

Machito at the Palladium, 1960
United Artists, United Kingdom, producer

Arthur Murray Favorites: Mambos Personally Recommended for Dancing by Arthur Murray, 1951
Capitol Records, Los Angeles, producer

Havana, 3 a.m., Pérez Prado and His Orchestra, 1956
RCA Victor, New York, producer

The Wolfsonian–FIU, The Vicki Gold Levi Collection, XC2016.01.1.1353, .1306, XC2002.11.4.357.5

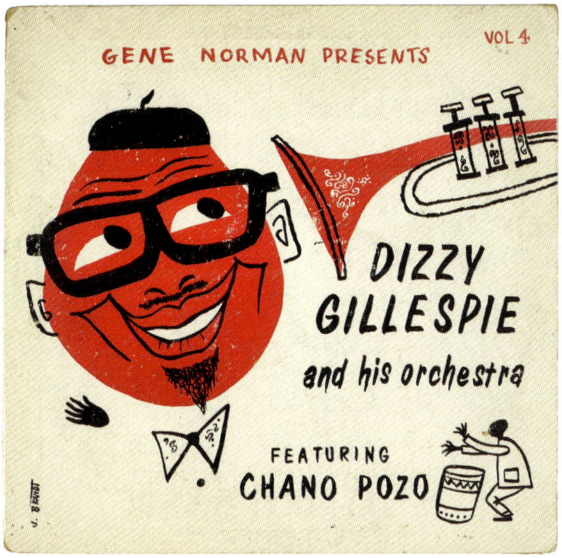

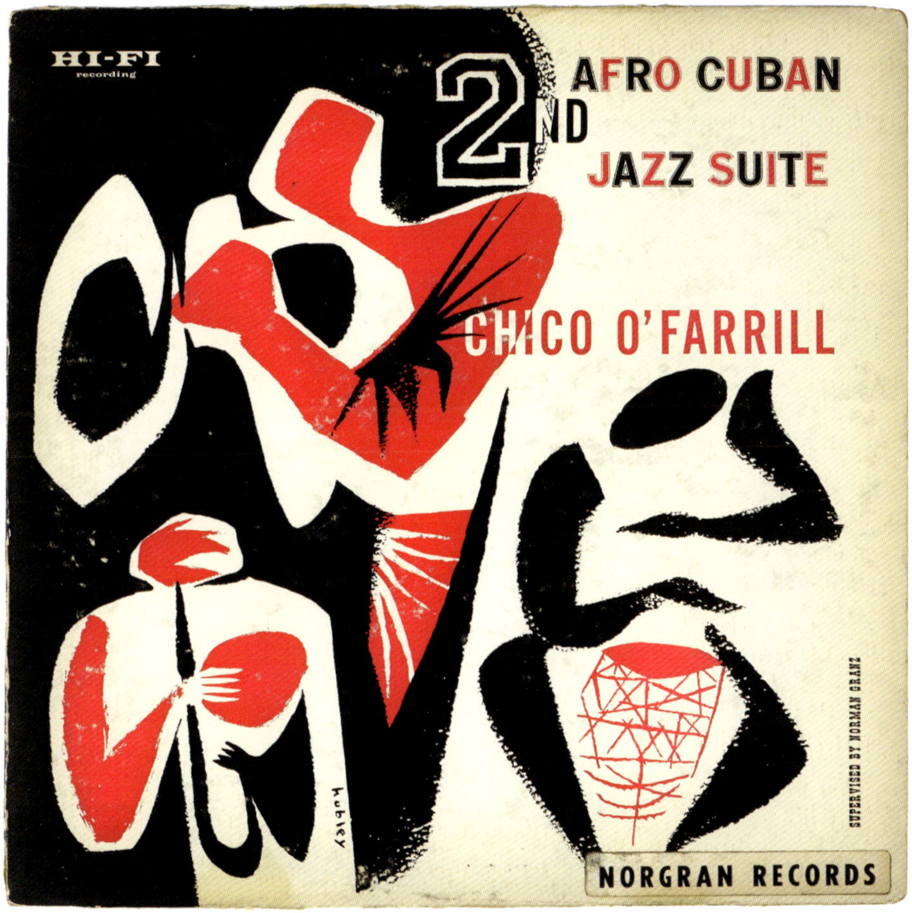

Album covers

Dizzy Gillespie and His Orchestra, Featuring Chano Pozo, 1954
John Brandt, cover designer
Gene Norman Presents, producer

2nd Afro Cuban Jazz Suite, Chico O'Farrill, c. 1952
Norgran Records, Los Angeles, producer

The Wolfsonian–FIU, The Vicki Gold Levi Collection, XC2016.01.1.1332, .1331

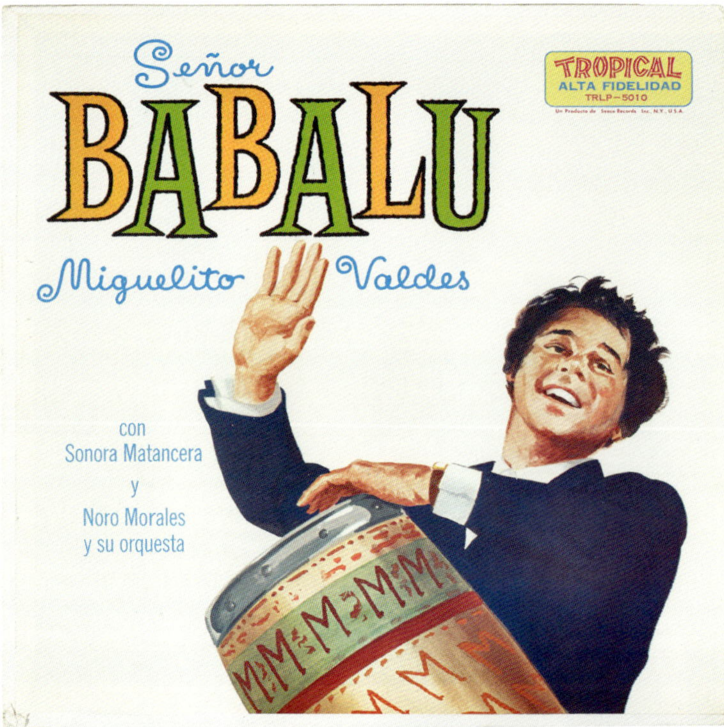

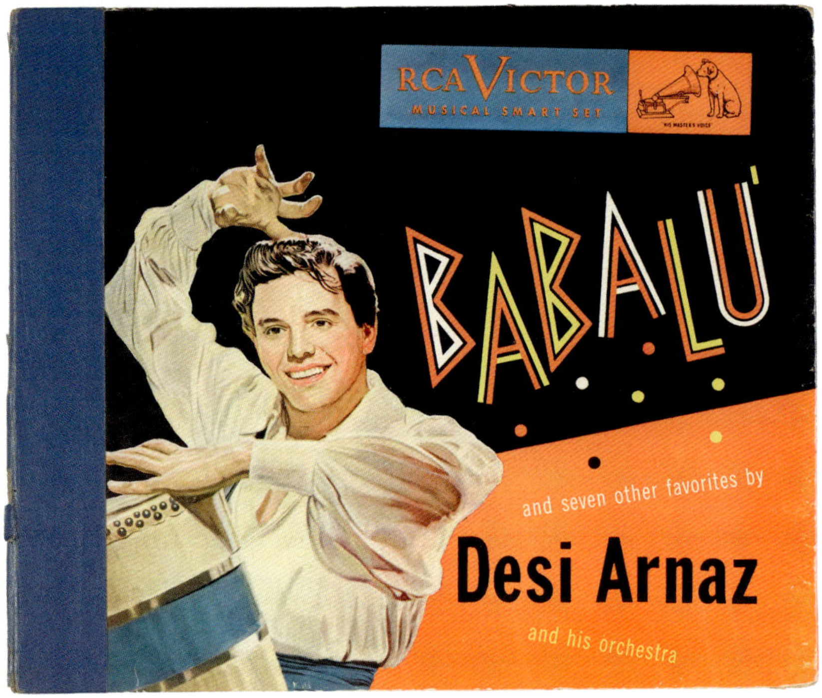

Album covers

Señor Babalu, Miguelito Valdes, c. 1950
Seeco Records, Inc., New York, producer

Babalú and Seven Other Favorites by Desi Arnaz and His Orchestra, 1953
RCA Victor, New York, producer

The Wolfsonian–FIU, The Vicki Gold Levi Collection, XC2016.01.1.1335, XC2002.11.4.357.1

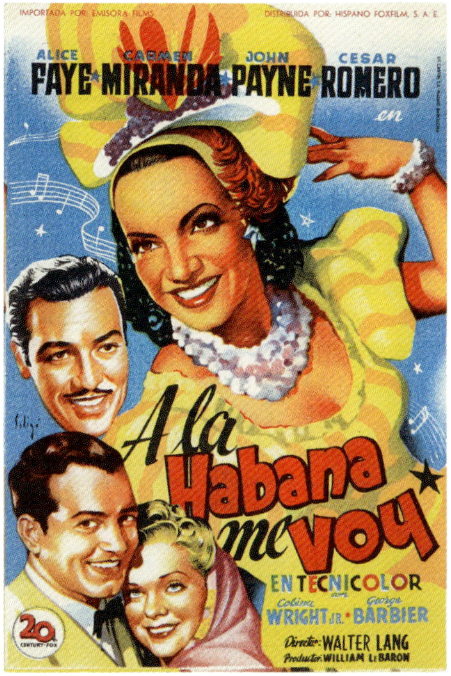

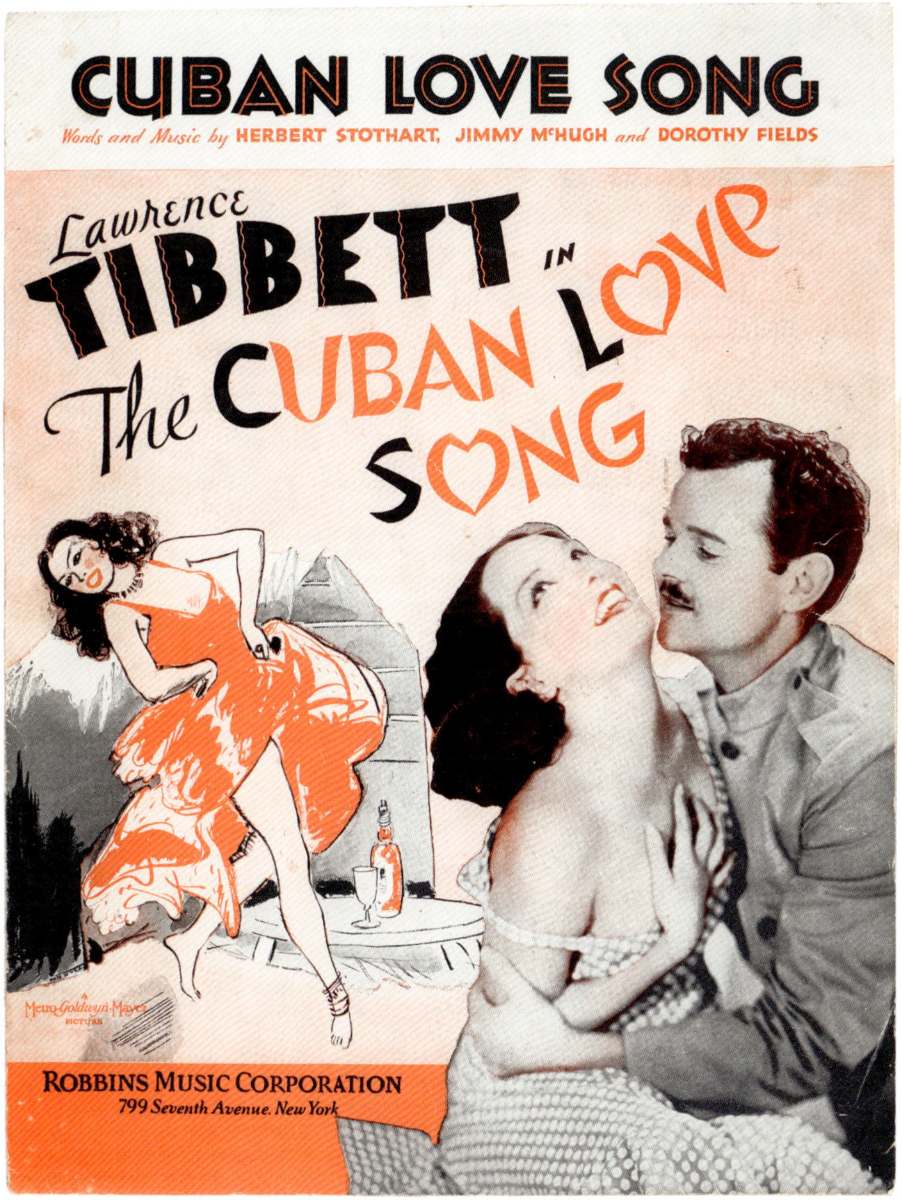

Advertising card, ***A la Habana me voy (Weekend in Havana)***, c. 1941
Lit. Cantin, S.A., Madrid, printer

The Wolfsonian–FIU, The Vicki Gold Levi Collection, XC2016.01.1.1243

Sheet music cover, ***Cuban Love Song***, 1931
Herbert Stothart, Jimmy McHugh, and Dorothy Fields, lyricists and composers
Robbins Music Corporation, New York, publisher

The Wolfsonian–FIU, The Vicki Gold Levi Collection, XC2002.11.4.162

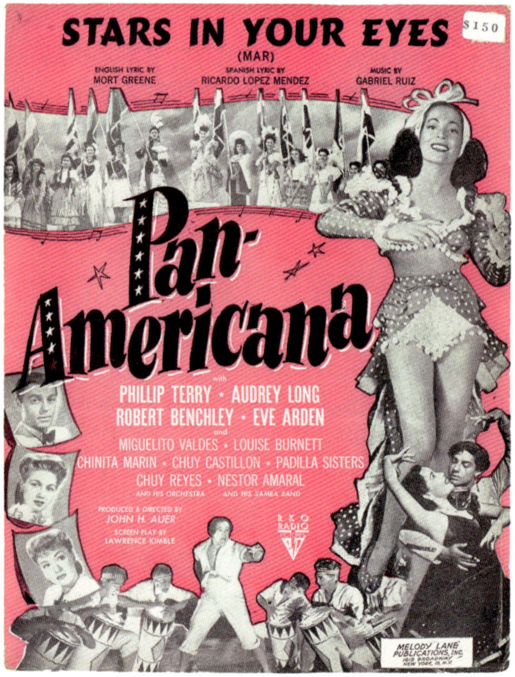

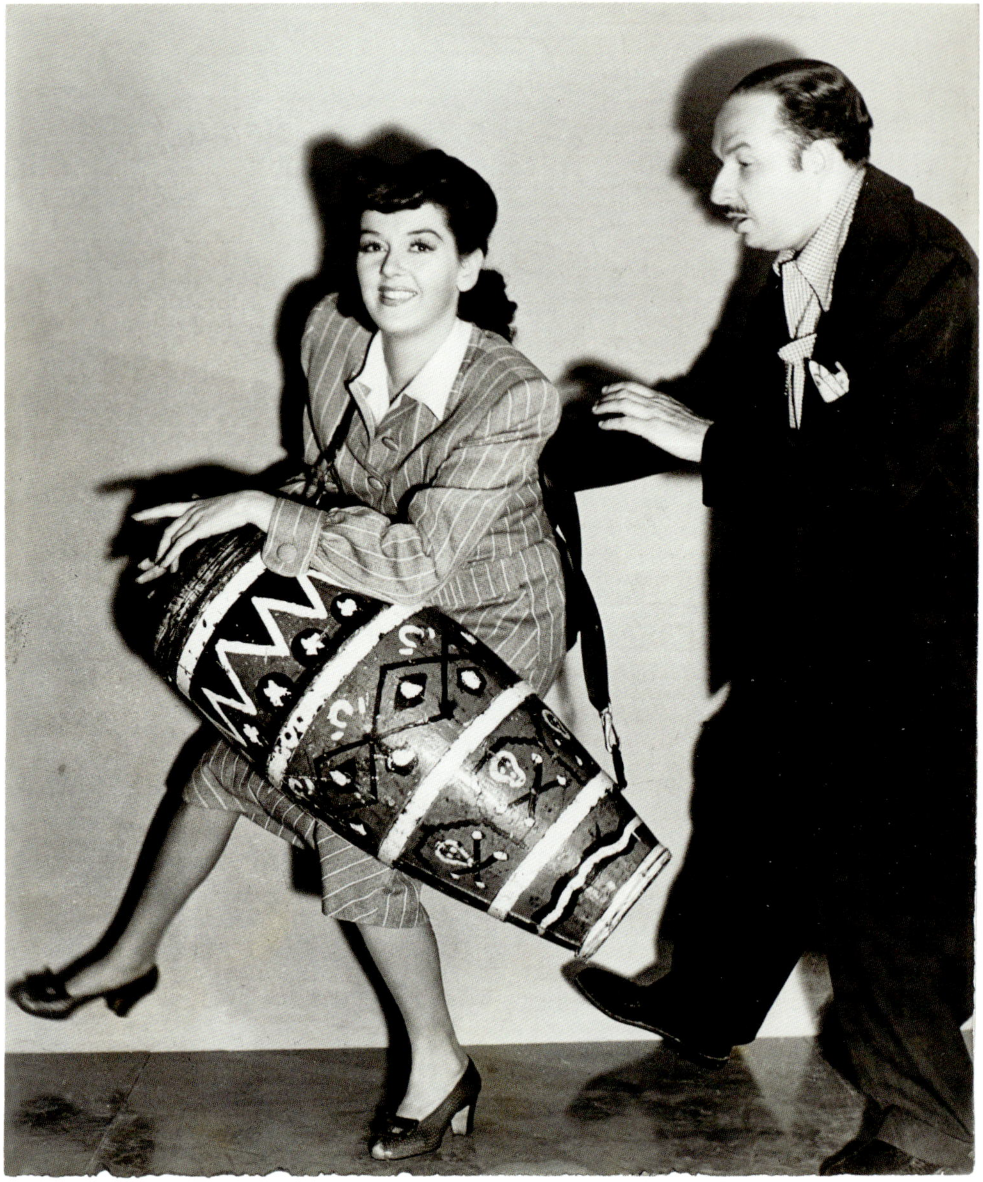

Sheet music cover, ***Stars in Your Eyes: Pan-Americana***, 1945
Mort Greene and Ricardo López Méndez, lyricists
Gabriel Ruiz, composer
Melody Lane Publishers, Inc., New York, publisher

The Wolfsonian–FIU, The Vicki Gold Levi Collection, XC2002.11.4.596

Photograph, ***Rhumba Runs Riot at Columbia***, c. 1954
Gelatin silver print

The caption reads: "Band leader Xavier Cugat leaves the Astaire-Hayworth dance musical to teach Rosalind Russell the songs, which she and Janet Blair will stamp out in a hilarious comedy scene in *My Sister Eileen*."

The Wolfsonian–FIU, The Vicki Gold Levi Collection, XC2016.01.1.893

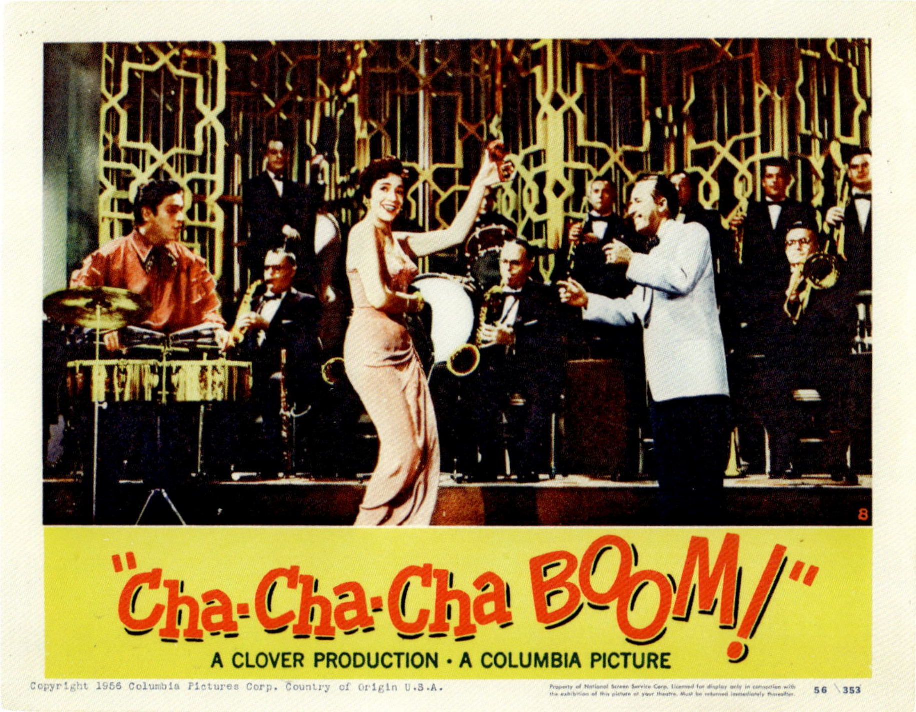

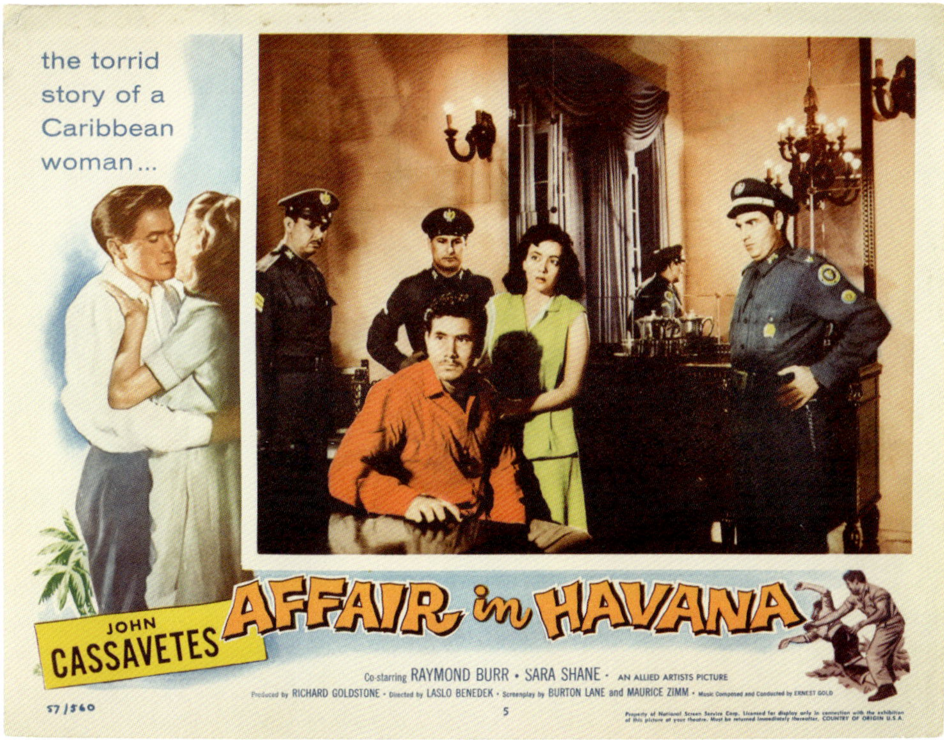

Lobby cards

"Cha-Cha-Cha Boom!"
Columbia Pictures Corporation, Los Angeles, publisher

Affair in Havana, 1957
Allied Artists Picture Corporation, Los Angeles
National Screen Service Corporation, publisher and printer

The Wolfsonian–FIU, The Vicki Gold Levi Collection, XC2016.01.1.911, .904

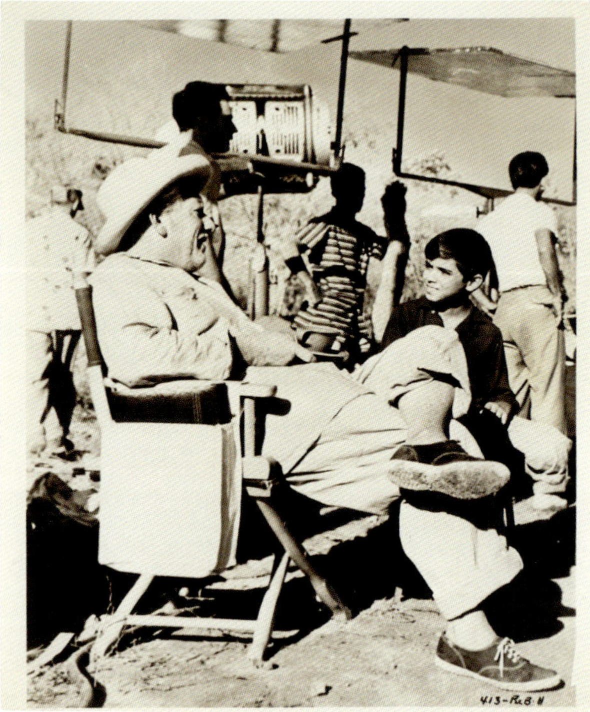

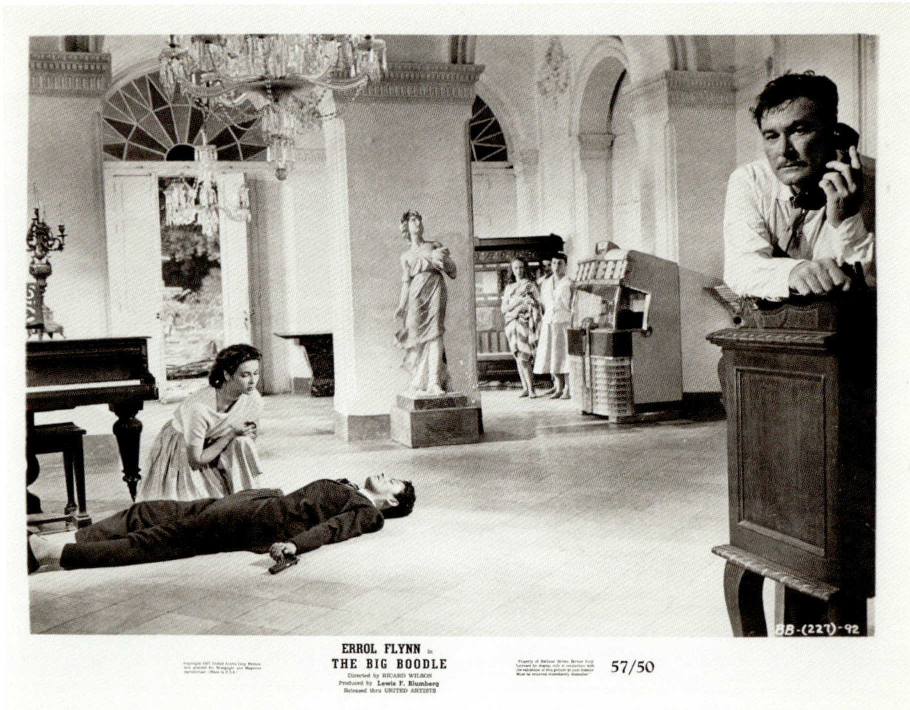

Photograph, **Spencer Tracy on the set of *The Old Man and the Sea***, July 1958
Gelatin silver print

The Wolfsonian–FIU, The Vicki Gold Levi Collection, XC2016.01.1.762

Film still, ***The Big Boodle***, 1957
United Artists Corporation, Los Angeles, photographer
Gelatin silver print

The Wolfsonian–FIU, The Vicki Gold Levi Collection, XC2016.01.1.3

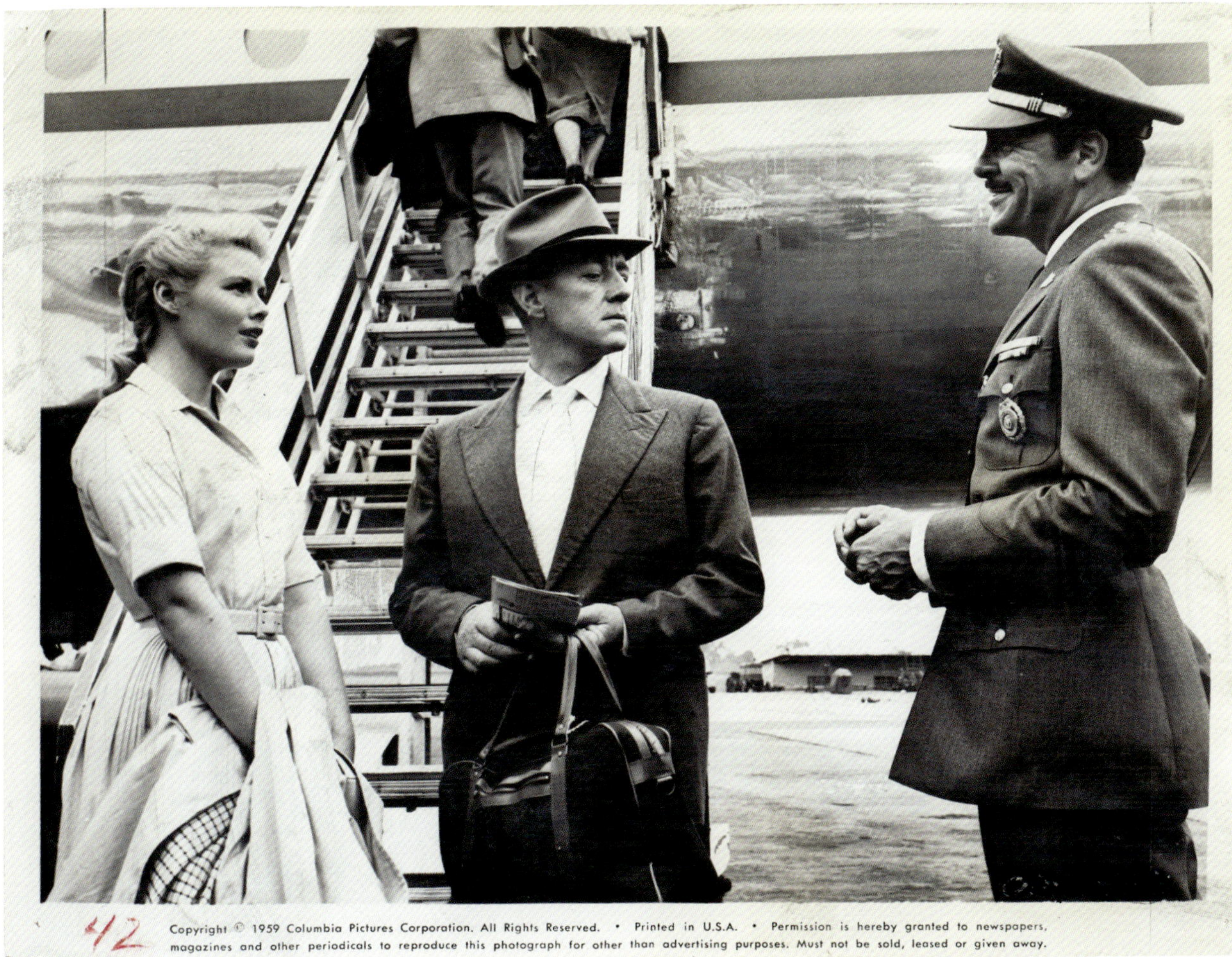

Film still, *Our Man in Havana*, 1959
Columbia Pictures Corporation, Los Angeles, photographer
Gelatin silver print

The Wolfsonian–FIU, The Vicki Gold Levi Collection, XC2016.01.1.916

FIU | The Wolfsonian